GRAND Lenormand

GRAND JEU Lenormand

The Grand Jeu Lenormand Fortune Telling Book

Fortune Telling with the Grand Jeu de Mlle Le Normand

(based on an original instruction booklet from 1845)

Andreas Nostra Dahm

Bibliographic information of the German National Library: The German National Library lists this publication in the German National Bibliography; detailed bibliographic data are available on the Internet via dnb.dnb.de.

English Edition - Translation by Dru Words.

Publisher: BoD • Books on Demand GmbH, In de Tarpen 42, 22848 Norderstedt
Printed by: Libri Plureos GmbH, Friedensallee 273, 22763 Hamburg

ISBN: 978-3-7597-3648-2

Prologue

Cartomancy

Something about the history of cartomancy

For many centuries, there has been a need for people to know more about their own future, more about their personal fate. For this purpose, in the past many people had used various methods of fortune telling and divination. Fortune telling with cards is nowadays a divination method that has become widespread but remains still covered in a mysterious tradition. Cartomancy, or divining the future with cards, is one of the most common divination methods and it has taken on a high place in fortune telling over the years.

There are many myths and legends about the origin of cartomancy: some talking about an origin in China, from the 7th century - others bring up today's Egypt when it is about the history of the origin of card reading - but one thing is certain: no matter where and when this oracle had its birth, it was already present a long time before cartomancy experienced a popular boom to the second half of the 18th century and then again in the 19th century in Europe. This time in Europe and the events that took place there are decisive for the current significance, the image, and the history of this art of divination. And it is an important fact that famous personalities, such as Etteilla (Alliette) and La Lenormand, made their contribution to this and built a part of the foundation that has not lost its influence until today. They have made cartomancy what it is today from its origins.

But as popular as the art of cartomancy is, it has always been accompanied by sceptics and doubters since its existence. Likewise, total opponents were those who were able to demonize, banish, and assign cartomancy to the charlatans and jugglers. Until today. And so many New Age movements gave and are still giving the sceptics another voice, even if at

the same time these movements made cartomancy once again more socially acceptable and made sure that this divination method could establish more itself in the 20th century. And even these days, the internet offers a great platform to spread knowledge of cartomancy but unfortunately the internet itself is at the same time the pyre of modern times.

But how does it work?

Even if, on the path from the early history to the modern age, cartomancy offers different facets and perspectives, one thought or intention remained always the same and true to mankind, namely this one to know when and how something is going to happen in future; human's desire is to use the cards to unravel the future and thus to reveal its secrets. Like many other oracles, the cards are capable of this, only someone who knows how to lift the veil of a more uncertain future with the cards is needed to get clarity. Cartography, cartomancy, or the art of reading cards is performed with different kinds of card decks and various methods (from traditional, classic, to modern). The most famous card decks for divination to date include the Tarot Cards, the Lenormand Cards, the Kipper Cards, the Gypsy Oracle Cards, and the Skat & Playing Cards. Each of these card decks is based on its own system of divining the future. But even if the meanings of the cards are always different, they have one fact in common: to do a reading, all the cards need to be laid out according to a certain scheme, a certain spread. And then, depending on the position of the cards, all cards get associated and interpreted with each other. And here the cards' own meanings take hold (always depending on which divination deck is used for fortune telling).

If you come to see someone who is to do cartomancy, the cards are usually first shuffled and then, as I said, laid out in a specific scheme, a spread, that is typical according to the card deck that is used by the card reader; followed by the most important part, the part of the interpretation of the cards, the fortune telling, the forecast. In the meantime, cartomancy has more to offer to society than just future predictions. Many people consult the cards as a support to make up decisions, as a guide, as a deeper look into the soul, and to explain certain circumstances or even the causes of situations. There are countless reasons for consulting the cards, and these are justified because the cards have answers to all questions that life creates. People want to know more about themselves and their future; they want to be prepared for upcoming events. In uncertain situations, people ask the cards for security, a form of support, a kind of help to decide, a taking away of fear, or asking for advice, hoping to get confirmation of their own assumptions or even the hint that those presumptions may lead them wrong. Some need to understand, need clarity about the past to finally leave it behind; others want to explore the present, the "why", the cause of a situation; and sometimes they just need to know whether everything is going to be fine and develops according to their own desires. Others want to know what other persons think or feel or whether a person will turn toward or away from them. In addition, those seeking advice would like to have quick and concrete answers to questions that they are currently unable to answer or will never be able to answer on their own. You can ask any question, no matter what concern you have, "from cradle to grave" - there are no wrong questions. An experienced fortune teller knows how to answer you because the cards cover all areas of life: the past, the present, and most importantly, the future. They know all the secrets; it only takes someone who knows how to reveal them. Because no matter how far card reading has arrived and been established in our modern age, it still has something mysterious - this mystical touch – that simply belongs to it. However, it is important that you ask a question; you must reach out to the cards; they do not come to contact you. And one thing is certain: the more accurate your question, the more accurate the answer that will be given to you will be. To cloud an issue does not make you move forward. Nowhere, not in life in

general nor in consulting the cards. At this point it should also be mentioned that the cards explain, they make statements and describe circumstances and backgrounds, they show a different perspective, and they also open the view into the future; in no way are the cards are there to make decisions or to take responsibility from or over someone. They don't pretend; they don't command, they don't show the way; they only name facts and things. How, what the Querent is going to do with the message of the cards is up to him.

During a reading, the cards will therefore make clear statements about the question of the Querent, which the fortune teller passes on, based on the position of the fortune telling cards to each other and in the respective spread. The fortune teller translates, so to speak, the language of the cards and thus has some function as a medium, a mediator between the oracle cards and the one who consults them. Every kind of question can be answered with each deck of cards, but there are of course also cartomancers, who prefer certain card decks for a certain situation or question. Some also intuitively select a deck of cards in an initial dialog with the client; various procedures can also be found and explained here. Also, card readers differ in whether they interpret the cards in a traditional, conservative way or in a more modern way, in which the cards are sometimes unfortunately too alienated, and some quickly get lost during their interpretations. That is a reason why some predictions unfortunately do not come true, because it is by far also a matter of interpretation style, knowledge, talent, and experience in how the cards are to be translated. Nowadays, reading cards is so widespread that you can believe that you can learn this art easily and quickly. It is a fact that his option is available to everyone, but it is also true, that the art of reading fortunes in cards is a craft that needs to be mastered, especially if you offer it. The cards, it is said, are always right; we are those who tend to be sometimes misguided in the interpretation. Think of it like poetry: You will already be able, with some knowledge, to recognize a poem exactly in its framework and in its structure, but this alone will never explain the meaning or intention of the poem's words. You need to be able to see the heart of the poem. And it also requires an additional ability to see inside the cards and to read them in relation to the different life issues, because when you do divination with oracle cards, you are with the cards and only with the cards - it does not need anything else. You do not need clairvoyance, no contact with the spiritual world or spirit guides, nor does it require any intuition; for a card reading you simply need to know the cards and put yourself completely into their hands. Thus, everyone can learn how to interpret cards, but whether he has the skills or the gift to practice this art will only be revealed with time.

The different decks of cards

To master this craft, a professional and serious card reader needs the knowledge about the cards and their various meanings and countless facets. This knowledge is simply gained with a lot of experience, and everyone should also know the historical background of the divination tool, to avoid misinterpretations. You need to know what you are doing and with what you are working! Know your divination tool! Previously, the popular decks were already mentioned in a few words; but here we look at them again a little bit closer:

Tarot Cards

The Tarot is one of the most famous and perhaps oldest card decks that is used for fortune telling, and until today many motifs of the classic and popular Tarot Cards are based on the motifs in their origin, which, by the way, is very important for the correct interpretation of an oracle card and the recognition of the essential meaning of the cards of each deck, that is used for fortune telling. One of the earliest versions, the Tarot of Eteilla, is gradually being added to the Tarot Card Hall of Fame, as are other well-known decks: the well-known Tarot de Marseille or the ever popular and famous Rider Waite Tarot

with the enchanting illustrations of Pamela Colman Smith can be found among many friends of Tarot. The Tarot of Aleister Crowley is a bit outstanding: the creator's reputation of being fonder of the dark side of fortune telling casts until today a little shadow over this variant of Tarot Cards (also A. E. Waite was, but the very popular, nice, and colorful style of the pictures of his Tarot made this fact being more irrelevant and nearly forgotten). Two very famous spreads with the Tarot are the Celtic Cross and the Small Cross. A deck of Tarot contains 78 cards, whereby 22 of these cards, numbered from 0 - 21, are assigned to the so-called Great Arcana (secret/ arcanum lat.). These are, for example, the popular cards of the Lovers, the Fool, and the World; the other 56 cards are assigned to the Small Arcana as suit cards: four suits each, 10 numbered cards (Ace to 10) and four so-called court cards (Jack, Knight, Queen, and King). The colors are represented by the four suits: Pentacles, Cups, Wands, and Swords. Even today these colors and suits can still be found on playing cards in Spain and Italy, for example, and they are giving rise to the assumption that the playing cards were derived from the Tarot. In Germany, the colors and suits became the Bells, Leaves, Acorns, and Hearts, and in France, the cards were provided with the suits of Diamonds, Hearts, Clubs, and Spades, which leads us to the next group of fortune telling cards:

Playing Cards (Skat, Poker, - Schafkopf Cards)

Using an ordinary card deck is a great way to unravel the future. Particularly if no other cards are available, you will always surprise the others with that. But in history, these cards were used very often for this: it was forbidden to do cartomancy and was tolerated in society even less than today, and thus some ladies pretended to be playing a Patience or Solitaire, but they did divination instead. It was also said that even Mlle. Lenormand, who used different methods of divination, knew how to see the future in Piquet Cards. And even in the famous opera Carmen, it was the 7 of Spades that forecasts great misfortune. But no matter which kind of playing cards are used - whether Skat, Poker, Schafkopf Cards, the Baraja Espanola from Spain or the Carte Napoletane or Piacentine from Italy - they are all a perfect divination tool. With their simplicity, the playing cards reach into depths and have an astonishing significance. Since there are no pictures or symbols to focus on, divination with these cards is often considered very difficult to learn, but it is one of the methods with the longest history & tradition. Here, too, the possibilities and ways of interpretation vary from country to country and from region to region. For example, in ancient German tradition, the Clubs were the suit with the darkest message of all, although in other traditions this is more associated with the suit of Spades. Since, logically, none of the mentioned playing cards had an instruction booklet to explain fortune telling, there is no guideline for an interpretation and the doors to any kind of interpretation are almost all open – cartomancers refer to the knowledge that was previously often only passed on by verbal tradition. What is represented in the playing cards by numbers and suits is represented in other fortune telling cards by words, images, or common symbols, depending on which card deck is selected. Now we move on and see what cards are used for divination, too:

Kipper Cards

Around 1890, in the middle of the time when the art of fortune telling with cards experienced a strong boom in Europe, the Kipperkarten were born in Germany, published by Matthias Seidlein in Munich (which is still can be seen in the illustrations of the cards showing contemporary, local architecture: for example, a local sign to Simbach refers to the proximity of Munich, too). In an accompanying booklet, which served as a guide to fortune telling with these cards, they were identified as those of Ms. Kipper. To this day, the Kipper Cards are available with the images from that time – with the only difference being that the cards are now printed mirrored! This

happened with the transfer of copyrights to the company FX Schmid. The Kipper cards are a set of 36 cards, all of which are laid out all at once for divination; these 36 cards are all numbered and because of that they have a fixed sequence. Each card has a name and a title that serves as a headline to describe it. The Kipper Cards represent an oracle based on pictures. The pictures show people and situations from contemporary everyday life, and fortune is told by them. The fact that many people are part of this deck is very welcome to some card readers. The amount of Person Cards is clearly a difference to many other decks. The Kipper Oracle and its statement are therefore not based on symbols but on situations, describing events and persons, comparable to Oracle Cards, such as the Sibilla Oracle, Biedermeier Aufschlage Cards or the Gypsy Oracle.

Aufschlage Cards

The Aufschlage Cards are a kind of umbrella term for various oracle cards, which have a place in the history of cartomancy, too. Those cards might seem like each other, but they are not the same. These include, among others, the Biedermeier Aufschlage Cards, the Sibilla Cards or the Gypsy Oracle Cards. All of these have something in common, even if the number of cards in each deck is different. Like the Kipper Cards, these cards also talk by using images as their language. The illustrations show events, happenings, situations, or various people. Each card is titled with a name, too. And to read the fortune, as usual, the cards are laid out according to certain spreads and get connected to each other. These cards have their origin mainly in the countries of Austria, Hungary, and Italy. This made them look very similar sometimes. Nevertheless, and this also applies in general to cartomancy: each deck of cards should be associated only with its own system to avoid mistakes and wrong predictions due to incorrect mixing. To this day, when buying one of those Oracle

Cards, often small instruction booklets are included, which should make it easier to get started with the cards.

But there are also cards that talk through mysterious or secret symbols that are drawn on them, and within this group of cards you find the Lenormand Fortune Telling Cards.

Lenormand Cards

These cards are among the most popular Oracle Cards, partly because they are believed to be the easiest to learn to read and thus provide a quick start in card reading. But as popular as this card deck is, it is really underestimated, and especially nowadays many people move only on its surface and too much on paths that have little in common with the real inside of the cards. Already, about the history and origins of these cards, there are so many inconsistent or false statements that are not visible to the majority, or they are just not really interested in. When we talk about Lenormand Cards, we need to distinguish within these three card decks: the classic Lenormand Fortune Telling Cards from Germany, the Petit Lenormand published by Grimaud in France and the Grand Jeu Le Normand, by Grimaud in France.

And this book tells you all about the Grand Jeu Le Normand.

Prologue

A warm welcome.

It has always been a need for people to know more about their own future by consulting an oracle, especially a card oracle. And there have always been countless ways to pass on this knowledge to learn divination with cards. Through family traditions, verbal transmissions, ancient mystical writings, or some notes that someone secretly kept in a secretary. There are countless books that are used by people as a kind of dictionary, trying to translate the language of the Lenormand Cards and to bring themselves closer together. There are so many ways to do divination with cards, each has its own system and guide. Just as there are different languages and dialects in other countries different languages and dialects exist - the language of the Lenormand Cards is often slightly different from country to country, from region to region, and has changed in the many years since cartomancy already exist. An unfortunate fate of today's Oracle Cards, however, is that they unfortunately suffered some kind of progress: they have evolved, and unfortunately, they were sometimes a bit too alienated; they became victims of the New Age spirituality, and more and more made into a coaching or a pseudo-psychological lifestyle object in line with society. Predicting the future, fortune telling with cards, the actual task that the cards have in their tradition, is often only minor matters because, on the one hand, it does not welcome modern society and the cards are preferred as a tool for other things. It is also no longer possible for many to read the future from the cards despite study because the connection to the origin of the cards has not always been passed on correctly over the years and has been lost. Because cartomancy is still an art, and it needs a true artist.

I see myself in the tradition of card readers, and it is important to pass on old and valuable knowledge about cartomancy to wrest this knowledge from oblivion. So, it is also important for me to share my knowledge about the Grand Lenormand Cards with you in this book, because when I read one or the other of what is told today about the Lenormand Fortune Telling Cards as well as about the Petit Lenormand or the Grand Lenormand, my traditional card reader's heart bleeds and my soul is sad.

People have forgotten to recognize the soul of these cards...

But if you are now ready to hide your previous knowledge or even ready to take the step to learn how to read cards correctly, then you are right here at my side and have chosen the perfect book about the Grand Lenormand Cards! The system of interpretation differs from all others. For it is that which has remained faithful to tradition, has it strictly as a basis, and has nevertheless adapted over the years to our modern time, without losing the soul, without losing the face, without losing the origins. It is the true way to interpret the Grand Lenormand Cards; this is how the "Grand Jeu" is played. This book is therefore an unprecedented "tell-all" about the Grand Jeu Lenormand. Free yourself from everything you already know about it and get ready to finally discover the real secrets of the "Grand Jeu de Mlle. Le Normand". Because if you haven't understood the cards yet with the knowledge that you have about them, then this is not up to you, but because your previous information about them was bad, you will not understand them in the future if you carry on with this inconsistent knowledge. If you intend to successfully predict the future with this oracle, then the only true and correct way is to learn it as it was once practiced and taught.

Personally, I was taught the "Gand Jeu" at a young age, and with this ancient way of fortune telling, the cards have always remained true & honest to me to this day. They have always been able to answer all my questions and thus assist me, and I am always grateful to my cards and to those who taught me how to read cards in my youth.

The "Grand Jeu" is the supreme discipline in cartomancy, something very special, and mastering this method of fortune telling also makes you something very special.

Now enjoy reading this book and enjoy the "Grand Jeu Lenormand".

Andreas

INTRODUCTION

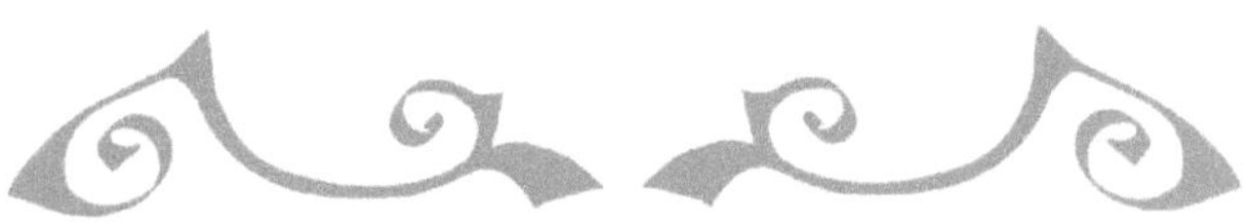

First steps...

What is to do now? You are curious and interested and you want to know everything about these cards? Then buy your own Grand Lenormand Cards if you do not have them yet! If the cards are now with you by your side, they should no longer leave your side. Do not let go of them, always carry them with you. They should be your companion from now on, your assistant, your confidant, always & everywhere. This is important. So, the cards recognize that they belong to you & only to you.

Shuffle the cards, feel the material, and get to know them – make them your daily companion, your friend, your confidant and, very important, always protect your cards, because they are much more than just paper. Never give away your cards – no one else should touch them. Only then the cards will speak to you. They recognize and feel immediately, if you treat them neglected.

Now the 54 cards are with you, and you want to learn and know everything about them as soon as possible, but you must be patient. Give yourself time, and you will see how deep you get into the cards. With my book and the method of fortune telling explained in it, I give you a full insight into the "Grand Jeu" as it has never been given before. Of course, you will personalize and expand your knowledge; that's good, and that's how it should be because we all have our own handwriting. But one thing must be certain so that you can be successful with cartomancy: the foundation of your system of divination must be solid and stable; you should not try to make a system out of different systems, because then you lose yourself in the interpretation of the cards. You will not be able to see or recognize their true meaning. If you have created a solid foundation, then try to expand or supplement it if you still feel the need for it, but always remember: the foundation must be stable and solid. Do not build on sand, and do not unconditionally combine tradition with modernity, because often they do not fit together properly. It must make some sense; the modern words must be recognizable in the traditional words. Stay authentic and choose what you can identify with and feel comfortable with. And remove yourself from your thoughts and intuition when reading cards, because both unfortunately lead to the loss of every true message of the cards. The cards have their native language, and they can only be interpreted correctly if base our interpretation on this language and concentrate on the core meanings of the cards during the reading.

Know your divination tool

Know your cards - master your craft – be a master in cartomancy.

Each oracle has its own history. So it is very important that before we dive deep into the Grand Lenormand Cards, we take a closer look at the history of these cards, because if you want to be able to see the future in them, be it for yourself, for friends or even for clients you should know exactly which Oracle Cards you work with and exactly what you are doing, and for this, you must also have knowledge of the origin of the Grand Lenormand Cards.

Looking back in time, we have now gained the certainty that the 54 Grand Lenormand Cards are the cards that are demonstrably closest to those that Mlle Le Normand once used for divination. And in this book, you finally learn where the Grand Lenormand Cards find their roots, their origins and thus also something about their real background and their true history: with this knowledge, you can say that you now not only know your cards by their true meanings but also by their whole true origin. You know their soul and their nature, and therefore you know exactly what you are doing when you use

the Grand Lenormand Cards for fortune telling. This is important to fully master this craft and wherever you will go and present yourself with your Grand Lenormand Cards, you will always make this as correct and authentic as no one else does.

The roots of Lenormand Cards

The Lenormand Fortune Telling Cards

The Lenormand Wahrsagekarten (Lenormand Fortune Telling Cards), which are known as such, consist out of 36 different cards, all of which have their origin in Germany. By looking back into the past, we have now gained the certainty that the 36 small Lenormand Cards do not correspond to those which Mlle Le Normand used for divination. Around 1845 the Lenormand Cards, as we know them today, were available for purchase to those interested in fortune telling with cards. At that time, a booklet explaining how to interpret these cards was supposed to credibly underline the connection to Mlle Lenormand, since the booklet was not written by anyone other than Philippe, the heir of Lenormand. To date, only this guide contains the true and correct meanings of these 36 cards and describes the only real method of fortune telling with these cards.

But the cards do not come from the heritage of Mlle. Lenormand, nor do they come from the ideas of design and meaning. The creators of the Lenormand Cards used a brand name and designed the cards in the style of an old dice game, which was composed of 36 cards with motifs to form a large game board. The so-called Game of Hope by Mr. Johann Kaspar Hechtel, published in 1799, in the year of Mr. Hechtel's death, served as a template for the illustrations of the cards. The true meanings of the Lenormand Cards, however, come from the pen of a German writer and his book, which dealt with the Arab art of reading coffee grounds and cartomancy. The true way of using these cards is based on the Oracle Cards mentioned in it, the so-called Coffee Card Deck, a real card game that first appeared in 1796 and is said to have been used by the German empress and at the court of Vienna for fortune telling. The instruction of these cards was the basis for Philippe's instruction sheet, which was attached to the famous Lenormand Cards. This old template was only changed in very few parts and details, so all this was not part of Mlle. Lenormand.

The Petit Lenormand

The Petit Lenormand is one of the two Lenormand Cards Decks from France published by the publisher Grimaud. It is a 37-card deck, and it is a shortened version of the Grand Jeu Le Normand. It contains 37 cards, which were the finest selection from the 54 and thus resulted in a smaller version of the card deck. Also, the 37 cards of the Petit Lenormand do not practice the "Great Game"; with the attached instructions, these cards have been assigned a different way of presenting and interpreting the future. This Petit Lenormand (as well as the Great Lenormand) is completely different in its cards, in its design, and in its spread, as well as in the meanings of each card, from the 36 Lenormand Fortune Telling Cards, which today are one of the most common oracles. (If you are interested in which cards were taken for the Petit Lenormand from the 54 cards, you will find a list on page 252).

The Grand Lenormand

The Grand Lenormand/Le Grand Jeu Lenormand by Grimaud is the other of the two Lenormand Card decks that really come from France. And it is the more familiar of these two decks of cards. In the European area, especially in the German-speaking area, these cards are also known as the "Astro – Mythologischen Lenormandkarten."

We're going back in time, during Mlle. Lenormand's lifetime it has always been said about her, that she used previously

unknown cards; some eyewitnesses speak of cards with images from ancient mythology, and others said she had used Etteilla's Tarot or Piquet cards. We also know that she was not only a card reader but also mixed many other traditional techniques of fortune telling with each other. She knew alchemy, kabbalah, and reading coffee grounds; she saw the future in eggs or water; and she was familiar with many other ancient methods of divination, such as palmistry and scrying (especially with mirrors). Mlle. Lenormand also taught her methods of fortune telling, but never in writing; she taught them to others only by words, but someone wrote them down.

In 1845, two years after the death of Mlle Lenormand, under the pseudonym Mme la Comtesse de ***, several books were published. It was said that this collection of books also included the astrology, Astro - mythological cards, and other divination methods explained by Mlle Lenormand. In fact, the books were published together with a set of cards, and the content of the books was about methods of divination such as astrology, palmistry, Kabbalah, and more. But the authenticity of these "secret techniques" was doubted by society, and they disappeared or almost fell into oblivion. Until later, fortune telling cards appeared on a flea market in Paris, and then in 1865, these books were republished in a second edition by the mysterious author Comtesse X. The first publisher was without a name and was only associated with one address: Rue Vievienne 46. This time, however, the author, Comtesse X, revealed herself as Madame Breteau, the wife of a publisher in Paris. She claimed to be a former student of Mlle. Lenormand (a rumor says that these books are still in the National Library of Paris).

We don't know the exact story anymore, and its fragments that create a logical picture, like a puzzle. A puzzle, but one that, even if it is a little incomplete, gives an idea of a meaningful overall picture, for it has become possible to sum up through all these fragments what kind of cards the cards were not that

Mlle Lenormand used to interpret the future. And it is also possible to say from historical and autobiographical knowledge that the Grand Lenormand Cards are probably those cards whose roots are really in France and at least correspond to a deck of cards, that Mlle Lenormand used, and several of Mlle Lenormand's methods of fortune telling are combined on the cards of the Grand Jeu. And also in some writings about the fortune teller, eyewitnesses mentioned themselves that Mlle Lenormad played the Grand Jeu for some of her clients, and it was also known that in addition to the name of the client, he also had to tell the fortune teller which flower was preferred because of its beauty and which flower because of the fragrance (in the later chapters, you will see to what this is connected to).

In the original French edition of these cards, 54 cards were always part of the game: 52 playing cards and another 2 additional cards, each with a male and a female person card. On the cards were scenes from mythology, star constellations, geomantic symbols, letters, playing cards inserts, one bigger and two smaller pictures, and various flowers to be part of the oracle, the Grand Jeu.

It is important to mention that these cards also tried to spread in Germany. They have been illustrated in various editions by the editor R. F. August Reiff in Koblenz. The difference in these versions is that the star constellation is not printed, and the arrangement of the flowers and the images is different. In the upper part of the cards, you can see the flowers; in the middle, often the small pictures; and below, the big picture. The images in Reiff's edition were still close to ancient mythology; only a later German version of these cards tried to adapt some images in a more contemporary style to bring this game closer to society, but in Germany this failed. In Germany, the 36 Lenormand Fortune Telling Cards were the real star, who was born in 1845. If you have one of these card games by August

Reiff, you can easily determine the time of a copy of this deck: If Koblenz is written like Coblenz, you can be sure that the card deck or. the pictures were designed and printed for the first time in Germany before 1920.

But now your 54 Grand Lenormand Cards journey begins. Become a master of the Grand Jeu Le Normand and learn to play the Grand Jeu. Learn now the supreme discipline of cartomancy!

A little anecdote on the side: These cards have made it very far, and they have become famous. It's amazing that these rare cards make an appearance in one of the music videos of our pop queen, Madonna. The music video for the 90s hit "Deeper and Deeper" contains a sequence in which the cards of the Grand Jeu Le Normand are used for fortune telling.

Grand Jeu de Société

et

Pratiques Secretes

de

Mademoiselle Le Normand

Grand Game of Society

and

Secrets Techniques

of

Mademoiselle Le Normand

PART I

Explanation & Use
of the
Astro – Mythological – Hermetic
cards

followed by

PART II

an addition with lot of examples:

the Great Spread of 48

the Aphorism of Flowers

and

the Voices of the Animals

the Achievements

by

Mlle. Le Normand

1845

CHAPTER I

Explanation and Meanings of the Cards

What is what?! - a Grand Lenormand Card's structure

Before you start, you should know the structure of a Grand Lenormand Card. You should know what can be found on it and why: When you look at the card you see many pictures, stars, symbols, a playing card, a letter… But what do all these pictures mean? Why is the card so detailed? Do not get confused; everything is based on one system, and the more you get to know the structure and the system of the cards, the more you will recognize the card's message.

Take a card, look at the card and now get to know the structure of the card:

1. Playing Card Insert
2. Firmament
3. Letter
4. Geomantic Symbol
5. Big Picture
6. Small Picture, left
7. Small Picture, right
8. Flowers

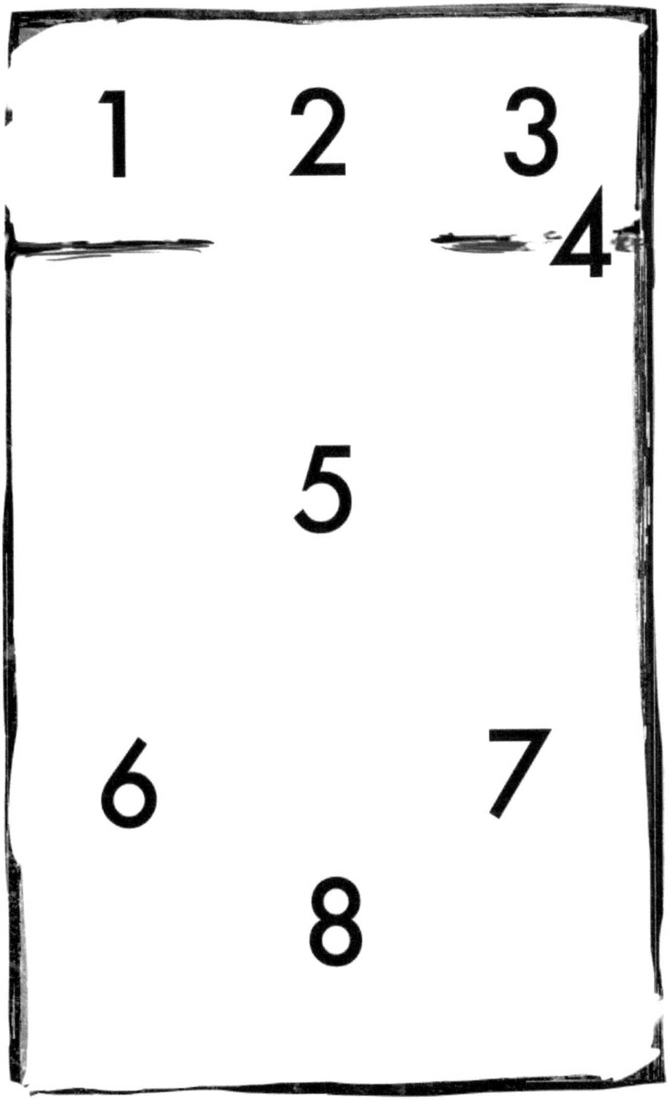

1 2 3
4

5

6 7
8

1. The Playing Card insert

The original instructions do not assign any direct meaning to the playing card, nor do you need any general meaning for the playing card. Theoretically, the general, original main meaning of the card can be assigned to the playing card symbol, but that would only be a heading of the whole card, because it carries many symbols. The playing card is also a kind of navigation system that guides you in one direction through the cards to keep them in an order based on the original order of the known playing cards. But be careful, because this order of cards does not coincide with the actual logical order of the cards given to the cards in their origin. Here and there, the court cards (King, Queen, Jack) and other person cards can be a helping hand to let you know, depending on the context, that there may be another person who is important in the spread or answering the question. But in general, the playing cards and their color are not given any significant meaning, and they have no value during the Grand Jeu. So, they have only one meaning in relation to persons and a general meaning, they are to be put aside above all.

2. The Stars, the Sky of the Card

Look into the stars, and you will know where the path leads. Here, in the upper part of the card, you can see several star constellations. Some are no longer common in today's astrology and astronomy, and some modern constellations are missing. And since the stars were used in ancient times as a kind of map or navigation system, you will also see that the stars can give you important hints on your journey with the Grand Lenormand cards. Among the 54 cards, there are eight cards with a "colored" star, which has an important and special influence on the Main Character and their situation. These are the so-called Star cards, which will be of great importance in the "Great Spread of 48." Only these eight stars are assigned a verifiable meaning and role in the old tradition of the Grand Lenormand; the other constellations, if you stick to the original instructions, are not important; there they are not even mentioned. That's why even these stars are not printed in some variants of the Grand Lenormand Cards. These are usually variants of the cards created by the German publisher Reiff. To assign a fundamental meaning to the constellations corresponds to the modern tradition of interpreting these cards.

The well-known cards of the zodiac signs are also not included here; they are shown elsewhere.

3. The Letter of the Alphabet

The main task of the alphabet in the Grand Lenormand is to show how successful an undertaking will be or whether a desired situation will arrive or not. In the chapter on achievements, this will be explained to you. Each letter has a numerical value that helps to calculate the quality of the result. According to the old tradition, the letter has no other meaning.

Again, it can be said that assigning the alphabet a meaning beyond the calculation of the achievements belongs to the modern tradition of interpreting these cards. In modern tradition, the values of letters can be used to recognize a certain time value. The numerical value of the letter helps in determining the time. There is little information about this timing system, and it is not so common. The same applies to the assignment of a certain keyword to each letter, which can have an influence on the actual topic; all this is not in the original instructions and therefore does not belong to the origin of the Grand Jeu.

4. The Geomantic Symbol:

Usually known and used as a separate oracle, once by Miss Lenormand. The Geomantic Symbols are visible on 22 cards in the deck. Two other Geomantic Symbols are also represented

by the Main Character's cards. A symbol is assigned a total of 24 cards. Here, too, the following applies: to assign a fundamental meaning to the Geomantic Symbol corresponds to the modern tradition of interpreting these cards. The symbols represent either a negative, positive, or neutral figure that has the corresponding effect on the spread. In modern tradition, Geomantic Symbols are also important for the timing. These techniques, both the influence of time and the influence of a symbol on the Main Character and his situation, are not part of the original way of reading these cards. They also came with the passage of time. But why are there some symbols on the cards that are not really related to the actual Grand Jeu, according to the original instructions? They are all oracles and methods of fortune telling, once used by Mlle. Lenormand, and it was considered important to present them together.

NOTE Additions to the interpretation added by modern times probably only make sense if they are in a logical connection to the origin and do not alienate the card.

The Pictures

The greatest attention is always paid to the three pictures. They are the essence of each card: the main ambassador and most important parts of the card to use for interpretation.

5. The Big Picture

The big picture. It is the main picture, the heart of the card. During the interpretation of the cards, one looks at it & pays most attention to its statement, as long as the rules of divination do not give the order to look at one of the other pictures or to consider something else for the interpretation of the card. The big picture always tells a story with a message that is reflected in the meaning of the oracle card. Most of the stories are rooted in ancient mythology, legends, or they are based on life situations or allegories.

6. The Small Picture to the left

This is important for your interpretation if the card touches one of the Main Character card's, refers to another card that represents a person, or is generally related to a person. More on that later.

7. The Small Picture to the right

This is important for your interpretation if the card touches one of the Main Character card's, refers to another card that represents a person, or is generally related to a person. More on that later.

NOTE If you are lucky enough to be in possession of an old German deck of cards of the Grand Jeu Lenormand by Reiff, you will find the smaller pictures together with the flowers in the upper half of the card and the big picture below.

8. The Flowers

In ancient times, various flowers were used to convey hidden messages to people so that they were not visible to others. Just like a secret language. On the cards, you can see a bouquet of different flowers or plants that were common and very well-known at that time. Wrongly, many use the influence of flowers as an additional clue in their interpretation of each card. This procedure is unfortunately wrong and leads to misinformation in the interpretation of the cards. The flower oracle "the Aphorism of Flowers" is a separate step during the Grand Jeu. This statement then is to connect with the oracle, but just look up the message of the flowers and attach it to a card within a spread is to avoid if you decide to play the "Grand Jeu Le Normand" according to its original rules.

Explanation of the pictures and meanings of each card

Now you know the structure of the card, and the next step leads you to the stories told by the pictures on the cards: the stories of the big picture in the middle and the two smaller pictures; later, the other symbols are added. Just in case you already know some of the meanings of the cards, it's time to let them go and hide them as well. If you intend to learn the Grand Lenormand properly, you must focus on the meanings given here in my book. I generally always recommend sticking to one system and not mixing anything; this often leads to confusion and is not particularly effective; too many cooks spoil the broth, they say in my culture.

In this chapter, you will first read the original meaning of the card, followed by an explanation of the big picture consisting of the title and a summary of the story that tells this big picture. Then the original meaning and several keywords are mentioned for further possible interpretation with this card. The same applies to the smaller pictures left and right; they are also explained.

It is important that you only focus on the three pictures in this chapter, so nothing else is mentioned here. In the following chapters, you will get more information about the cards, learn step-by-step the whole Grand Jeu with all its facets, and learn to interpret these cards. And it will be amazing that you will be able to make the first steps in fortune telling with these cards only with knowledge of the meanings of the pictures.

NOTE The descriptions of the large & small pictures and their scenes mentioned in the book always refer to the pictures that were shown on the original Grand Lenormand card.

The Main Characters

The Gentleman & The Lady

The Suit of Clubs

King of Clubs

Original meaning

"A wise man with experience who is able to give wise & clever advice."

(possible person card)

Big Picture

Phineus.

Story

You see Phineus, an old man, the king of Thrace. This man is blind, but he knows the wisdom of life, because he had his own sad fate. His wicked wife Idea told him that his son Plexipos wanted to replace him on the throne. Phineus, believing his wife's words without proof that these words of Idea were true, and so he stabbed his innocent son's eyes.
The Gods took revenge for this injustice and punished Phineus with blindness, they took away his ability to see. Then the Gods send the Harpies to destroy his food before he could eat it. He could not see the Harpies because of his blindness, but he knew his own fate, he knew he had done wrong, and he knew it was a punishment of the Gods. And from then on, he could answer the life questions of others with a wise mind, even if he could not live his own life with wise advice. He was able to give. With the help of Phineus, Jason, the Argonauts receive the important clue how to reach the island of Colchis, where the Golden Fleece was hidden. They had to pass the dangerous Symplegades, two rocks that moved towards each other every time someone wanted to pass the water between them to get to the island. Phineus, ordered them to send a dove through these rocks to set them in motion. The moment the rocks moved back was the moment the Argonauts themselves could

pass this dangerous spot. He gave helpful advice, but he was unable to give advice to himself.

Original meaning

"In every way, follow the advice of an old man you need to consult."

Interpretation

- advice
- advice is needed
- follow the advice
- important advice
- real advice
- experience
- support
- helping hand for others
- blindness
- "preaching water while drinking wine"

Smaller left picture

A dove passes a rock.

Story

To get to the island of Colchis, Jason and the Argonauts had to pass the Symplegades, two moving rocks that collided when a ship wanted to pass them. The ship of the Argonauts would be destroyed by the rocks. Phineus advised them to send a dove forward, because they could do nothing to the dove so that the rocks would set in motion, and the ship could pass afterwards. This picture shows the dove passing by the rock.

Original meaning

"Safety in business and travel."

Interpretation

- success
- an undertaking, a project will be successful
- the challenge is mastered
- relief
- no danger is imminent
- danger is over

Smaller right picture

A dove must pass rocks.

Story

It is the same story, but the difference is, that the dove has not passed the rocks yet, it still must pass. The dangerous situation is still ahead for the Argonauts.

Original meaning

"Mistrust & precautions are to be taken in relation to a trip."

Interpretation

- to face the challenge
- upcoming, unavoidable obstacles
- attention
- danger
- a dangerous situation
- focus on the task and situation
- no time to stop

F

Queen of Clubs

Original meaning

"A friendly, generous, helpful, fun-loving and carefree woman."

(possible person card)

Big Picture

Three of seven Hesperides.

Story

The picture shows the eternally blooming garden where the tree of golden apples can be found. It is said to be the garden of paradise, somewhere between heaven and earth. Three women are there, three Hesperides, three of the daughters of the evening star, called Aigle, Erytheia and Hespere. They live in the garden to guard the tree with the golden apples. These apples must be guarded strictly, for the legends of the Gods say that whoever eats one of these apples was given eternal life, and this should not be given to men, it was reserved only for the Gods. Once Hercules stole some golden apples with the support of Atlas. For a moment he took off the weight of the heavens on Atlas' shoulders. But the Gods managed to return the apples to the Garden of Paradise and the Hesperides guarded them even more strictly and conscientiously from that moment on.

Original meaning

"Woman of less serious character, problematic existence, poetic, artistic, loves entertainment, play, music and carelessness."

Interpretation

- easiness, lightness, carefree
- thoughtlessness
- carelessness causes trouble
- a warning to be reckless
- difficulties due to careless lifestyle
- a person of a naive, not serious character
- more dreamy than realistic
- immature
- lovers of arts, music, and beauty
- enjoy beautiful sides of life (sometimes too much)
- positive: friendly, generous, and accommodating

Smaller left picture

A panther.

Story

A panther looking into a mirror and seeing his own reflection (but the reflection is different).

Original meaning

"Lavish, debauched woman."

Interpretation

- being too careless has negative consequences
- without responsibility
- financial problems
- unreliability
- see themselves differently, disguise themselves
- hide from the truth

Smaller right picture

A woman.

Story

A woman with a fan in her hand (The original old picture depicted a woman standing next to a golden chair).

Original meaning

"Woman of good company, with good manners, pleasing by her nature and whose company one seeks."

Interpretation

- woman in & of good company
- sometimes loose manners
- open-minded
- someone who is not serious, but whose company is wanted
- someone gets recognition despite ease
- someone to spend beautiful, entertaining moments with
- desired company

K

Jack of Clubs

Original meaning

"A young man, gallant with ladies, skillful, persistent, using all means to achieve his goal."

(possible person card)

Big Picture

Hippomenes & Atalanta.

Story

Atalanta was the daughter of a king of Boeotia and Arcadia and was abandoned as a newborn because her father always wanted to have a son. So, he left the unwanted daughter alone in the wild forest. From that day on, the Gods who witnessed the king's terrible act guarded the baby and it was raised in the forest by a wild bear. Later, hunters found the girl and raised her in their tradition. As a young woman, but due to her fate and the influence of the hunters, she was a more masculine type of woman. Once she returned to the realm of her father, who now appreciated her more for her masculine nature. She did not want to marry and was considered a virgin, and her father allowed her to make a condition to the admirers: they should compete with her in a race; if the admirer would win, he could marry her. If he lost, he would be killed. So, Atalanta, who was always faster than everyone else, lived quite carefree until one day Hippomenes fell in love with her because they both shared the love of nature. And he asked Venus for help, and the goddess Venus saw Atalanta's behavior with great aversion, for everyone should love and be loved. So, she gave Hippomenes three of the golden apples from the garden of the Hesperides. During the race he dropped the apples and Atalanta stopped to pick them up because she was impressed by the shine of the golden apples.

As a result, she lost time and Hippomenes won the race and was allowed to marry her.

Original meaning

"Only with skill and tactics will it be possible to get there."

Interpretation

- trick
- skill
- cunning
- clever action
- you will only achieve something if you use skill and artistry
- list
- sophistication
- intelligence
- scammed
- charm

Smaller left picture

Venus.

Story

Venus sits in her chariot, which is pulled by birds through the clouds.

Original meaning

"You pursue a thought that torments you: Use art & seduction."

Interpretation

- you pursue an idea with love and passion
- use the art of seduction
- passion finds its way and its goal
- pressure to find a way

Smaller right picture

A man & a woman.

Story

An old man in the company of a young girl, making beautiful promises to her.

Original meaning

"You will receive the object of your desire only out of your own interest."

Interpretation

- warning, someone will do anything to get the object of their desire.
- warning of cunning and tricks
- egoism, self-interest
- flattering
- false compliments

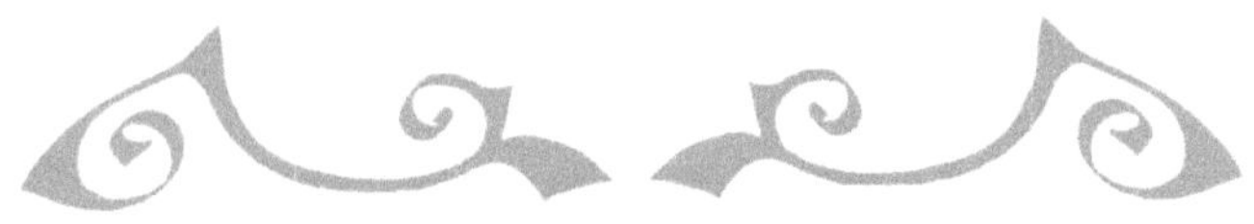

10 of Clubs

Original meaning

"Success in a risky enterprise."

Big Picture

Odysseus & Diomedes.

Story

You see Odysseus and Diomedes together, they defeated King Rhesus, king of Thrace. Rhesus was an ally of the Trojans and thus he was also their opponent. With Odysseus and Diomedes are the wonderful white horses of King Rhesus. To be able to take the horses, they had to run across the battlefield, because it was the only way to escape this situation, there is no other way out, they walked over the dead bodies", (They did not shy away from anything).

Original meaning

„Third Fatality. Great courage that will make you risk your life to take an enemy a degree of strength. The talisman of Mars makes you invulnerable."

(later the background to the seven fatalities and the talismans are mentioned).

Interpretation

- you must face the obstacle and the challenge
- go with courage and strength, if you do not have this, rethink the plan and better stop
- to face the challenge because it will be a success
- this card shows that you can do something difficult
- grow with vigor
- show no fear, be fearless

- overcome themselves
- there is support
- have an ally
- risky ventures
- a risk in general

Smaller left picture

Grapes.

Story

A branch with several grapes, representing joy, celebration, and passion. This is the prediction of imminent peace and silence.

Original meaning

"After the successes, skills and strength are still required."

Interpretation

- after success you still must be strong
- imminent peace
- forthcoming silence
- there will be reason to celebrate
- success, even if it is a risky situation

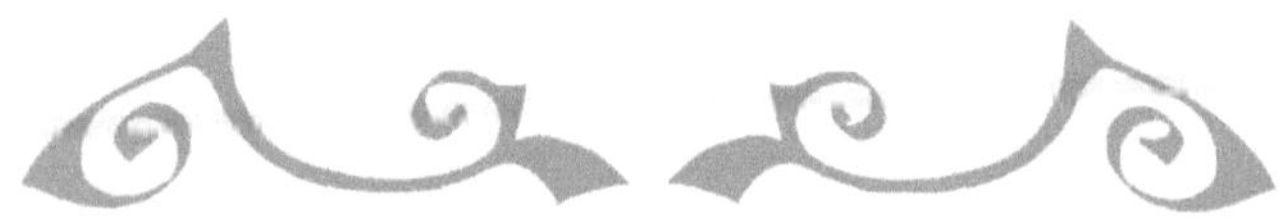

Smaller right picture

Patroclus.

Story

Patroclus has been injured by Hector; he is in his struggle for survival. The war is not over yet.

Original meaning

"Setback in the midst of success."

Interpretation

- setback in success
- don't be too sure of your position you're still vulnerable
- victory is not yet yours
- there is still a risk
- still a risky situation
- strong enemies
- strong obstacles

9 of Clubs

Original meaning

„This card announces success to a merchant; if a person is married, he will be widowed prematurely; a man without good status in society and without assets. If he is adaptable and skillful, he will still earn money, but only by serving the wicked machinations and whims of the great. "

Big Picture

Hercules & Hydra.

Story

You see Hercules fighting the Hydra of Lerna, and each time he severed one of their heads, two new heads grew. But Hercules could win this hopeless battle, because almost all the animals helped him to defeat the dangerous Hydra. Only the cancer did not support Hercules because he was very attached to Hera. Since the day of Hercules' birth in Olympus, Hera felt a deep hatred for her husband Zeus's illegitimate son. Hercules grew up in Olympus and gained immortal power through the cunning Zeus: while Hera slept, Zeus put him to her breast to breastfeed him and Hercules drank the divine milk. Hera was therefore full of hatred and as revenge for this betrayal, she cursed Hercules' soul, which led him to kill his own children. As an atonement, he had to pass 12 trials, including the fight against the Hydra. During the fight, Hera felt the deep devotion of the Cancer to her and therefore made the animal benefit for her malicious intentions: she sent him to bite Hercules - so the Cancer bit Hercules in his toe during the fight, but without success. The cancer was not strong enough and sacrificed his life because of the evil Hera. And although the help of Cancer was not successful, she was deeply sad in her heart about the loss of the animal but also so grateful for the strong devotion of the Cancer, which she learned from no one

else, that she gave the Cancer an eternal place in the sky at night through his own zodiac sign.

Original meaning

"Messenger with intentions and personal interests."

Interpretation

- emotional reactions can cause misfortune
- be attentive and protect yourself
- emotions can be a threat to business
- you can be successful despite making mistakes
- use someone for personal interests
- financial success
- deserved success
- self-awareness, admit mistakes and make amends

Smaller left picture

A merchant on a market.

Story

The picture shows a foreign merchant with his stall, he sells goods in a bazaar to earn money for his living.

Original meaning

"Success, profit."

Interpretation

- good business
- financial success
- profit
- employment

- hard work
- working class

Smaller right picture

A man with money.

Story

The picture shows a man who has a higher position in society - a business owner or a salesman who counts his money, his earnings.

Original meaning

"High- yield loan."

Interpretation

- financial support
- you will have money
- you will get money
- know the terms of this deal
- income
- earnings
- higher position

D

8 of Clubs

Original meaning

"Wedding, marriage."

Big Picture

The alchemist between two test tubes, one of which contains hard and the other volatile material.

Story

The alchemist works and experiments with chemistry in his laboratory, with two test tubes, retorts, to his left and right. The scenery is the mixture of hard and volatile material, the so-called "wedding of Beya and Gabertin". At this point in his experiment, the materials are about to change and transform; two parts that belong to each other and will complement each other can be seen here. This can be equated with the image of "Ying and Yang".

Original meaning

"You want a marriage to come about, it will happen."

Interpretation

- the change needed to come together
- a wedding
- marriage
- the realization of a marriage
- there will be a connection
- connection
- a relationship
- duality

Original meaning

"If you're not careful, your marriage will fall apart."

Interpretation

- no secure and stable relationship
- there is a risk that someone can come into the relationship and endanger it, for example a third party can become annoying
- thread from outside of the relationship
- it's a little careless
- if you are not careful, the private relationship will be broken
- two that are not connected

G

7 of Clubs

Original meaning

"An artist, poet or musician, seduces with his talents, his voice and his nature."

(possible person card)

Big Picture

The Giant & Pan.

Story

Pan is a son of Hermes, the messenger of the Gods, who brought divine inspiration into the world. People worshipped him not only because he was a healer and prophet, but also because of his musical talent, which he demonstrated with the pan flute - this he bequeathed to the Greeks. Known for his love of sex and intimacy, Pan was in a strong love affair with the nymphs - the water fairies. Later, people gave him the appearance and characteristics of the goat as a kind of allegory of the devil and sins, especially because of his sexual pleasures: his countless sexual affairs later caused him trouble. In the picture, we see Pan fleeing from a giant and only escaping it by climbing up the sky to save himself, to maintain the secured and eternal position in the zodiac as Capricorn.

Original meaning

"The person accompanying this card must beware of a seducer."

Interpretation

- success for any kind of artist
- but before seduction, so always keep your head free
- the person accompanied by this card must beware of emotional traps and learn to resist seduction
- seduction, to seduce or getting seduced
- the arts
- creativity
- sensitivity

Smaller left picture

Flames.

Story

You see a fire, a lot of flames burning in a furnace, a fireplace with dangerous sparks.

Original meaning

"Deceptive promises of gifts and wealth."

Interpretation

- false expectations, too high expectations
- false hopes raised by others
- attention is required: deceptive promises of gifts and riches.

Smaller right picture

A man.

Story

You see a craftsman with his tools in his hand - a craftsman holding an object of mechanical form in his hands.
At that time, he belonged to the lower part of society, he belonged to the proletariat, the workers' people.

Original meaning

"An inventive genius who will accumulate fame but little wealth."

Interpretation

- intelligence and craftsmanship
- recognition by others for the work done
- work with your own hands for others, but for less money
- lower compensation
- art can be good, but not always profitable
- inventive genius who knows how to gain fame, but will still have little wealth

H

6 of Clubs

Original meaning

"False reconciliation of two enemies."

Big Picture

Paris & Menelaus.

Story

A scene of the Trojan War: Paris and Menelaus before on the battlefield, preparing for battle. They sacrifice lambs and consult the priest. There is a strong tension between the two and in the whole situation; something will happen, but still nothing seems to be final, even if one already knows that the Gods have doomed Troy.

Original meaning

"You are about to settle a dispute, settle a disagreement or a complicated matter: none of this will happen."

Interpretation

- conflict
- discord
- imminent unrest and fighting
- tension
- any rash action will make it worse
- it is better to be patient and act wisely
- there is a dispute to be settled or an obscure matter to be resolved, but none of this will really be done
- the appearance is deceptive

Smaller left picture

Achilles.

Story

The picture shows Achilles playing a harp, and it is said that Paris was the one who killed Achilles. The image of the harp and its music indicates a deceptive peace.

Original meaning

"Forgetting oneself, boredom, sorrow, madness."

Interpretation

- forget yourself
- insane
- distraction, inattention
- boredom
- sorrow
- despair
- depression
- false peace, deceptive silence

Smaller right picture

Odysseus & Diomedes/ a statue.

Story

Odysseus and Diomedes kidnap the statue of Pallas Athena, the Palladium was considered the heart of Troy. With this statue the security and the existence of Troy was given. With the kidnapping of the statue of the goddess of fortune, however, the downfall of Troy was inevitable. In this small picture you can see that in the scene of the big picture there is not really a situation of decisive consequences, it is just a moment of immense tension. The real downfall of Troy has its origin in the kidnapping the statue of Pallas Athena. And so, the small picture on the right speaks more of an action that has decisive consequences.

Original meaning

"Fourth Fatality. You will gain another measure of power to reach the goal you have set for yourself; if you take the talisman of the sun as an aegis, you will gain honor."

Interpretation

- victory for one, loss for another
- exercise power
- take what you want
- you will gain a certain amount of strength to achieve the goal you are pursuing
- a decisive action with consequences

T

5 of Clubs

Original meaning

"This card announces that someone will betray the trust of their friend by taking what is most expensive & dearest to them."

Big Picture

Helena & Paris.

Story

Helena, who is married to Menelaus, leaves her husband together with Paris, caused by the intrigues of the Gods. Because of her promise of love, the goddess Aphrodite sent Helena (who was the human image of the goddess Aphrodite) into the arms of Paris: so, Helena, who was married to Menelaus, fell in love immortally in Paris. The betrayal kindled by the revenge of the gods is shown here and the victims were human. It is a situation full of conflicts, aggression and tensions, hurt feelings, false pride and by no means a card of love. Helena and Paris were forced to flee to live their love. There was no other way, they were associated with betrayal and deceit and the deceived wanted revenge.

Original meaning

"Bad deed committed within a family."

Interpretation

- mistrust
- betrayal
- breach of trust, but all people are close here
- usually a reference to a triangular relationship or a deception in a relationship with a close friend
- a woman between two men
- someone between two people

- an act of jealousy and envy.
- loss of trust
- treacherous
- separation
- despair
- play someone off against someone

Smaller left picture

A woman praying.

Story

Here is a praying woman: It is Helena, alone and desperate, begging the Gods for help.

Original meaning

"Repentant woman."

Interpretation

- to regret
- remorse
- of the mind and its power
- there is hope, even if it is a desperate situation and everything seems hopeless
- there is a solution

Smaller right picture

Two men.

Story

In the picture you can see Menelaus with Agamemnon. He was betrayed by Helena and insisted on taking revenge.

Original meaning

"Preparations for revenge; family agrees to severe punishment."

Interpretation

- a scam is obvious
- the victim knows everything
- the betrayal was revealed
- the betrayal can no longer remain hidden
- lies come to light
- revenge
- hate
- punishment

4 of Clubs

Original meaning

"Vain, loud, quick-tempered woman - a marriage that does not meet the conditions of desirable happiness."

(possible person card)

Big Picture

The alchemist looks at how the material changes.

Story

In his laboratory, the alchemist looks focused and curious only about what is happening at this moment in his experiment. He focuses on himself and his work without noticing what is happening around him, and the material is still dissolving. He listens to the sound and watches the progress.

Original meaning

"A man subordinates himself to the whims of a woman."

Interpretation

- being trapped in the situation
- being spellbound
- one is subordinate to the whims of the other
- just accept something
- to let something happen
- selfishness
- self-confidence
- proud
- in love relationships, this is always a card that addresses complicated circumstances and times

Smaller left picture

A young woman writing.

Story

In this picture you see a woman writing. She works but seems to belong to a higher social class (on the cards you can often see this on the clothes people wear). She must always focus on her work (writing) to maintain her living standards.

Original meaning

"Educated woman with more fame than really deserved."

Interpretation

- always working, but never enough
- fast fame that will be hard to get
- someone has more prestige than really deserved
- undeserved recognition
- heavy relationship
- hard relationship life

Smaller right picture

A man and a woman.

Story

A "grisette", in French tradition once called a young, unmarried woman, receives the visit of a businessman or a man from the upper class. She reaches out her open hand to receive something from him.

Original meaning

"Woman of pleasure, coquettish."

Interpretation

- someone takes advantage of each other's situation
- self-interest
- emotional abuse
- only give to receive something in return
- a deal
- an agreement
- a kind of affair
- services to have pleasures
- be coquettish

3 of Clubs

Original meaning

"A joyful surprise in a moment of grief."

Big Picture

The alchemist (kneels and) looks at the material in the test tube over the fire.

Story

The alchemist looks expectantly at his test tube over the fireplace, what happens to the material after it is combined with heat? You see the glass bottle with the material that will be dissolved by the heat; the alchemist examines the progress of his experiment, and he now knows that everything has been done right, and there will be a positive change.

Original meaning

"This state of the material is the symbol of a mixed/ connected existence, laboriously worked out, which is soon present in abundance through an honorable marriage."

Interpretation

- something gets stronger and more stable, connects
- the bond of a relationship will be as solid as the bond of a marriage
- in uncertain situations, this card brings peace and security
- after the effort comes the reward, the appreciation you deserve
- this state of matter is the symbol of an exhausting existence in the beginning, which will soon be an enrichment
- togetherness

Smaller left picture

Three younger women.

Story

The three women are the daughters of the Egyptian god Anubis, who was responsible for the well-being of the deceased. In ancient Egypt, the deceased received many gifts for life after death. The daughters of Anubis helped to take care of the deceased and are therefore often shown with goods at a market. The daughters were also responsible for earthly connections and were also responsible for marriages.

Original meaning

"Good anticipation."

Interpretation

- good providence
- good prospects
- good fate
- an emotional and material opportunity
- recovery
- caring
- a sign of someone having more children

Smaller right picture

A goddess with a woman reading a letter.

Story

The goddess in the picture is Martea, she represents the goddess of inheritance, next to her is a woman, a will is read.

Original meaning

"Change of position, inheritance."

Interpretation

- change
- change of position,
- a situation becomes better or more stable through financial, material aspects (inheritance, financial contribution, professional promotion)
- financial contribution by another person, partner
- a contract
- an official document, will
- a private document

2 of Clubs

Original meaning

"Gold will come to you, either by inheritance or gift."

Big Picture

Women on a riverbank.

Story

In this scene you can see women drawing gold from the river Pactolus. One of the legends surrounding this river says: King Midas saved Dionysus' lover, Silena, from the captivity of the Phrygians. God Dionysus was so grateful to him that he decided to fulfill one of the greatest wishes of Midas. But Midas was unfortunately not very smart (so also show him some pictures with the ears of a donkey), and he wished that everything he would touch from now on would turn into pure gold. He was overwhelmed by this idea. At first it was amazing, and the euphoria was great, but even Midas quickly realized the misfortune that came with this gift: he could not even eat, because his food became gold as soon as he touched it. Close people and friends fled for fear, because they did not want to be touched by him. Therefore, Midas asked Dionysus to remove this spell from him. Dionysus told him that the only way to get rid of this spell was to take a bath in the river Pactolus, which Midas did. Since then, gold has been flowing in these waters.

Original meaning

"In an unexpected situation, you will meet a man who will provide you with a lot of gold."

Interpretation

- abundance
- financial success
- material success
- reward
- debts will be paid
- under unexpected circumstances you meet a person who supports you materially
- money & financial matters

Smaller left picture

A bird and a rock.

Story

A bird sitting on a rock. The bird sits here on the top of the rock (compared to the other picture, the bird has already climbed on the rock). He's upstairs, resting and looking out.

Original meaning

"Wealth with name, title and fame."

Interpretation

- famous
- riches, make a name for yourself
- come to high honors
- title of fame, official title, official title
- abundance
- recognition
- price
- award
- have achieved something

Smaller right picture

A bird and a rock.

Story

A bird sitting on the ground below in front of a rock, ready to climb, ready to fly on the rocks. But he still must do this in this picture, and he is not yet at the top of the rock.

Original meaning

"Wealth without name and title."

Interpretation

- no fame, no glory
- riches without great prestige in society
- success will always come only through own work and efforts
- nothing is given to you
- there's still a lot to do
- striving for recognition and wealth
- trying to achieve a goal
- the beginning

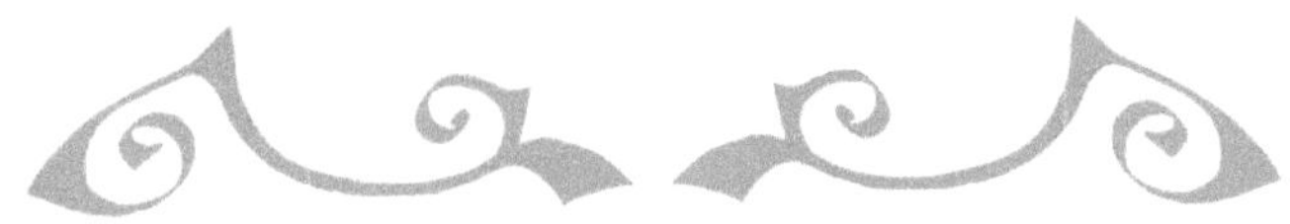

Smaller left picture

A test tube, retort filled with material.

Story

In this picture you can see how the elements connect in the test tube and form a mixture of solid and volatile.

Original meaning

"You'll be happily married."

Interpretation

- two becomes one
- strong and secure relationship
- unification
- fusion
- marriage
- happy family life

Smaller right picture

Again, a test tube, retort filled with material.

Story

In this picture you can see the hard material on the ground and the volatile in the air. Two materials that do not bond, the hard and the volatile, remain separated from each other.

Ace of Clubs

Original meaning

"Wealth and fame are won by an unusual deal."

Big Picture

Jason & the Golden Fleece.

Story

The scene is still the island of Colchis, and you can see Jason in the sacred forests. He is already the owner of the Golden Fleece, which now hangs behind him in a tree. Even if this success was not brought about by him alone, because he was only able to master all challenges with the help of the king's daughter and priestess Medea. But why did Jason conquer the Golden Fleece? His father was dethroned by his own brother Pelias. And to reclaim the throne, Jason was to bring the Golden Fleece to Pelias, who wanted it in his possession. But the truth was that Pelias awaited Jason's death on this journey. But Pelias was proved wrong by Jason's success and his return. In the picture you can see Jason defending the fleece in the last battle, but it is already certain that the conquest is over - he also won this battle. There is no challenge for him now, only to return home.

Original meaning

"Great success."

Interpretation

- success in all areas
- success through a deal
- success with the support of others, with allies
- escape a ruse, an intrigue
- no sacrifice

Smaller left picture

A man & a woman on a ship.

Story

The man and the woman in the picture are Jason and Medea on the ship, the Argo. The journey is over, and Jason and Medea return home together.

Original meaning

"Return from a journey."

Interpretation

- a return
- a comeback (after a successful trip)
- good news
- homecoming
- luck & success
- fortune
- one of the best cards in the game
- win someone over

Smaller right picture

A man & a woman on a festival event.

Story

The man and the woman in the picture are Jason and Medea at a celebration. Jason had become Medea's secret love during his ventures, she loved him so much - here they are together at a social event. However, they were forced to hide their relationship and wait until they could finally leave the island of Colchis together. The departure from the island seems to be an escape, a liberation for both, but the social occasion less so.

Original meaning

"Amidst opulence, pleasure, dissatisfaction and compulsion."

Interpretation

- social duties can distract, therefore be careful and not distract
- don't lose focus on what you want
- hiding Intentions
- hide feelings
- hiding plans
- play a game
- keeping secrets
- do not share intentions and plans with the public

The Suit of Hearts

King of Hearts

Original meaning

"A rich, wise man will obey you if you follow his example and advice in every way."

(possible person card)

Big Picture

An older man.

Story

The picture shows an older man sitting in his library, thinking, looking back on his life, his experiences, but also looking forward - because he knows he has still a lot to do here on earth, he still has tasks to do. Even if it is only to help someone with words and deeds. The traditional card also features a clock near a globe in the background. This is the symbol that he still has time to fulfill the tasks of life. But whatever this person will do, it will be well planned, well thought out and always fully prepared. Since this man makes wise decisions, he knows life, but only because he has already had many painful experiences.

Original meaning

"Prudence and wisdom in all steps, desires and undertakings of life."

Interpretation

- a well-thought-out plan will be successful
- Wisdom and wisdom in all steps, decisions, or undertakings of life
- experience
- wisdom

- advice
- there is still time to start or to continue
- this card is the equivalent of the King of Clubs, who also made terrible mistakes to get to his wisdom, but did not learn from it for himself

Smaller left picture

An open book.

Story

An open book on a desk, the Book of the Laws of Solomon.

Original meaning

"Enlightened, learned, profound mind."

Interpretation

- enlightened
- educated
- profound
- down-to-earth
- realistically
- the science
- the laws of science
- the laws of justice

Smaller right picture:

An open book.

Story

Another picture with an open book on a desk, this time the book is the Bible.

Original meaning

"Peaceful life, in charity and in religion."

Interpretation

- spiritual or religious person
- be connected to spirit
- to be connected to the spiritual world
- peaceful living
- everything is done out of charity, because of faith and religion
- the faith, the religion
- a person trusts in God and religion
- spiritual or religious education

E

Queen of Hearts

Original Meaning

"A woman of utmost gentleness, of excellent heart, from whom you will receive great services."

(possible person card)

Big Picture

(Zeus &) Astraea.

Story

The picture shows Astraea, the daughter of Zeus and Themis, who is sometimes considered the goddess of justice and the laws of nature. Once upon a time people on earth lived in deep harmony with the immortal Gods, but the years passed and were subject to change: times became rougher and more evil. The once golden age became the iron age. And in the meantime, the Gods had gradually abandoned the people and the earth. Only Astraea lived on earth, with the great hope of bringing justice, goodness, and harmony to the people. Disappointed, Astraea lost patience and hope passed away. So, she also left the earth and with it the chance for people to live in harmony and peace with nature. From then on there was no more justice and peace among the people. In gratitude and admiration for the commitment of his daughter, her father Zeus gave his daughter a new heavenly domicile with the constellation Virgo.

Original Meaning

"You need protection from weakness, though the purity of your heart and the elevation of your soul will likely guarantee it; but be sure to avoid bad company."

Interpretation

- seeing with the heart and purity
- see positive aspects
- believe in the good (in a person)
- good intentions
- sometimes need of help and support
- you need protection from weakness, though the purity of your heart and your pure soul can guarantee you
- be careful and avoid bad company
- kindness
- sincere and good intentions
- innocence
- naivety

Smaller left picture

A woman watching a bird.

Story

The woman you see here is a nun, watching a bird of paradise flying in the sky.

Original Meaning

"Virtuous woman who cannot distract from her duties."

Interpretation

- living in hope
- living in prayer
- having faith
- living in solitude
- retreating
- escape or stay away from conventional life or pleasure
- virtuous person who cannot distract from their duties

- yearning
- renunciation

Smaller right picture

A woman playing organ.

Story

The picture shows a young woman playing the organ.

Original Meaning

"Good inspiration will give you wise protection, you will achieve the good."

Interpretation

- love
- devotion
- inspiration
- the arts show the way and guide these people
- good inspirations will put you under wise protection, protect
- you will feel comfortable, safe and healthy

Jack of Hearts

Original Meaning

"You will make the acquaintance of a young man with whom you will befriend and receive services."

(possible person card)

Big Picture

Dionysus & Zeus.

Story

The scenery shows us Dionysus, the son of Zeus and Semele, on his way through the ancient world. He wandered a lot and is now thirsty, but at first no fountain was visible on his way and so his father Zeus appeared to him from a cloud in the form of a man with the head of a ram to show him the way to a fountain (It can be said that the fountain of youth is meant, because Dionysus was always described as a very young man). Zeus, as so often, was in the company of an eagle as a sign of peace and love (in the Christian tradition, the eagle was replaced by a dove).

Original Meaning

"A man ashamed of his troubles, looking everywhere for someone to do him a favor."

Interpretation

- help & support in general
- help & support at the right time
- accept that you need help
- the help & support brings you to the goal
- alone it is not possible to advance
- lack of independence

- depending on others
- youth, beauty
- gift

Smaller left picture

Moths.

Story

The picture shows moths searching for the light, flying around a candle.

Original Meaning

"In a society in which you are invited and in which you go with the intention of taking the opportunity to talk about your difficulties, promises are made to you that are never kept. "

Interpretation

- promises not kept by others
- false reassurance
- false protection
- illusion
- company of others only in good times

Smaller right picture

A cornucopia.

Story

The picture shows a bulging cornucopia on a table.

Original Meaning

"If it is a gentleman, he will receive great help from young ladies. A young lady, if she is wise, she will marry a young gentleman whom she did not expect."

Interpretation

- support in abundance
- abundance in general
- you get the helping hand you need, material, emotional (money, food)
- when it comes to a Gentleman, he will get a lot of help from a young (married or tied) woman.
- when it comes to a Lady, when she makes a wise choice, the husband or partner will be a well-off young man
- a situation where you don't have to compete
- gift
- good fate

E

10 of Hearts

Original meaning

"Young girl, sincere and without will."

(possible person card)

Big Picture

The alchemist is observing the results of his work so far.

Story

The picture shows the alchemist in his laboratory. Still at work, here currently with crossed arms, observing how the light grey material continues to transform during the process. These are the final steps of the experiment, and it seems to be successful. This successful step is described by a small white foam crown on the grey stone; it is like the birth of Venus from the foam, the sea - so this card is just as often about love things & heart matters.

Original meaning

"A man looks with joy at the merits and benefits of a woman."

Interpretation

- love
- new love that brings happiness
- new successful projects
- new ways
- one looks with joy and without envy at the graces, the gifts of life and merits of someone else
- the beginning of something
- the start

Smaller left picture

A woman.

Story

On the traditional card you see a woman playing the piano, full of emotion and passion.

Original meaning

"You are looking for a rich worker who deals only with art and amenities."

Interpretation

- to do what you do, always with joy and passion (spirituality & art)
- free of pressure
- without obligation
- the work, even if it is so hard and exhausting, is only for entertainment and personal pleasure and not for the income or support of life
- in the negative sense: unprofitable art

Smaller right picture

A woman.

Story

On the traditional illustration you see a woman with an embroidery hoop. The woman works with her own hands and hard work for others. Others see the result, but not the effort associated with this handiwork.

Original meaning

"You are looking for a hardworking, young girl from an honest family."

Interpretation

- diligence
- talent
- diligent with sincere family or private background
- lack of appreciation by others
- effort of work is ignored by others
- profit from others and feeling good with it but not reward them fairly

P

9 of Hearts

Original meaning

"In every position we will have the respect and friendship of all."

(possible person card)

Big Picture

Hercules and the Nemean Lion.

Story

The picture shows Hercules fighting a lion - It is known from ancient mythology that Hercules had to survive 12 challenges to get rid of the sin he committed by murdering his children. Caused by the jealous Hera, he murdered in a sacred ceremony his own children instead of the animals. This was not the first time that Hera felt deepest hatred and jealousy. Hercules was the real son of Alcmene, and Zeus wanted Hercules to be promised great things even before his birth. So, he wanted to bequeath a kingdom to the firstborn - Hera delayed this birth with all her power and another child became firstborn. The second fraud against Hera was by secretly breastfeeding Hercules on her breast. The fight against the lion was his first challenge, which had to be mastered: The lion, whose skin was made of metal and stone, drove its mischief near the city of Nemea and frightened entire villages and their inhabitants. Hera sent this lion there, and after a long battle, Hercules succeeded in strangling the lion with his bare hands. The lion's skin, which from then on was worn as a cape, served Hercules from then on as protection from enemies. This animal also found its place in the firmament in the form of the constellation, because as well as the Cancer, Hera was also owed thanks to the lion.

Original meaning

"A useful, courageous man exposed to all dangers for the peace of his country."

Interpretation

- fight with success through your own bravery, courage and strength
- Use of courage and strength, also for others and not only for yourself
- bravely
- strength
- commitment that pays off
- struggles for recognition
- fight for friendships
- great efforts

Smaller left picture

A woman & a man.

Story

A woman is crowned, honored, and distinguished by a man.

Original meaning

"A hardworking and wise girl (young woman) that everyone protects and respects."

Interpretation

- recognition
- official recognition
- be honored by others
- diligent and wise person who everyone appreciates and respects
- recognition based on personal nature and character

Smaller right picture

Two men.

Story

Here the traditional image of this card refers to Napoleon handing a medal to one of his soldiers as a reward for his commitment and loyalty.

Original meaning

"Bravery, merit, reward."

Interpretation

- recognition by deserved honor and deserved respect due to deeds
- success is coming soon
- success through bravery and courageous action
- success through risk tolerance
- success through cohesion
- stand up for someone
- merit
- reward

R

8 of Hearts

Original meaning

"Secret joy, success in something you have long wished for."

Big Picture

An eagle.

Story

The picture shows an eagle flying away with a toad in his claws and crossing a pond. The eagle is the king of birds, the king of the skies and it is reported that only he can look at the sun without blinking. The eagle is depicted here as a powerful being capable of eliminating evil. in this scene the evil is unfortunately represented by the little toad, which is due to a contemporary symbolism. The water is a symbol for the feelings and the soul of a man and the bad leaves the soul and will no longer cause any harm from now on, so that the loss equals a healing.

Original meaning

"Loss or removal of a known person or family that has caused you harm."

Interpretation

- loss or removal of someone known to or related to
- loss and removal of someone who was harmful
- something will happen that turns the bad situation into a good one
- a misfortune will become a fortune
- a change (positive change)
- a kind of happiness in an unpleasant situation
- often only visible in retrospective

- looking back in time, and realizing misfortune was greatest happiness.
- to let go
- letting go
- a wish is fulfilled
- release
- relief that someone disappears
- relief and joy that a bad influence, a burden will be gone

Smaller left picture

A tomb.

Story

There is a grave in this picture and a flame fluttering over it and the grave is gently touched by a plant.

Original meaning

"Heritage of minor importance."

Interpretation

- a gift (even if it is small, it is a gift)
- a farewell gift
- a heritage of low value
- a small legacy
- something remains
- only a memory

Smaller right picture

A woman.

Story

A woman stands at a grave and cries bitterly.

Original meaning

"You have a rival, but soon you won't have him."

Interpretation

- there's a rival, but soon the rival will disappear
- one who caused harm is left behind, yet the soul must heal
- the soul must recover, but it will recover
- it takes time for joy to return
- patience
- time is needed

7 of Hearts

Original Meaning

"There is a deep friendship in this card that you have no idea about; however, you will learn with sorrow about marrying someone else."

Big Picture

The Alchemist adds something to the material.

Story

In the alchemist's laboratory, you can now see that the material in the bottle has hardened again, almost like a stone. Something is needed to change the condition of the material. The alchemist therefore adds some liquid to the material that has become stone to create a new reaction. What was once hard is now becoming soft, and the action of the solvent is necessary to make this change possible.

Original Meaning

"The stone arrived at this stage represents the entrance and exit, and indicates visits of all kinds."

Interpretation

- this indicates visits of all kinds, meetings
- come and go
- move, movement
- activity, initiative
- messages, news, messages
- new effects, impulses, new impulses
- get things started, the first step
- it is important to pay more attention to the loved one
- change is inevitable, is necessary

- twists and turns in (relationship) life
- uncertain outcome

Smaller left picture

Two men.

Story

The picture shows a postman and a man, the postman delivering a parcel to the man, a message.

Original Meaning

"Unpleasant visits, painful news."

Interpretation

- this image stands for disturbing and disappointing news
- unpleasant visits
- unpleasant encounters
- painful news

Smaller right picture

A man and a woman.

Story

This picture shows a postman and a woman, the postman handing over a letter to the woman.

Original Meaning

"You will receive a visit that will make you feel happy."

Interpretation

- an invitation
- good news
- a gift,
- visit is pleasant, joyful
- pleasant encounter
- pleasant meeting
- an event, a visit, a message will make you happy

NOTE on the traditional card you can see on the left picture the gentleman with the postman and the package and on the right picture the postman who hands the letter to the lady.

According to the instructions from 1845, the bad and the good news are also assigned to the left picture with the only difference that the instructions reversed the motives of these pictures. Even if the card on the left shows the picture of the two men, the instruction on the left described a picture of a lady and a letter, with the interpretation of bad news and on the right the instruction described a picture with a man and a package, that contains good news.

The message of the pictures from the point of view of the positions is therefore the same, but the pictures exchanged: The lady receives the bad messages with the letter and the gentleman the good with the package.

6 of Hearts

Original meaning

"Nobility, honors, high position."

This card promises a couple a happy time.

Big Picture

The alchemist has completed his work.

Story

The alchemist at the end of his work, it is the last step of his experiment in the alchemist's laboratory. But the alchemist is tired of his work, he sits in his chair. Now it is time to rest. He has got the certainty that his work was successful. He was able to assemble the materials and turn them into real gold (he found the philosopher's stone). This success is the work of a long road that was difficult to walk, but he did it. Many attempts and criticism made him not to stop and persevere, because he believed in his success. No one and no situation could ever stop him.

Original meaning

"This state, in which the stone turns into gold, is the symbol of a long, happy career."

Interpretation

- this state of the "gold turned stone" is the symbol of a long successful career
- luck
- fortune
- honor
- to succeed

- success
- money, wealth
- true love
- living a dream
- fulfilment of wishes

Smaller left picture

A couple.

Story

The picture shows a couple. An old rich lady with a young man near her; a man is in search of love and finds love with this lady (she seems to be older - this was not usual this time).

Original meaning

"Marriage proposal."

Interpretation

- one loves and will be lucky and both have advantages within this relationship, be it in social position and in personal desires
- an offer
- a marriage proposal
- a marriage in a high position
- an unusual connection
- a younger person prefers an older person
- a relationship not accepted by society

Smaller right picture

A couple.

Story

Again, the picture shows a couple, but this time the man seems to be older, and this was common for that time. He confesses a love and proposes to the lady. An elderly man who does everything unconditionally for a young lady: he gives his life, his heart, his fortune to her.

Original meaning

"A woman courted by a gentleman."

Interpretation

- they one loves and will be lucky and both have advantages within this relationship, be it in social position and personal desires
- an offer
- a marriage proposal
- a marriage in a high position
- an older person prefers a younger person
- a relationship accepted by society

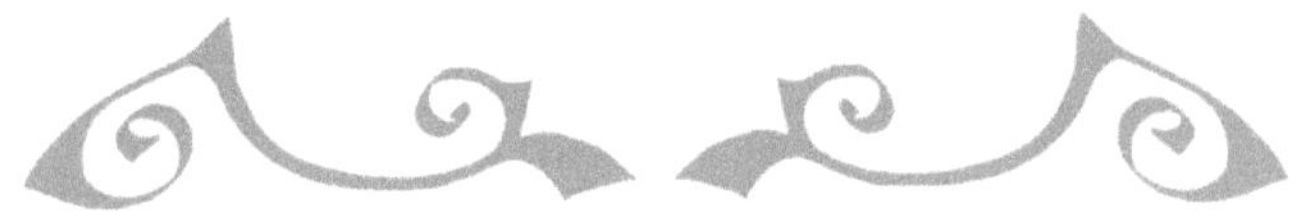

N

5 of Hearts

Original meaning

"A statesman receives proposals from extraordinary envoys - interests to be protected."

Big Picture

Three men.

Story

The traditional big picture shows three men in a palace: a king, a statesman or a governor receives two men for audience. The different, foreign styles of men's clothing are the indications that people of different countries or cultures meet. They wear traditional clothing from their countries of origin.

Original meaning

"Great personalities from foreign nations came to take care of the affairs of their country."

Interpretation

- negotiations
- diplomacy
- politics
- state affairs
- business (executive floor)
- abroad
- foreign countries and foreign cultures
- colorful society
- group of different cultures (salad bowl or melting pot)

Smaller left picture

A parrot.

Story

A parrot is kept as a pet and is chained so that it cannot fly away.

(Due to the exotic animal at that time, the meaning of the map in relation to distant and foreign countries is underlined here as a whole)

Original meaning

"Loss of freedom."

Interpretation

- loss of freedom
- limited possibilities
- restrictions
- setbacks
- be dependent
- the weaker part
- adverse situation

Smaller right picture

A tree.

Story

An orange tree with its flowers, which partly already bears fruit.

(The exotic fruit of that time also underlines the importance of the card in relation to distant and foreign countries).

Original meaning

"Loyal but cunning and skillful statesman."

Interpretation

- fruits of success
- successful business or negotiations
- bear responsibility
- loyal companion/ companion, but nevertheless cunning and skillful
- advantageous, favored situation
- good conditions
- diplomacy
- politics
- business matters
- foreign countries

F

4 of Hearts

Original meaning

"Harmful advice."

Big Picture

Venus & Cupid.

Story

You can see two dolphins in the picture; these animals were seen as soul bearers/ soul companions. They accompany you from here to the other side, it is a scenery in the river Euphrates. There are two important people who ride the dolphin: Venus and Cupid. Venus, the goddess of love, Venus protects people in rough times of emotional life, and her son who brings love into the world. But not only in a positive way, because it is love that also causes the greatest pain. Also, Cupid sometimes makes a person react because of his natural sex drive and lust and therefore this card can also show affairs. It should be noted that since Venus, born from the foam of water, the card represents a protection on difficult journeys to the sea.

Original meaning

"Escape from the paternal roof."

Interpretation

- unplanned, unexpected departure
- an escape
- escape from the "paternal roof"
- escape from home
- difficulties are not overcome well
- uncertain life situations
- emotional conflicts

- unbridled passion
- follow the passion & desire
- passion
- infidelity
- trip
- short trip

Smaller left picture

A man and two women.

Story

A man is with his wife, his partner, and yet another woman stands by his side. Secretly, the man passes on a message to the other woman.

Original meaning

"The first consequence of bad advice is a couple's quarrel."

Interpretation

- scammed
- treacherous
- dishonesty
- unfaithful
- one person between two other
- a relationship threatens to break
- another person harms a relationship

Smaller right picture

A soldier.

Story

On the picture of the traditional card is a soldier - he guards a ship.

Original meaning

"Escape the company of people who are able to give harmful advice."

Interpretation

- difficulties threaten if there are no well-prepared activities (for example, a trip)
- it is important to pay attention to other people around you: not everyone will give good advice
- be careful, someone tends to do harm
- refraining from people who set a bad or harmful example is important and necessary
- you should only rely on what you know & see
- it is important to protect yourself and your belongings
- the whole situation calls for caution

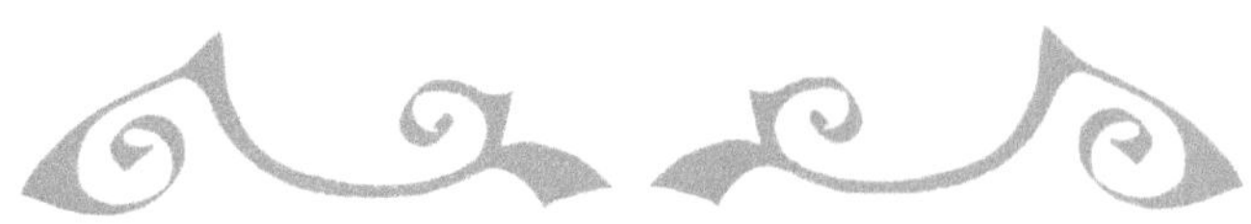

F

3 of Hearts

Original meaning

"A genius."

(possible person card)

Big Picture

The Cynocephale.

Story

The picture shows a Cynocephales, a dog-headed mythical creature. In one hand he holds a scroll and in the other hand a stick with which he writes sacred words of fate in the sand. There are many myths about this card: it is also said that it is Anubis on that card, Anubis was the god of the deceased, he took care of them and led them to the other world. Traditionally, a papyrus with the deceased's name was placed on the mummy's chest so that the deceased could find spiritual peace. This interpretation was supported by the spiritual meaning of this card. But in the origin and in the way the Cynocephale is represented und the drawing of the environment on the card excludes the connection to Egypt. The Cynocephales were seen differently depending on the region and the culture of that region. Here the man with a dog's head takes a religious, peaceful, and very wise position.

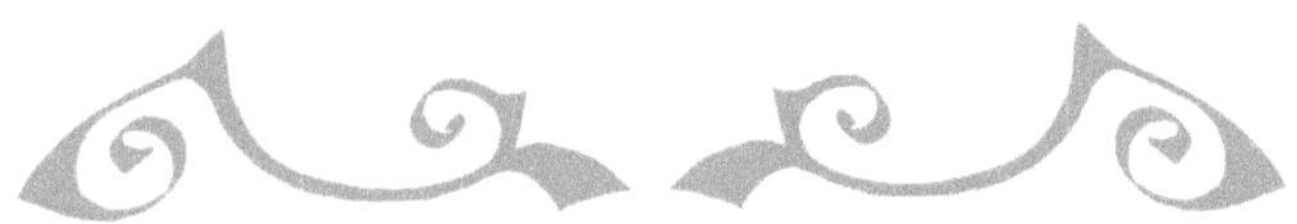

Original meaning

"Invention, mental work."

Interpretation

- intentions
- important thoughts
- (spiritual) science
- knowledge
- intelligence
- spirituality
- spiritual consciousness
- religion, believes
- success in the occult profession
- card of the Spirit
- one of the best cards in the Grand Lenormand

Smaller left picture

A man.

Story

A man stands next to a sundial, but the hands of the clock are still in the shade.

Original meaning

"Unrecognized genius who suffers from the injustice of his rivals."

Interpretation

- unknown genius
- unrecognized genius
- the injustice of the lack of recognition and understanding of others

- you are in the shade
- success is "overshadowed", hard to enjoy success

Smaller right picture

A man.

Story

The traditional small right image of the card shows a man burning a laurel branch.

Original meaning

"A brilliant man, to whom all bow."

Interpretation

- recognition for own work
- recognition
- high recognition, high honors
- genius man everyone admires
- but you don't really believe in yourself or trust yourself without any doubt

2 of Hearts

Original meaning

"Man of integrity, selfless."

(possible person card)

Big Picture

A dog.

Story

The picture shows a lawn, with some trees on the edge, possibly a forest begins here, and the meadow is an open space in front of it; a group of partridges fly away, they are followed by a dog - he has very probably chased them away. Forests were often considered sacred in ancient tradition and this picture shows a kind of idyll. Unfortunately, disturbed by the cute partridges - once they were a symbol of grace and desire, but unfortunately this later changed into the symbol of temptation and so the birds became a bad metaphor. In this scene, the temptation (the partridges) is deterred by the truth and loyalty (the dog). There is no room for temptation in a "holy place". The dog was already considered by Mlle. Lenormand herself as a friend and faithful companion of people and associated with those values.

Original meaning

"Administrator, honest official, just, faithful, slave to his word."

Interpretation

- sincere
- sincerity
- fair
- faithful

- fidelity
- honest
- honesty
- loyal
- loyalty
- resist the temptation
- trust
- trustworthy
- friendship

Smaller left picture

A hermit.

Story

A hermit sits in front of his hut.

Original meaning

"No vile flattery will echo in your head."

Interpretation

- incorruptible
- reliable
- no flattery affects the mind
- withdrawn
- balanced
- inner calmness
- inner peace

Smaller right picture

A fountain.

Story

A fountain surrounded by greenery, perhaps in a park, with a beautiful water feature.

Original meaning

"You are surrounded by flatterers; your integrity is shaken."

Interpretation

- unreliable
- unreliability
- you are surrounded by flatterers
- someone's integrity is fragile
- unfaithful acquaintances
- lightness
- lack of seriousness
- superficiality
- superficial friendship
- only acquaintances
- not being true friends

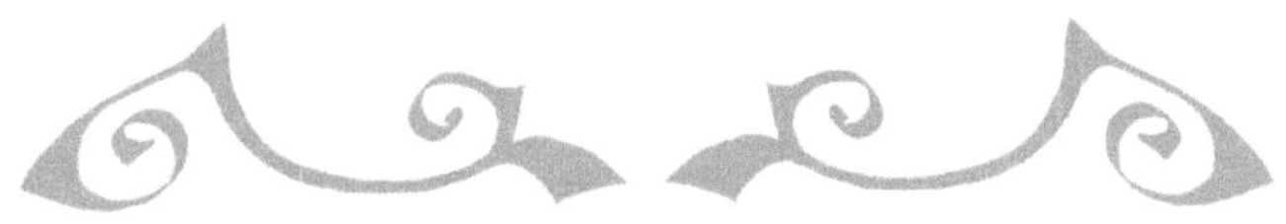

Z

Ace of Hearts

Original meanings

"Relatives."

Big Picture

Danaos and his daughters.

Story

The picture shows the family of the Danaides, Danaos with his 50 daughters. Danaos was at odds with his brother Aigyptos, the father of fifty sons. One day Aigyptos decided to reconcile himself with his brother and proposed to marry their children together to reunite the families. Danaos agreed, but it was a ruse, for he ordered each of his daughters to kill their men on the wedding night. The daughters followed the father's orders and murdered their men, except for one of the daughters, Hypermnestra did not follow her father's orders. A conflict ends terribly, and Aigyptos fled from Greece to Aroe and died shortly thereafter.

Original meanings

"Family."

Interpretation

- family
- relatives
- kinship
- the family environment
- closer circle
- the private environment
- everything that happens in the home
- unification

- celebration
- festivity
- apartment, property, real estate

Smaller left picture

An incense burner.

Story

The picture shows an incense burner, with this is smoked, potpourri is burned.

Original meanings

"Family with ambiguous morality, disagreement, society that is dangerous to frequent."

Interpretation

- family with double morality
- disagreement
- discord
- distance between family members
- distance between each other
- do not live together
- be divided
- treating people with caution
- people with bad influence

Smaller right picture

A spacious columned hall, a hallway, part of a cathedral.

Story

The columns are the supporting columns of a large cathedral, church, where people pray, where you can find peace, silence, and protection.

Original meanings

"United family, protection."

Interpretation

- peaceful family life
- peaceful coexistence
- family reunion
- a meeting
- belonging
- protection
- mutual protection
- safety net
- security

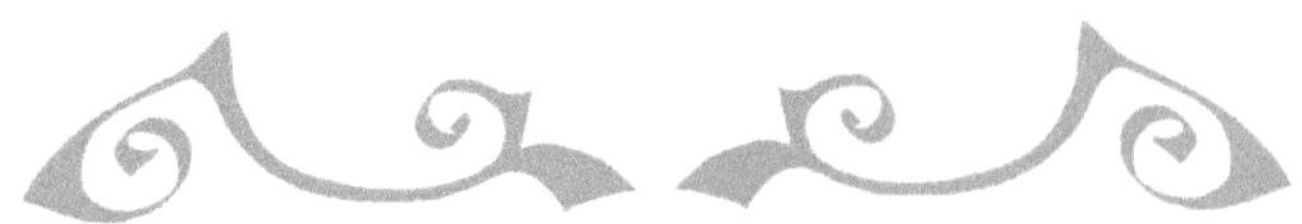

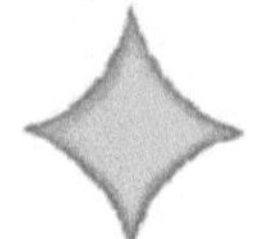

The Suit of Diamonds

King of Diamonds

Original meaning

"A helpful man, without fuss, courageous, open-hearted, for whom one must take care."

(possible person card)

Big Picture

Cadmus & Minerva.

Story

Cadmus was a prince and the brother of Europa who was kidnapped by Zeus. Her father sent his son Cadmus and his other two sons and his one daughter to search for their sister Europa throughout the ancient world. The siblings of Cadmus gave up, but Cadmus continued to wander the world tirelessly, asking everywhere for his sister. One day he finally reached Rhodes. The goddess Athena admired Cadmus for his perseverance and commitment and told him that the island of Rhodes would soon be plagued by a snake plague and that he should flee to protect himself. At that time, Minerva ruled over the island of Rhodes, and he helped Minerva protect her empire by giving her a hidden message: he gave Minerva a vase with the inscription that the island of Rhodes will soon be devastated by snakes.

Original meaning

"Services offered by an unknown."

Interpretation

- help
- support
- help from a stranger

- help from a stranger
- surprising, unexpected help
- help in exchange for favors
- ambitious
- activity
- commitment
- to have an open heart
- to be without prejudices towards others

Smaller left picture

A woman & a scarab.

Story

The small picture on the left shows a woman holding a scarab with outstretched wings.

Original meaning

"Service in exchange for favors."

Interpretation

- service in exchange for favors
- helping each other
- get something in return for the help you give
- offer money as support
- one hand washes the other

Smaller right picture

A pig under a tree.

Story

A crow sits in a tree and drops the fruits of the tree, a pig under the tree eats these fruits.

Original meaning

"Service to someone lower than yourself."

Interpretation

- a humble person does you a great service
- an action helps someone who has less than you
- have the benefit of something that someone else no longer needs
- value used things
- value things others do disrespect
- partnership of convenience

Queen of Diamonds

Original meaning

"Slanderous, evil woman who only enjoys doing evil."

(possible person card)

Big Picture

Eris.

Story

This is where it all began: It is the wedding of Peleus and the goddess Thetis. Eris, the goddess of discord and strife, was not invited because of her vicious character. But she did not accept that she was excluded from this event, and so she nevertheless appeared at the wedding. With her very personal gift: she threw an apple on the table with the dedication: "the most beautiful". Here lie the roots of the Trojan War, the scenery to which this card belongs. Still at the festival, Aphrodite, Hera, and Athena began to argue over the "bone of contention". To put an end to this disaster, Zeus caused Paris to make the decision which of the goddesses was the most beautiful. He should then hand over the apple. And Paris gave the apple to Aphrodite, for it was she who had promised in exchange to give him eternal love with the most beautiful woman on earth; this later proved fatal. Helena, the promised lady, was already married to Menelaus. Thus, Paris kidnapped Helena and the beginning of the war for Troy was made (the prophets said that Paris was the one who would bring about the downfall of Troy). Meanwhile, Eris was also on the side of the winners: discord was born and even the marriage between Peleus and Thetis will break due to a misunderstanding after the birth of her son Achilles.

Original meaning

"An event that will lead to debates between several ladies."

Interpretation

- jealousy
- envy
- resentment
- rivalry
- something that creates conflicts between people
- gloating
- self-interest
- malicious intentions

Smaller left picture

A snake.

Story

A snake on a tree, in a nest there are eggs from a bird; the snake will eat them.

Original meaning

"Threat of revenge."

Interpretation

- threat of revenge
- harms
- loss
- danger
- rejection
- malicious intentions

Smaller right picture

Paris & Aphrodite.

Story

Paris has made his choice, and he hands over the apple to Aphrodite.

Original meaning

"A woman is happy about an award."

Interpretation

- honor
- recognition
- beauty
- admiration
- compliments
- a kind of award
- a bonus
- a reward
- make someone happy
- flatter someone

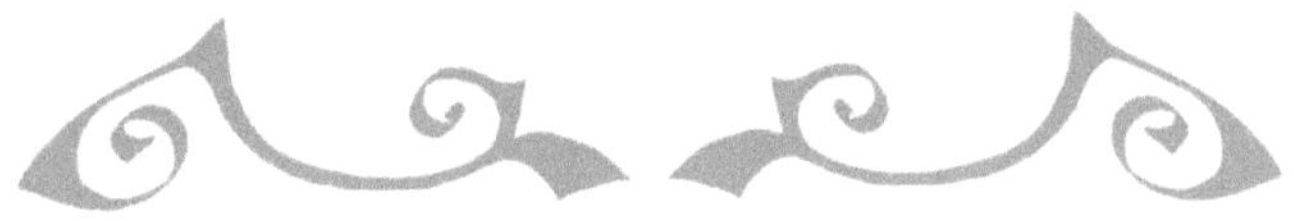

T

Jack of Diamonds

Original meaning

"A cunning and skillful young man who brings an important message."

(possible person card)

Big Picture

Odysseus at the palace of Lycomedes.

Story

The story goes that Menelaus began planning his war against Troy after losing his relationship with Helena and the breach of trust his wife had committed. He needed soldiers, an army. Odysseus was a part of it, but they also needed the support of Achilles to finally win. They had gained this knowledge when they questioned the seer Calchas, so they went in search of Achilles. An oracle told the mother of Achilles that Achilles one day will be very famous, but also that he will die at a young age, so his mother Thetis tried to make her son immortal by diving him in the Styx, a river of the underworld - this made him invulnerable. But his heel, where she held him, was not wetted and so this place remained the only vulnerable - she also heard that Menelaus sent Odysseus to seek soldiers to build his army. So, she and her son went to the palace of the Lycomedes, where he hid as a woman. However, through the seer Calchas, Odysseus knew the hiding place of Achilles. He entered the palace dressed as a merchant and showed the women jewels & fabrics and dresses. Meanwhile, Odysseus blew the horn as a call to war: the women ran away fearfully, but Achilles immediately took his sword and shield. He was unmasked and followed Odysseus to join the army and the war.

Original meaning

"Useful discovery for an activity you intend to do."

Interpretation

- disguise, show yourself different than you are
- to hide something
- a hidden message
- a hidden sign
- mystery, secret
- a secret is/ will be revealed
- a secret cannot remain hidden
- an important revelation
- a realization will be helpful
- a discovery
- a stranger
- sophistication
- trick

Smaller left picture

Hera.

Story

Hera up in a cloud, watching the events around Troy, ready to help in the war against Troy. The help of Hera and Athena was important to win this fight. The ambition of the ladies was the fact that Paris had decided against both and handed over the apple to Aphrodite.

Original meaning

"Courage! You will not lack help!"

Interpretation

- courage is required
- a real force is helping
- a helping hand
- you will receive support & help
- you are not alone, so you should dare to do something

Smaller right picture

Soldiers.

Story

A row of armed soldiers stands trellis.

Original meaning

"Superior forces."

Interpretation

- superior power
- a powerful enemy - this is important to know, avoid the enemy, because he could be stronger
- protect yourself, set boundaries
- know how to defend yourself
- be able to defend yourself
- must defend yourself
- be prepared for everything

D

10 of Diamonds

Original meaning

"Insidious advice, travel plans."

Big Picture

Jason & Pelias.

Story

You see Jason & Pelias together in the throne room of the castle of Pelias. Jason, the nephew of Pelias, however, was the real heir of this throne, which Pelias took over in a cruel way. Pelias knew nothing of Jason, the rightful heir to the throne, but already the oracle of Delphi gave him a dark and mysterious forecast about his downfall. Jason was taken away after his birth and raised by the centaur Chiron. Now he returned to take over throne and let justice and goodness reign again in his land. He asked Pelias only for the throne and not for all his wealth and gold, this should be able to keep Pelias. Pelias harbored malicious intent and accepted but asked Jason for a favor: He asked Jason - before he began to rule - to get the Golden Fleece from the distant land of the Colchians, because with the possession of this Golden Fleece it was possible to destroy a curse, who was weighing on their ancestors (cursed for fraudulent behavior) - secretly, however, Pelias expected that Jason would not return from this dangerous journey.

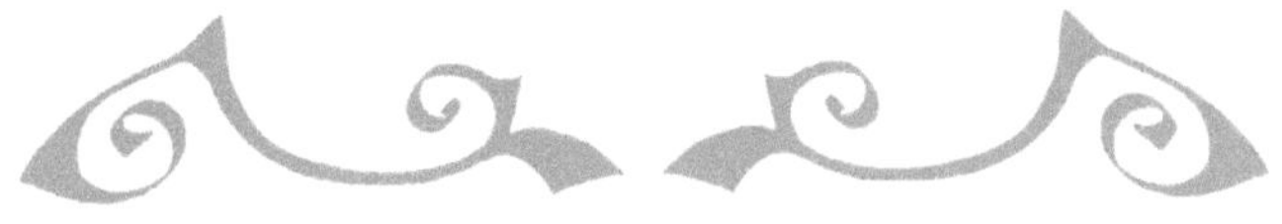

Original meaning

"A young man who listens to advice with joy and without suspicion."

Interpretation

- false advice
- fraudulent intentions
- bad advice
- insidious advice
- a journey, a project will be dangerous and risky
- it is important to prepare everything before acting
- not trust all promises and hints/advice
- skepticism is appropriate
- journey

Smaller left picture

Jason.

Story

Jason is in the sacred woods, in the holy oak grove of Dodona (an oracle site) - here the connection is made to Zeus, who sends Jason visions & Hera, who also supports Jason.

Original meaning

"A young man is afraid of the intentions he meditates on. "

Interpretation

- trust yourself
- trust your inner voice
- have confidence and be relaxed
- inspiration

- visions
- advice that is supportive and helpful

Smaller right picture

A man and a drawing of a ship.

Story

The goddess Athena supports the preparation of this responsible and dangerous journey. For Argos, the architect of the Argo, she is the muse for his last inspiration to finish the plans for the ship called Argo. All the interaction of these forces is stronger than the Pelias' fraudulent intentions.

Original meaning

"Travel arrangements."

Interpretation

- best preparations
- it is a journey with good prospects
- something is under a "good star"
- a good omen
- deception is not successful
- a fraud will not succeed

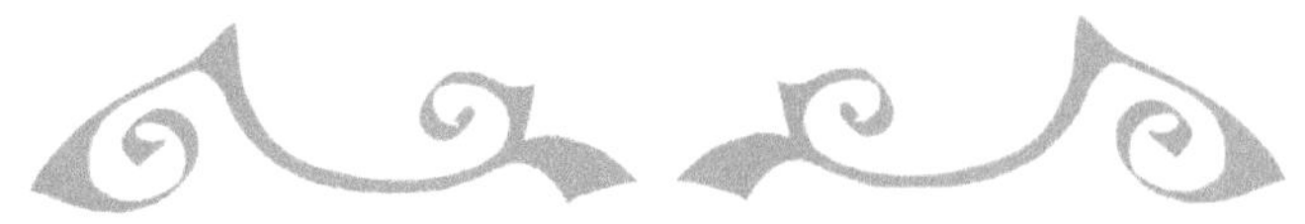

N

9 of Diamonds

Original meaning

"Actions, worries, preparations for departure to a distant trip."

Big Picture

The ship, the Argo on which the Argonauts are on board.

Story

It is the image of the ship called Argo; the fabulously fast ship built by Argos with the help of Athena. All preparations have now been made and the journey is about to begin. Jason has an amazing team of more than 50 men behind him. Among them were Hercules, Peleus, Telamon, Theseus, Castor and Pollux, Odysseus, Orpheus, the sons of the North Winds, Acastos, the son of Pelias, who became Jason's friend, and Idmon, a prophet, to name just some of the famous names from ancient mythology. Before departure, gifts and offerings were made to the gods, thus creating the best conditions and circumstances for the journey. The project was, so to speak, under a favorable star.

Original meaning

"Journey."

Interpretation

- an important journey
- preparation of the journey
- long journey
- changes
- movement
- move
- confidence

- optimism
- spirit of optimism

Smaller left picture

The Argonauts.

Story

The crew of the Argo, the Argonauts, gets their food for the journey; they load the Argo with the necessary provisions, which shows the preparations that must be made so that everything goes according to plan later. To get this, a price must be paid, but it is worth it, because only then will the journey pass safely.

Original meaning

„Happy journey."

Interpretation

- material loss (but you get a value for it)
- good trip
- enterprise, projects without problems
- preparations are necessary
- it is better to be safe than sorry
- what is now thought of pays off later

Smaller right picture

The Argonauts.

Story

This picture also shows a scene of preparation: the crew brings the Argo to water to make the ship ready for departure. Carrying the ship on your shoulders may not be so easy and it takes some time, but the ship will reach its place in the water.

Original meaning

"Obstacles on the way."

Interpretation

- delay of departure
- a delay
- delays
- additional time required
- patience
- to wait
- no easy journey
- no smooth start
- nothing is fixed
- obstacles on the way

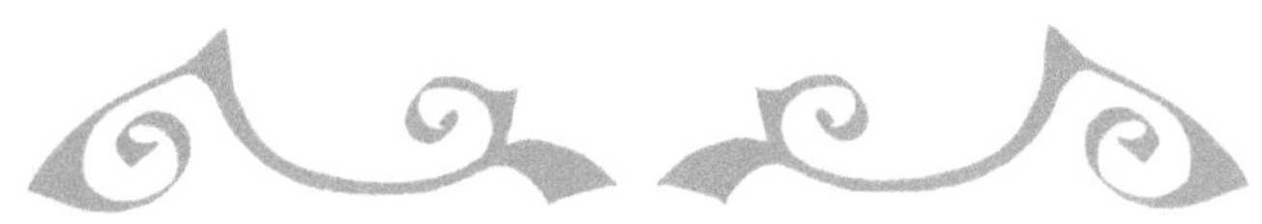

A

ABCDE

8 of Diamonds

Original meaning

"Actions of a good, helpful person to find employment."

Big Picture

Ganymede.

Story

We see a scene in Olympus - all the Gods are together; on the traditional picture of the card, you see as a highlight Neptune with his trident in the middle (as a reference to the sign of Aquarius). The center of the scenery, however, is the young & pretty Ganymede, who gives out ambrosia and nectar to the Gods. It was an honorable task that he had, and that Zeus had given him - Zeus loved Ganymede very much and felt drawn to his nature, his youth and beauty. He was most handsome of the mortals. Once again, Zeus took what he wanted and approached Ganymede in the form of a falcon and took him to Olympus. To justify presence and make it permanent, he bequeathed this comfortable and protected position of the cupbearer of the Gods to the young man.

Original meaning

"Secure position."

Interpretation

- safe position
- safe workplace
- safe environment
- the right job
- the right work
- the right task
- permanent work

- permanent employment
- work theme in general
- patrons & sponsors
- positive reputation
- duty
- mission

Smaller left picture

A female teacher.

Story

A woman teaches students, this scene is about teaching, learning, transmitting knowledge to others. On the traditional card, this is depicted above with the scene of the teacher with her students.

Original meaning

"Admitted orphan."

Interpretation

- education
- a profession in pedagogy
- a social work
- ensure a good education
- to form, to educate
- provide accommodation
- caring for or taking care of someone
- responsibility

Smaller right picture

A man with a book.

Story

The picture tells the story of a student learning with his book.

Original meaning

"Bad reputation, lack of perseverance."

Interpretation

- studies
- good training
- vocational training
- learned profession
- further training
- education
- without diligence no price
- without effort and endurance you will get nothing, and you will fail

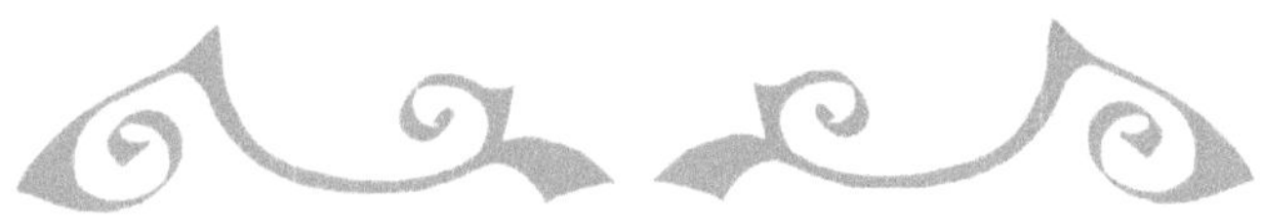

L

7 of Diamonds

Original meaning

"Vicissitudes."

Big Picture

Pandora.

Story

Like many other Gods, the titan Prometheus was subject to the rule of Zeus. In an animal sacrifice, he fraudulently deceived Zeus by handing over the best meat not to the father of the Gods, but to humans, his protégés. As a punishment, Zeus denied humans fire. Prometheus then stole the fire and brought it to the people on earth against the will of Zeus. Full of anger, Zeus punished Prometheus, tied him to a rock and exposed him to the eagles. But the revenge was not yet over: the Gods created the beautiful Pandora and sent her to earth to Epimetheus - he was the brother of Prometheus. Since Prometheus was regarded as the clever forward-thinking, the cause was sought in Epimetheus, the unwise thinker. And so, the punishment was also for him. He married Pandora, although his brother Prometheus warned him never to accept a gift from the Gods. Pandora also took a sealed vase to earth, which Zeus forbade her to open, as it was a gift exclusively for humans. The contents of this vase were all the evils of the world and hope, but Zeus knew that Pandora would not keep to the rule. And he was right: She opened the vase and escaped from the vase all vices and evils and from then on spread to the world, where they had not existed before. Pandora was shocked and quickly closed the vase before the hope of the vase could escape. From now on, the earth was a desolate place.

Original meaning

"Punishment of all kinds."

Interpretation

- pain of all kinds
- trouble & problems in all kinds of matters
- rash action
- not thinking before acting
- action with bad consequences
- misfortune
- hopeless situation
- punishment

Smaller left picture

A man.

Story

The story tells of a man who must beg, a beggar.

Original meaning

"Misery."

Interpretation

- misery
- bad business
- poor financial situation
- loss of money
- bankrupt
- broke

- unfortunately, no (financial) improvement in the long term
- poverty
- insolvency

Smaller right picture

A man.

Story

A man is desperate because of the situation he is in.

Original meaning

"Bad business."

Interpretation

- bad situation
- hopeless situation
- hopelessly
- loss of money
- temporary setbacks

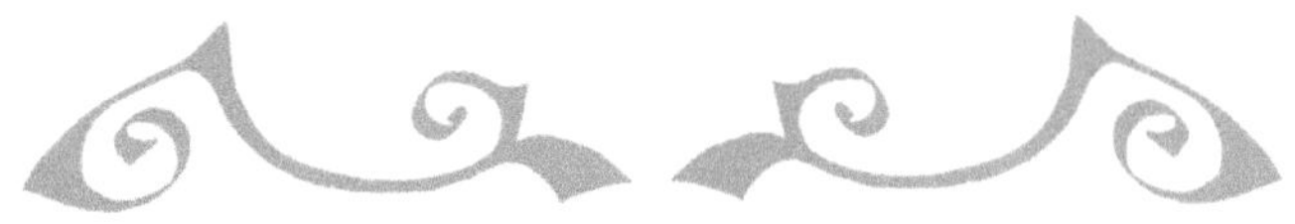

M

6 of Diamonds

Original meaning

"This card can even expose a criminal; as it points to darkness."

(possible person card).

Big Picture

The Crocodile & the Ichneumon.

Story

The Ichneumon was considered a sacred animal in ancient Egyptian culture. In the tombs of the pharaohs, embalmed remains of this animal, also called Pharaoh's Rat (especially in the French-speaking area) were found. After death, the animals were embalmed and buried in holy places. The crocodile, a strong and powerful animal, did not have so many natural enemies and was therefore considered very dangerous - but in the ancient popular belief of Egypt, the Ichneumon was a real danger to the crocodile. The animal was said to crawl into the mouth of sleeping crocodiles, then eat their hearts out of their bodies and kill them. A small thing can destroy something powerful and great.

Original meaning

"A perverse person who knows how to use all possibilities to realize the wickedness he pursues."

Interpretation

- danger
- betrayal
- treacherous
- scam
- deceit
- malicious person who knows exactly what to do
- dangerous person
- malicious intentions
- harming someone
- ambushed
- dangerous situation

Smaller left picture

A man & a woman.

Story

On the Card of the traditional Grand Jeu, a woman plays the guitar, and a man beats the drum - they play different instruments, each for themselves and not together. But the malicious intentions they have in common.

Original meaning

"Disunity, dangerous men and women, inclined to evil."

Interpretation

- disagreement
- quarrel
- split pair
- enticement
- seduction

- dangerous man and woman open "doors to evil", they pull you into their bad affairs
- money for entertainment
- waste of money

Smaller right picture

A star.

Story

A star falling on earth, a comet.

Original meaning

"A man corrupted by dealing with villains."

Interpretation

- attention, negative person in your own environment
- be careful of your surroundings
- your reputation is in danger "a man falls to the ground when he surrounds himself with villains"
- bad company
- bad handling damages your own image
- lose reputation
- lose face

B

5 of Diamonds

Original meaning

"Stubborn, proud, slanderous."

Big Picture

Phaeton.

Story

We see Phaeton driving along the horizon with the chariot of sun, Phaeton being the son of the sun god Helios. Helios created day and night by riding his chariot through the sky. Phaeton was so conceited because of his origin: to be the son of the famous and important Helios, a reason for him to consider himself better. But his companions wanted Phaeton to prove his origins, for they suspected boasting behind all this appearance. Phaeton asked his father to drive the chariot, but he refused, as his son lacked experience. Stubbornly, the son resisted the father and did it anyway, which ended in disaster. Whether the goddess Artemis sent a scorpion to distract Phaeton is different depending on tradition. The fact is, however, that the horses of the Sun Chariot were frightened at the sight of the Scorpion of Heaven, spun and Phaeton lost control and the chariot fell towards earth. The picture tells of the moment when Phaeton saw what was happening and he knew that he could no longer control the situation, the scorpion was very close to the horses, raised its sting and the horses became wild and Phaeton had no power, to hold the reins of the horses. The chariot came too close to the earth and a fire was lit that could stop Zeus by killing Phaeton with a thunder, and the horses rode back into the sky, where the scorpion is still visible today as a constellation in the night sky.

Original meaning

"Bad advice, not willing to listen to the advice of prudence."

Interpretation

- bad not to follow or to ignore any advice
- not be willing to listen to any of the advice of caution
- "pride comes before a fall"
- not being careful, inexperienced, superficial, not listening, only bad experiences will be a lesson
- arrogant, arrogance
- stubbornness
- boasting, showing off
- false pride
- haughtiness
- too proud
- without ambitions

Smaller left picture

A man.

Story

The story shows a former guard (uniform) sitting at a table and he seems to listen to the conversations in the room (in our century this could be a policeman).

Original meaning

"A person who puts wrongdoing, reprehensible ideas or a bad thought in the hands of the police."

Interpretation

- trouble with official institutions
- trouble with authorities
- taking responsibility for bad behavior
- inconveniences
- reprehensible ideas or a bad thought lead into the hands of the law

Smaller right picture

Two women.

Story

The two women who can be seen here argue with each other; they seem to be in a market in public.

Original meaning

"Loss of the job because you have slandered your superiors."

Interpretation

- be careful what you get into
- discussions
- false words and rumors are not helpful and inappropriate, especially in public with others or at work - there may be consequences
- conflicts with people
- talk falls back on yourself
- gossip

4 of Diamonds

Original meaning

"Through love you will gain wealth and fame."

(possible person card)

Big Picture

Medea & Jason

Story

Jason arrived at Colchis, the island where Aietes lived, the owner of the Golden Fleece, in the sacred grove of the god Ares. There Aietes had hung the golden fleece in a tree, and it was guarded by a dragon, which was huge like a ship and never slept. Aietes only gave the fleece to Jason if he managed to pass two tests: he was to defeat the fire-breathing bulls and the dragon. Medea, the daughter of Aiete, educated in magic work, fell in love with Jason, gave him a potion and a powder to survive the challenges Aietes had imposed on Jason. Only with the help of Medea could Jason be successful.

Original meaning

"Mighty protection."

Interpretation

- protection
- powerful protection
- support from someone who is powerful
- success, but not without the help of others
- success with support of someone
- you need someone to succeed
- the support comes because you are protected and loved

- cohesion
- help, advice
- being strong, but only together and not alone

Smaller left picture

Jason and the bull.

Story

Jason is afraid, but he must face the challenge and fight the fire-breathing bulls- he pours magic water that Medea helped him to, on the bulls - without the help of Medea, Jason would have been lost in this fight.

Original meaning

"Fear."

Interpretation

- facing the fear, the challenge
- nervousness (Jason's first challenge)
- it cannot be done without support
- lack of self-confidence
- doubt

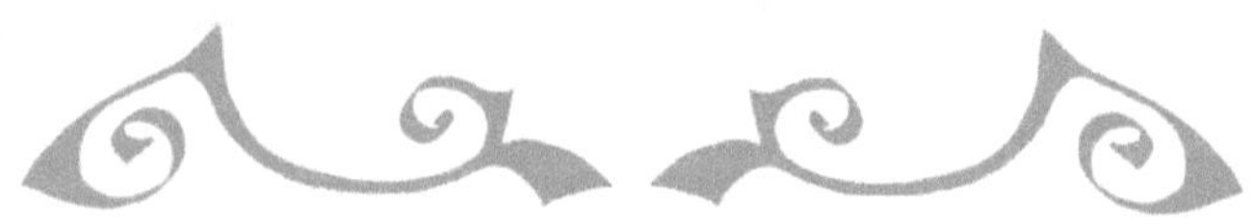

Smaller right picture

Jason and the dragon.

Story

After the first challenge passed, Jason is now more confident and powerful than ever, and he is without fear to face the challenge and fight the dragon. He used the magic powder that had helped him defeat the dragon. Again, Jason would have been lost in this fight without the help of Medea.

Original meaning

"Security."

Interpretation

- self-confidence
- certainty
- confidence (since it's not Jason's first challenge)
- to know that the target is safe
- trust in own abilities
- victorious
- despite everything, it is not possible without help

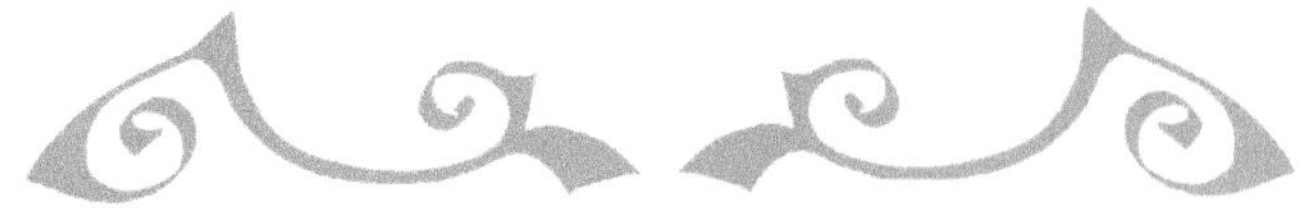

E

3 of Diamonds

Original meaning

"Affection, crossed union."

Big Picture

Castor & Pollux.

Story

Zeus was once in love with Leda and had two children with her: A son named Pollux and a daughter named Helena. Both as children of the god Zeus were thus demigods and were immortal. At the same time, the mortal Castor was born of Leda. However, his father was not Zeus, but Tyndareus, a mortal, and thus Castor was also mortally born. The half-brothers resembled each other very much and were also seen as twin brothers of Helena. The Dioscuri Castor and Pollux, however, had a particularly intimate relationship with each other and were very connected. they were always together, together they accompanied even Jason on the Argo. One day the inevitable happened: the mortal Castor was injured and dying. Pollux desperately asked his father Zeus for help; he did not want to be separated from Castor. He asked his father to allow him to be in Hades (realm of the dead) at Castor during the day and to bring Castor to Olympus at night. Zeus fulfilled his son's dearest wish. So, you can still see Castor & Pollux in the night sky in their eternal connection to each other in the sign of the twin.

Original meaning

"Friendship, family ties."

Interpretation

- friendship
- family cohesion
- deep (inner) connection
- a connection that cannot be lived - sometimes due to external influences
- two connected souls, that must still be separate
- fateful connection, fateful affection
- connected souls
- connection until after death
- an inevitable separation, but souls remain connected
- gloomy romanticism

Smaller left picture

Two palm trees.

Story

You see two palms, the leaves seem to be touching carefully, secretly, but the palms are still apart. They are separated from each other.

Original meaning

"Unhappy friendship, no hope of union."

Interpretation

- a kind of sadness
- two that are not together, but belong to each other

- longing for someone you can't be with or with whom you won't be
- no strength to overcome the separation
- unhappy friendship
- no hope of union or reunification
- two remain separated
- something becomes unattainable
- something will be a memory

Smaller right picture

A man and a horse.

Story

A man riding alone on a horse, considering the theme of this card, the man is in search of comfort and love in life. For this he rides away to find it.

Original meaning

"After a pain in the heart, a trip is the best thing to do."

Interpretation

- after lovesick, taking distance is the best thing to do, because distance brings healing
- moving on to find real love
- on new shores
- leave something behind
- time heals wounds
- distance heals wounds
- the new way brings happiness
- now be for yourself, at least for a while

P

2 of Diamonds

Original meaning

"Ambiguous behavior, birth, new beginnings, sexuality."

Big Picture

A child sits on a goat.

Story

The story shows a child riding on a goat through nature. With the goat, a picture of the god Pan, son of Hermes, is again symbolized on a card. Pan enchanted many people, especially the women, with his flute playing. Pan was also known for his love of sex and intimacy and lived his sexuality intensely. He was in a strong love relationship with the nymphs - the water fairies. In later centuries, people no longer tended too much to sexual pleasures, and therefore Pan became a devilish figure, often depicted with ears of a goat and a horse's hoof. Or people also gave him the appearance and characteristics of the goat as a kind of allegory of the devil and the sins, especially because of his sexual escapades. The child is a sign of innocence and of pregnancy because of sexuality.

Original meaning

"Fertility, birth."

Interpretation

- sexuality
- pregnancy
- birth
- fertility
- lust
- drifted
- innocence

- closeness to nature
- child
- offspring
- nature instinct, people are who they are

Smaller left picture

Two women.

Story

On the traditional card you see a young, sad girl with an evil fairy. This picture tells the story of pregnancy and fertility.

Original meaning

"A young girl cries for an irreparable mistake."

Interpretation

- negative consequences
- can't handle the consequences
- young person crying over his own fate
- no support
- be alone (in pregnancy)
- unwanted pregnancy
- unwanted fate
- unwanted situation
- unwanted outcome

Smaller right picture

Two women.

Story

On the traditional card you see a young, sad girl with a good fairy. This picture also tells the story of pregnancy and fertility, but as a counterpart to the other smaller picture with a positive effect.

Original meaning

"A young girl is proud to be able to make up for her mistake."

Interpretation

- positive consequences
- cope with consequences
- young person who is strong and proud and confidently faces fate
- young person gets support
- not to be alone in pregnancy
- intended pregnancy
- intended fate
- auspicious situation
- auspicious outcome

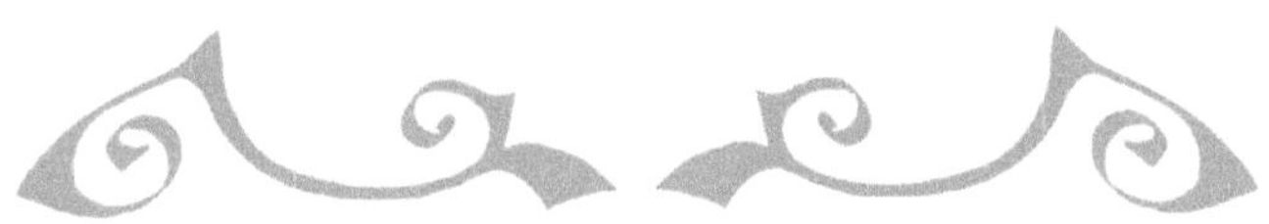

S

Ace of Diamonds

Original meaning

"Letter or message."

Big Picture

Harpocrates & Hermes.

Story

Harpocrates (the Greek god for Egyptian Horus) was a very powerful God, in the form of a falcon he stretched his wings around the sky and his eyes were the moon and the sun. He had a deep inner connection with his parents Osiris and Isis and even though he is grown up, powerful and wise, he was always the loving son. The scene shows him sitting on a lotus flower, placing a finger on his mouth, and giving a message to Hermes. The traditions of Plutarch interpreted the finger on the mouth as a symbol of silence, of silence, and so Harpokrates was seen, according to Plutarch, as the God of silence and discretion. Without words, he passes the message on to Hermes, who was seen, among other things, as the God of eloquence, of messages, of communication (including divination). This was the background at the time of the creation of the cards and therefore affects all images of this card. Later the interpretation of the Plutarch was refuted and the deep connection to his parents Osiris and Isis and he the eternal beloved son emphasize very much the childlike and the interpretation that Harpokrates is equated with a childlike God comes into focus, likewise, the gesture of the finger is seen as a very childlike gesture. However, this is not noticeable in the meaning of the card.

Original meaning

"Messenger, trust."

Interpretation

- messenger, transmitter
- familiar, confidant, trusted person
- trust
- discretion
- news
- message
- information
- letters
- communication
- plans
- confessions
- secret confessions

Smaller left picture

Argus.

Story

This picture tells the story of the giant Argus, the giant with his 100 eyes. When 50 of his eyes were asleep, the other 50 were always open so he could see everything. He reads a letter - like a spy and thus things will be revealed.

Original meaning

"Indiscreet messenger/ confidant."

Interpretation

- gossip
- indiscretion

- no trusted person in the environment
- indiscreet messenger
- you are observed, so you should act secretly and carefully
- unpleasant news
- a secret comes to light
- a secret is not in good hands
- lack of loyalty

Smaller right picture

A Cynocephale.

Story

A Cynocephale guards a sacred papyrus roll, this scene is a symbol of reliability.

Original meaning

"Safe and discreet confidant."

Interpretation

- reliable and honest contact/s
- trusted person
- reliable person
- trusted friend
- ally
- safe and secret
- good news
- to keep a secret
- a secret is certain
- a secret will remain a secret

The Suit of Spades

King of Spades

Original meaning

"A man of the law with whom you have to settle matters."

(possible person card)

Big Picture

A court scene.

Story

The picture tells the story of Menes; it is said that he was the first king of Egypt; he once built the city of Memphis. He protected the city with a huge white wall from the water of the Nile. Here he leads the court and so the card is often in combination with a judgment, consequences, and some kind of possible loss.

Original meaning

"Process."

Interpretation

- first card of legal processes
- official procedures
- authority, state authority
- affairs with authorities or communities
- official affairs
- a process
- laws, justice, legal matters
- conflicts with the law
- the separated man, the divorced man, the widower

Smaller left picture

A man.

Story

It is the story of a man behind bars, a prisoner in a prison cell.

Original meaning

"Criminal process."

Interpretation

- serious problems
- dangerous matters
- serious conflicts
- criminal process
- lost process
- slander
- harshness of the law
- disingenuous action with just consequences

Smaller right picture

Two men / a document.

Story

A servant of court or from today's perspective, a bailiff submits a letter of judgment to another person.

Original meaning

"Civil and economic process."

Interpretation

- civil process
- divorce
- court order (often in money matters)
- seizure
- formal document
- official document
- formal correspondence
- official correspondence

U

Queen of Spades

Original meaning

"Abandonment or widowhood."

(possible person card)

Big Picture

Isis.

Story

This is the story of Isis, the goddess of birth, rebirth, and magic. Isis was the mother of protection from the loving people, the farmers, sailors, and healers. Isis & Osiris have always loved each other and became a couple as adults. Seth, the brother of Osiris, married Nephthys, the sister of Isis. But Seth could not love, he as a counterpart to Osiris was filled with hatred from birth. One night, Nephthys pretended to be Isis and loved Osiris, from which Anubis was born. Isis took the boy away to hide the child and the truth from Seth. But Seth already knew, and he murdered Osiris because of jealousy and envy, dismembering his body and distributing it throughout the land. The grieving Isis sought every single part of Osiris to finally reassemble it with the spell and magic - she was still so in love with him. And with her power of love, her power of magic and the help of the Gods, she was given a son with Osiris, Horus. And with the death of Osiris, the hereafter was born, and he ruled it, and Isis was the chosen one of the Gods who could form a bridge from this world to the hereafter. Her son, Horus, became an adult and the fate of his parents was unforgettable for him, and the day came when he took revenge and killed Seth.

Original meaning

"A woman mourns her husband."

Interpretation

- sadness
- accept the grief
- willpower
- mental strength
- defeat the terrible fate
- to live with fate
- to regain hope after something bad
- never give up, keep going
- someone who mourns the loss of a loved one
- struggle with grief and loss, but there will be healing of the soul
- the separated woman, the divorced woman, the widow
- the beyond, the hereafter

Smaller left picture

A man, an oil lamp.

Story

A man fills a lamp with oil so that there is light in the dark again.

Original meaning

"Loss of a friend."

Interpretation

- loss of a friend
- abandonment
- hatred of fate

- grief
- grieve alone
- finding comfort will be difficult
- loneliness
- sadness
- moving on with life, carry on
- continue living and keep memories alive
- grow with the situation

Smaller right picture

Two women.

Story

Here Isis is shown in a scene during her search for Osiris' body, sharing with a lady, an older woman. Some traditions say that the helping lady is Queen Astarte, but there is no more tangible evidence.

Original meaning

"Consolation."

Interpretation

- consolation
- understanding
- sympathy
- empathy
- encouragement
- someone shared the same fate
- shared suffering

L

Jack of Spades

Original meaning

"A man of knowledge who is instructed in the laws and all matters of justice."

(possible person card)

Big Picture

A man with a scale.

Story

In ancient Roman history, justice was more of a man's thing, but we all know that the goddess of justice, Justitia, is a woman. On this card we see a man, a philosopher, a scale in his hand; like the alchemist on the cards belonging to the group of hermetic science (later there will be more information about the groups), he also prepares his work, by balancing the right amount of ingredients against each other and finding the exact amount he needs for his work. Sometimes this is more of one than the other or it is the mediocrity - it is always subject to circumstances.

Original meaning

"Justice, equality."

Interpretation

- the second card of legal processes
- equality
- justice
- corrective justice
- justice will be spoken, justice will be
- it always depends on the Main Character whether this card is promising for the person or not.

Smaller left picture

Two men & a Judge.

Story

The traditional image of the card tells the scene where a judge interacts with two men - he announces his verdict, he communicates justice between them, he sometimes also arbitrates disputes.

Original meaning

"Agreement."

Interpretation

- agreement
- peace
- balance
- accept an offer
- a handshake
- settle a dispute
- after such an arbitration, often everyone goes the own way
- agreement, but no new beginning
- legal matters
- official matters

Smaller right picture

A man in front of a judge.

Story

In this scene, in the picture of the traditional card, the judge speaks only with one person, he holds up his hand, he has also here made his judgment and announces it.

Original meaning

"Accusations without result."

Interpretation

- the search/ hope for justice is without success
- blame
- false blame
- false assumptions
- false thoughts
- wrong decision

X

10 of Spades

Original meaning

"Theft, loss."

Big Picture

Laverna.

Story

Laverna was regarded as the goddess of cheaters and thieves and of the underworld, for she was not extremely turned to Olympus, in which the other Gods found themselves. At night she preferred to sneak around in the woods near the city of Rome with her foxes and wolves. The wolves and foxes were their faithful companions.

Original meaning

"You will experience a more or less significant theft, depending on what influence your fellow human beings have on you or what leeway you grant them. "

Interpretation

- theft
- loss
- losses of all kinds
- tears due to loss
- nocturnal events, the night
- dark events, dark chapters in life
- secret events
- secrecy
- disease
- misfortune
- deceit, betrayal

Smaller left picture

A fox.

Story

The scene is a farm, where a fox ambushed and stole a hen.

Original meaning

"Someone is watching your actions, trying to get inside to figure out how to deceive you."

Interpretation

- someone is watching your actions
- someone is waiting, trying to get close, to figure out how to fool you and to see where your weaknesses lies
- from the ambush
- become a victim

Smaller right picture

A woman.

Story

A woman steals an object from the drawer of a desk on the picture of the traditional card. Apparently, this is about stealing personal belongings.

Original meaning

"Theft of trust."

Interpretation

- abuse of trust
- heavy loss
- invade the privacy of others
- divulge private information
- the thief is in the private sphere
- taking advantage of foreign property

E

9 of Spades

Original meaning

"Grief, moral pain, it takes time to find back to inner peace."

Big Picture

Helena.

Story

The scene shows Helena in the company of her maids, there is war, and they know about it. Iris, the goddess of the rainbow, tells Helena that Paris was fighting with Menelaus on the battlefield - the men she loved became terrible enemies and found themselves in a deadly conflict. Like her father Zeus, Helena was very fond of falling easily in love - she couldn't help but fall in love with Paris and followed her heart. But during this war the love of Helena and Paris broke into. He was seriously injured and sought refuge with his first wife, but she refused to help him. Helena returned to Menelaus, who took her back again.

Original meaning

"Grief, emotional and moral grief, it takes time to return to inner peace."

Interpretation

- unpleasant news
- bad news
- despair
- restlessness, worries
- inability to interact, unable to act
- injury caused by a loved one/ close person
- injury to the person you love, you feel close to

- being responsible for someone's pain
- thinking about the misfortune you caused
- become/be aware of your own guilt
- admission of guilt
- remorse, regret
- bad conscience
- to return, to go back (often in old partnership)

Smaller left picture

Thetis & Achilles.

Story

Thetis hands over magical, enchanted weapons to her son Achilles, because since his birth she tried to protect him, but without success, because with the gift of weapons she rather supported him, and he was now ready to go to war, in which he finally died.

Original meaning

"Run to ruin."

Interpretation

- to get lost
- make a mistake
- deceive, deception
- wrong action with consequences
- think about to change ways, it's not too late

Smaller right picture

Arrows.

Story

Considering the mythological stories, these arrows refer to the powerful arrows of Hercules.

Original meaning

"A guilty woman, saved by the talisman of Venus."

Interpretation

- saved by love and faith
- unnatural forces can grow
- the impossible can become possible
- you can still react and change the situation for the better
- good end is still possible
- situation turns out to the good
- development to the good
- you still have the situation in your hands, you can influence it
- actively fight the evil, fight it

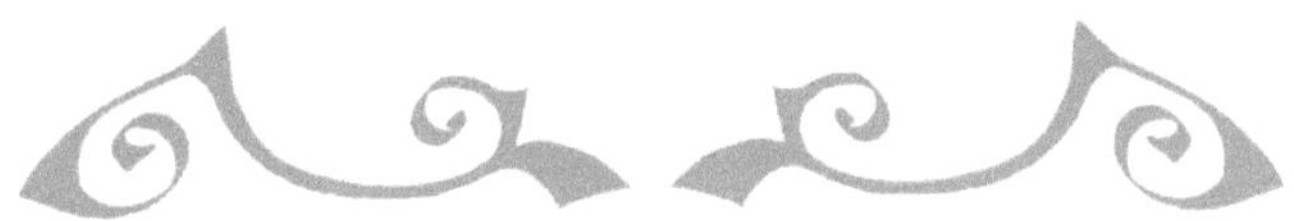

8 of Spades

Original meaning

"Tears and grief from the loss of a loved one."

Big Picture

Achilles.

Story

Achilles played a major role in the story of the Trojan War, assassinating Hector, a Trojan prince, in revenge. Achilles was full of hatred and revenge, for Hector had killed Patroclus, the cousin of Achilles, in battle. When he was dying, he asked Achilles to take him to the city so that he could die there, but Achilles maliciously denied him this request, he, on the other hand, tied his body behind a chariot and dragged him around the walls of the city and around the tomb of Patroclus, Zeus could not tolerate the cruel behavior of the otherwise so noble Achilles - he ordered Thetis, to bring their son to reason, and so he gave the body of Hector to wild beasts. Peace was created.

Original meaning

"Result of the revenge of an enemy."

Interpretation

- revenge
- hate
- cruelty
- low motivational and malicious or even hurt feelings cause pain and grief
- take care for others is needed, an act of kindness is important now
- loss causes pain and despair

- heartlessness
- madness
- hate

Smaller left picture

A woman, a grave.

Story

It is Andromache, the wife of Hector, who is here at the grave of her husband, who is now widowed and mourns for her late husband.

Original meaning

"Crying family."

Interpretation

- grieving relatives
- tears
- grief
- loss
- loss of a beloved person
- loss of a close friend
- loss of a deep connection

Smaller right picture

A skull, bones.

Story

Pelops' father, Tantalus, was invited by Zeus as a guest to be part of the divine table in Olympus. He stole ambrosia and nectar, he hid a golden dog in his home, which he took from Olympus - he denied these deeds. He also tested whether the gods were truly omniscient by sacrificing his youngest son and offering as a meal to the gods. But the gods recognized the outrage that he had murdered his own son, and so they sent Tantalus to hell to suffer torment from thirst and hunger - so-called "Tantalean Punishment" - the Moira Klotho gave Peplos a new life.

Original meaning

"Happy fate, an obstacle is overcome by the grace of the moon."

Interpretation

- the terrible times are over
- despair is gone
- a new beginning is created
- an obstacle is overcome
- the bad is banished from life
- you overcome a bad time and start again

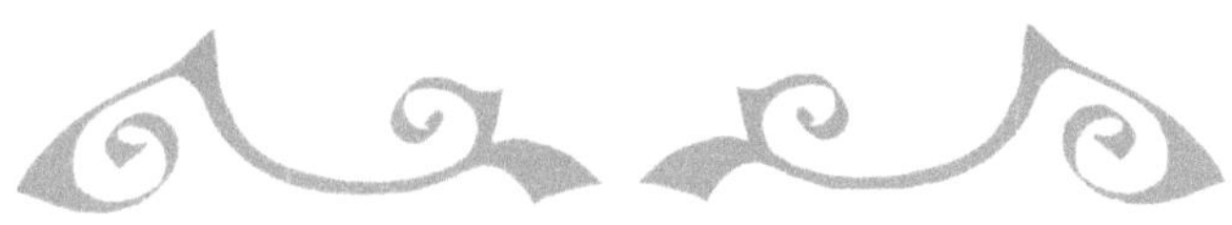

7 of Spades

Original Meaning

"Hope for the realization of an idea."

Big Picture

The alchemist starts his experiment.

Story

The scene on the card shows the alchemist in his laboratory. It is the beginning of his great experiment, which includes seven different steps. At the beginning, he fills some dark raw material into a test tube, seals the glass and heats the material over a fireplace. It is the beginning, and he is full of expectations, ambition, and joy. But he also feels confident: he is sure that his experiment will not fail. Everything will have a good start and end well - at least that's what is expected.

Interpretation

- beginning
- youth
- start (often in an emotional context; first feelings),
- wonderful time.
- first love
- new or first steps.
- a relationship that starts now can last a long time
- signs of a happy marriage.
- positive card, a situation becomes positive, even if the prospects are not so positive
- euphoria
- confidence
- optimism

Smaller left picture

A young woman.

Story

A simple, young girl (by her clothes you can establish a connection with the former layer of the working class), she walks through nature, she seems to be alone, but in her heart, she is not, because she is in love.

Original Meaning

"This woman is the object of your desire/ choice."

Interpretation

- first love
- first feelings of love
- to be in love with someone
- it's the woman of choice, someone you chose from the bottom of your heart

Smaller right picture

A couple.

Story

Here you see a young girl talking to a worker, maybe it's a young couple (both belong to the working class here). They can expect a bright future because they can work and afford life. The man has a job, so he's serious and trustworthy and offers security.

Original Meaning

"She believes she is loved and relies on the promises."

Interpretation

- someone believes/ feels loved and hopes to experience good times
- there is love, trust and harmony
- being together
- you start to a life together with someone
- cohabit
- security
- secure future
- fulfilled hopes and dreams
- and fulfilled hopes and dreams you had in your youth

R

6 of Spades

Original meaning

"Deception, which you will only recognize when there is no more time."

Big Picture

The Trojan Horse.

Story

The scene shows the famous Trojan horse - by now it was clear that it was not possible to defeat the Trojan soldiers by force and take the city. The seer Calchas also indicated that victory would only be possible through cunning and a cunning plan. This was only possible with the help of Zeus, Hera, and Athena and with the support of the Gods, the Greeks built a wooden horse in which the soldiers could hide. Odysseus pretended to withdraw with the army and the ships departed from the coast. Only a huge wooden horse remained, but the Greek soldiers had hidden in it. Due to the warnings of the priest Laocoön and Cassandra, who both said that the horse would bring the downfall of Troy, some of the Trojans became suspicious and wanted to drown the wooden horse in the water of the sea. But Athena prevented this by sending two terrible snakes on the water, which ate everyone who came too close to them. Thus, despite all warning, the horse was pulled into the city of Troy, believing that the horse was now a gift for the gods and the inhabitants celebrated a supposed victory. The following night, Greek soldiers stepped out of the horse and opened the gates of the city. The previously withdrawn soldiers, however, had returned, could enter the gates of the city, and bring Troy down. This happened partly in a cruel way, so that even the Gods angered and made the return of the Greeks more difficult, as the wanderings of Odysseus report.

Original meaning

"Catastrophic event."

Interpretation

- catastrophic events
- betrayal
- deceit
- treacherous
- treason
- wrongness
- danger
- misfortune
- unjustly
- ambushed
- threat
- the appearance is deceptive
- inappropriate trust
- heed warnings and don't miss them

Smaller left picture

A woman & a man.

Story

In the story we see a lady named Briseis, actually Hippodameia, who was Achilles' favorite slave and concubine. She kneels next to the deathbed of Patroclus that was murdered by Hector. She was very attached to Patroclus, to whom he assured her of a promising future as Achilles' wife.

Original meaning

"You will suffer the effects of a discord for which you are not to blame."

Interpretation

- to experience a suffering you did not caused
- grief because of others
- tears that were caused by others
- suffering due to external circumstances

Smaller right picture

A rider.

Story

In the scene Pyrrhus, the son of Achilles, is depicted, he resembles his father in appearance and strength, and he is one of those heroes who were in the Trojan horse. He contributed to the victory.

Original meaning

"Thanks to the Jupiter Talisman, you will achieve what you want."

Interpretation

- commitment pays off
- do not give up
- to copy someone, try to be someone else
- join others to succeed
- a twist of fate brings you closer to what you want

5 of Spades

Original meaning

"Your religious principles and acquired knowledge give you more hope."

(possible person card)

Big Picture

Chiron.

Story

The scene shows Chiron dying, Chiron visually belonged to the centaurs. They were half human, half horse - and were usually considered cruel creatures. But Chiron was different in his kind, possibly because he was partly of different origin. But because of his appearance, he was cast out by his mother Philyra and has lived in a cave ever since. Despite this fate, he did not lose his sense of goodness and he became a master in various arts: music, astrology, writing and archery. He was greatly appreciated by the Gods and many young men were sent to him to receive an excellent education (e.g. Castor, Pollux, Jason). Chiron was also a master in the art of healing, in this art he trained Asclepius, who later became the god of medicine. All this made Chiron immortal, but Chiron is still shown dying in the picture. At a time when the centaurs were being persecuted, he was accidentally injured by an arrow spilt with the Hydra's blood, and even Asclepius could not cure him. Because of his immortality, he was condemned to suffer forever. Chiron, however, gave his immortality to Prometheus, who was thus freed and would no longer be exposed to the eagles. The picture represents the moment of his death; he descends into heaven, there Zeus gave him the place of the zodiac sign Sagittarius on firmament.

Original meaning

"A wild, imaginative character, dominated by softness and carelessness, with great knowledge you remain without a future."

Interpretation

- even if there is potential here, if it is not promoted and if you are not diligent and honest, you will fail
- lost potential
- unused potential
- be careful not to be too lazy
- despite intelligence and knowledge, a secure future is uncertain or even unlikely
- carefree, not thinking about the future
- carelessness
- powerless
- succumb
- people with (hard) fate in the past
- people who can give much education and healing

Smaller left picture

A hunter.

Story

Here is a hunter, but not during the hunt and without a hunting trophy.

Original meaning

"Personalities of misfortune; success cannot achieve them."

Interpretation

- it's not the right time for success
- the time has not come yet
- do not be active, better wait
- the talent is not yet trained well enough
- stagnant situation
- unlucky persons, characters of misfortune - success can often not reach these people or if only in very difficult way

Smaller right picture

A man.

Story

A man on foot, balancing and trying to keep his equilibrium: with wings in one hand and a weight in the other.

Original meaning

"Insurmountable obstacles."

Interpretation

- emotionally unstable
- unbalanced
- missing balance
- no equality
- you need more confidence and experience
- don't be your own limit: you have wings to fly, but don't keep yourself on the ground
- you will not overcome the obstacle if you have the wrong attitude

4 of Spades

Original meaning

"Artificiality that suggests jealousy."

Big Picture

Hera & Semele.

Story

Hera, the wife of Zeus, shows her jealous side again in this story. Zeus loved the beautiful Semele, the daughter of Harmonia. He promised to fulfil her every wish and to be in love with her until death. When Hera uncovered the relationship, she grasped an insidious plan out of jealousy and sought out the young Semele. To gain access, Hera chose, in the form of the old nurse Beroe von Semele. She raised doubts in Semele because she told her that Zeus was not really Zeus. Therefore, she urged Semele to ask Zeus to prove his identity, to show himself to her in his divine form, as proof of his love. If he denied and denied her this wish, he would not love her and be a deceiver. Hera knew about the fact that Semele would not survive this, for the splendor would destroy her, as nothing earthly can exist if it comes too close to the sun. Semele kept to the words and asked Zeus to do so; he refused because he knew what would happen, but Semele insisted vehemently. Finally, he showed himself out of love in his natural form. And it happened as it was to happen, Semele died by the splendor of Zeus. However, the child, her son Dionysus, was saved by the gods.

Original meaning

"Malicious advice with the intention of getting rid of a rival."

Interpretation

- evil, sneaky advice
- advice from a jealous person
- jealousy as a drive for action
- malicious intentions
- pain and grief (caused by malicious behavior)
- insidiously
- blind trust (becomes a disaster)
- credulity (becomes a disaster)
- to take out a rival
- competition

Smaller left picture

A child, a fire.

Story

A pile of straw lit by a child; one sees the smoke, a fire lit.

Original meaning

"Unsatisfied jealousy."

Interpretation

- jealousy in default
- something is brewing
- heated up mood
- tense situation
- explosive content for disputes
- lack of care has consequences
- recklessness

Smaller right picture

A woman, lightning bolts.

Story

It is the night when Hera's evil plan is born, and Zeus shows himself to Semele in his divine form and therefore she dies. She was struck by Zeus' lightning.

Original meaning

"Satisfied jealousy."

Interpretation

- satisfied jealousy
- successful revenge
- "evil wins the day"
- an evil plan comes to life with cunning and treachery
- the consequences of taking bad advice

U

3 of Spades

Original meaning

"Serious illness, danger to life."

Big Picture

The Moirai.

Story

The card tells the story of fate and shows the three Fates, the Moirai. They are the personified fate of a person, and even the Gods could not avert a fate determined by the Moirai. Their names are Clotho (the spinner), Lachesis (the allotter) and Atropos (the inevitable). They determined the fate of the world, the Gods and the people and they stood above everything. The picture shows the three Moirai on a cloud and they do their work: "Clotho spins the thread of life, Lachesis ties it, and Atropos will cut it off when the time comes. They represented the circle of life, one can say that they stand for birth, life, and death.

Original meaning

"Uncertain existence."

Interpretation

- challenges of life
- fate (inevitable)
- destiny
- fate must be accepted
- fateful situation in life
- bad phase of life
- a dark hour
- hour of need

- a fate that affects you personally
- whatever happens now is fateful and therefore inevitable. Most of the time, these events are perceived as terrible and very stressful and painful
- this card appeared in origins as a card that meant deaths in the immediate personal environment or serious illness
- the worst card in the Grand Lenormand

Smaller left picture

Lachesis.

Story

Lachesis creates a thread of life that was previously spun by Clotho. Legend has it that golden wool was spun for the beautiful moments in life and black wool for the difficult times in life and the sequence of these was decided and knotted by Lachesis.

Original meaning

"Long and quiet life."

Interpretation

- only temporary danger
- short negative phase
- only temporary bad luck
- less dangerous situation
- long and pleasant life

Smaller right picture

Atropos.

Story

Atropos (the metaphor for death) is cutting off the thread of life

Original meaning

"Premature death."

Interpretation

- big change in life
- it's about big cuts in life
- changing stages of life
- something is coming to an end
- something is terminated (but not by itself)
- end
- no new beginning
- in the old tradition: premature death, death

U

2 of Spades

Original meaning

"Confidentiality, secrets you will use."

Big Picture

Calchas & Menelaus.

Story

Everything is prepared for war and the Greek heroes and soldiers sought out their seer, Calchas, to inquire about the course of events. There was a sacrificial ceremony to reveal the secrets of the future. A dragon appeared to the seer in the vision, and the dragon ate nine birds - now Calchas knew that the Trojan War will last nine years, and that Troy will fall. He also saw that they would need Achilles to win the war against the Trojan army. In addition, Odysseus needs help and a cunning plan - the city would not fall by force of arms alone.

Original meaning

"Healthy opinions."

Interpretation

- advice in a difficult situation
- the advice of a confidant, rely on it
- secret council
- useful advice
- secret
- secret meetings
- secret message
- secret clues
- secret hints
- gain an advantage

Smaller left picture

An urn.

Story

Here is an urn filled with ashes; in some traditions it is said to be the urn with the ashes of Laomedon, the second king of Troy. He was a man of broken words and promises; this behavior leads to his undoing: he became a victim of the wrath of the gods and other quarrels led him to his death.

Original meaning

"Saturn's talisman is a fortunate tool against any revenge."

Interpretation

- someone who is not to trust
- no real advice
- empty promises
- broken promises
- do not keep his word
- consequences of unreliability
- consequences of false trust
- a quarrel divides two people forever

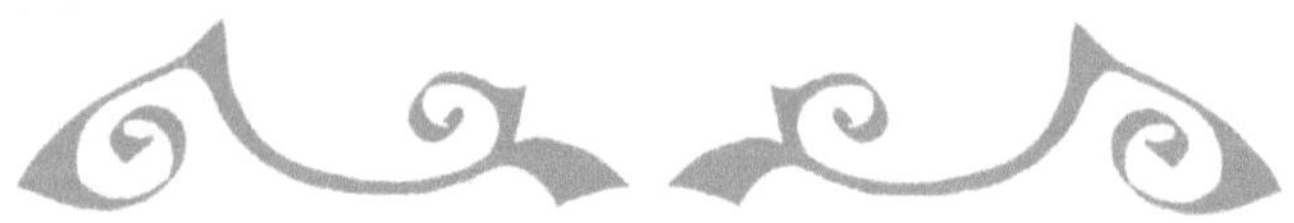

Smaller right picture

Shield & sword.

Story

The picture shows two swords with a shield, and it is a hint that a conflict is arising. It is obvious that there will be a battle, so fight and defend yourself.

Original meaning

"Beginning of hostilities."

Interpretation

- beginning of hostilities
- a conflict starts
- a conflict cannot be avoided
- a dispute
- trouble

Ace of Spades

Original meaning

"Ambiguous behavior, nocturnal rendezvous."

Big Picture

Europa.

Story

From ancient mythology we know that in this story Zeus turned into a white bull when he was under the loving influence of Venus to kidnap Europa, the beautiful daughter of Agenor. He was so in love with Europe and could not resist this passion. He took her in the form of a bull and carried her on his back across the wide sea to the island of Crete. After that, he lived for a long time together with Europa on the island of Crete, under a tree that is said to always have green leaves. In the older story, Zeus is not yet married to Hera on that occasion and is intended to marry Europa - only later versions bring in the marriage with Hera, the fraud on her, her jealousy, and her revenge. Regarding the significance of the card, the abduction of Europa by Zeus is placed in the context of affairs and secrecy.

Original meaning

"Despair in a family because of the injustice of a child, kidnapping of a girl."

Interpretation

- sexuality
- lust
- passion
- guilty pleasures
- (secret) pleasure

- (secret) vices
- secret affair
- secret relationship
- escape
- departure, hasty departure
- despair
- something that is taken away in a hurry

Smaller left picture

A woman.

Story

The scene of the original card shows a woman standing in the doorway, one can assume she is in her front door. She looks out, seems to be waiting for someone, a man for example, whether she grants him entry into her house?

Original meaning

"A young girl will lose herself/ will get lost."

Interpretation

- to act with caution
- not play with the fire
- risky game
- seduction
- risk of losing a good position, reputation
- think about who to engage with and why
- the lover who is second best
- always a card for the lover, never a card for the actual partner

Smaller right picture

A man.

Story

You see a man sitting alone at a table holding a glass, drinking alcohol in solitude.

Original meaning

"A depraved man."

Interpretation

- addiction
- drugs
- dependence
- addicted to… (in the bad sense)
- bad person
- weak person (mental)

NOTE It is advantageous if you remember the most positive cards and the most negative card of the Grand Jeu, to recognize them immediately during a reading.

In Grand Lenormand you will find three cards that we say are positive, like a joker in the card game for example. Three cards that have a strong positive influence and one that unfortunately has a very strong negative influence.

So, it is very important for the interpretation of your spread, for example, if one of these lucky cards appears, because if this is the case, the outcome of the situation will still be positive or in your favor, even if it looks unfavorable. Or a bad prognosis will be slightly weakened. The cards do not say that something unpleasant suddenly becomes amazing, but they take the heaviness out and sometimes let you know that something bad can still have good consequences for you.

So, it is always important to take a first look at whether you see one of these three cards in the display of the cards or if you see the worst card of the game, because their influence is also enormous on the outcome of things.

Lucky Charms & the Bad Omen

The Lucky Charms: the 3 best Grand Lenormand Cards

- Ace of Clubs: the success card
- 3 of Hearts: the card of the spirit
- 7 of Spades: the card of hope

One or more of these cards that appear are always a positive and happy sign.

The Bad Omen: the worst card in the Grand Lenormand

And it is quite natural that there is light, there is also shadow, so there will be readings in which you will see the worst of all cards:

- 3 of Spades: the fate card

This card in a reading means, among other things, that the situation must be considered with much caution and responsibility. Because this time the problem is a challenging destiny that needs to be solved, there is no way around it. The Queen of Spades, for example, also shows a confrontation with fate, and this is also not very welcome, but most often in this case the Queen of Spades appears when the bad turns into good - the reversal of fate. But the most important thing will always be the appearance of the card 3 of Spades. This card gives a darker and more serious note to other cards or to the whole spread; situations with the 3 of Spades should never be underestimated.

The energy of these four cards, the three strongest positive cards and the worst card, has a big impact on the other cards - so before you start interpreting the cards, look closely to see if you see any of these cards.

Excursion "Petit Lenormand"

The French Petit Lenormand is a game of 37 cards taken from the Grand Lenormand: visually with the three pictures, the flowers, and the playing card insert. And thematically almost with the same meaning, but the cards are designed according to their own system. Each position then determines which facet of the card is used for interpretation and the meanings are printed on the cards in the "Petit Lenormand".

The French Petit Lenormand contains the following 37 cards:

0 The female Main Character - named after Mlle. Lenormand

1. 9 of Hearts
2. 6 of Diamonds
3. 10 of Spades
4. King of Hearts
5. 7 of Hearts
6. King of Clubs
7. Queen of Clubs
8. 9 of Diamonds
9. Queen of Spades
10. Jack of Diamonds
11. Jack of Clubs
12. 7 of Diamonds
13. Jack of Spades
14. 9 of Clubs
15. 10 of Clubs
16. 6 of Hearts
17. Queen of Hearts
18. 10 of Hearts
19. 6 of Spades
20. 8 of Spades
21. 8 of Clubs
22. Queen of Diamonds
23. 7 of Clubs
24. Jack of Hearts
25. Ace of Clubs
26. 10 of Diamonds
27. 7 of Spades
28. Ace of Hearts
29. Ace of Spades
30. King of Spades
31. Ace of Diamonds
32. 8 of Hearts
33. 8 of Diamonds
34. King of Diamonds
35. 9 of Spades
36. 6 of Clubs

It is striking that the cards that were taken correspond exactly to the arrangement of playing cards, which can also be found on the German 36 Lenormand Fortune Telling Cards. Likewise, each card of the French Petit Lenormand is provided with a number and a title of the card, which also corresponds to the German Lenormand Fortune Telling Card. But these are the only parallels, because neither in interpretation of each individual card nor in the display of the cards these systems are the same. All my in-depth research has proven to exclude connections between these two decks of cards. They are supposed connections.

CHAPTER II

First Insights

Basic Rules

(The beginning of the Grand Jeu)

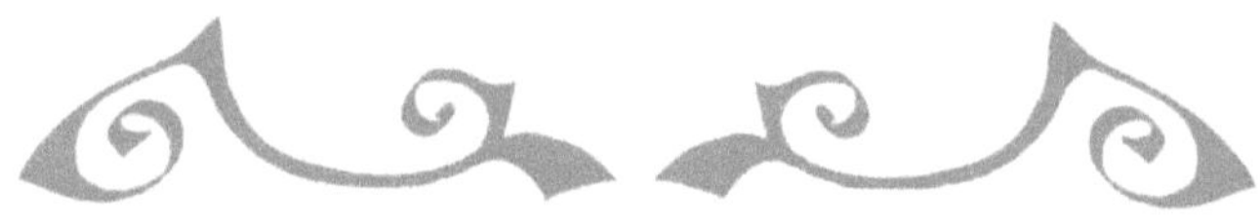

The 7 Basic Rules of Fortune Telling with the Grand Lenormand Cards

Now take a step back in time and read the cards as they were in 1845.

The explanation of the game, as presented in this book, corresponds to, and refers to the original instruction of divination with the Grand Jeu: the true, traditional way of fortune telling with these cards, as it once was done in the late 19th century.

You have now learned the meanings of the cards in the previous chapter, and you now know them inside out. Now you just need to know the rules you need to follow to read the cards according to the old traditional methods of 1845.

Whatever someone wants to know about what will happen in the future, you, as a card reader, must master the method of fortune telling with these cards perfectly. You must first shuffle the cards. Take the cards and then put them face down on the table. Take the number of cards from the deck you need for your spread. The number of cards you must take from the deck varies and always depends on the method you want to use. However, it is always important to take the odd number of Grand Lenormand Cards. Never do spreads with an even number of cards; you will see the reason why while reading this book.

First Rule If the Main Character card is not part of the cards that are drawn, the card in the middle represents the one who consults the card and its situation; this is the basis of the information that you seek.

Second Rule The cards on the left (from your perspective as a card reader) have a close connection to card in the middle;

they can affect it for better or worse, depending on whether they are positive or negative in their meaning. In the cards on the left, you can see the following: the habits of the Main Character, the current state, the morality, or even where it is missing, or where problems lie, important or less important personal facts. This means that you can see if the person is well or poor, has a marriage, or has a job. Here you will find all the information you need to know about the person who consults the cards.

The cards on the right determine the character, thoughts and the future of the person represented by the card in the middle. On this side, you can also see in the cards what the person likes most, what is desired and what can be difficult to have.
These cards to the right, therefore, have a great impact on the future of the person, more than others. If they are positive, it is an indication to the Querent that success is to be expected, but if they are negative and there are obstacles to be seen in future, it is a sure indication to the Querent to be able to mistrust or be careful.

Example (to imitate)

You should now know in general that with the Grand Lenormand Cards, the priority of the images you use for interpretation changes depending on the position of the card in the spread; and the card in the middle will be influenced by the smaller image on the right or left. I will describe this to you based on this spread of 5 cards as an example.

NOTE I always recommend that for each example explained in this book you take out the cards appearing in the example and then follow the explanation step by step not only theoretically, but also practically.

The following cards have been drawn:

King of Clubs. Jack of Clubs 9 of Clubs

Queen of Clubs 10 of Clubs

Now imagine a Gentleman consulting your cards, and you do not know what he wants to know right now; but based on the cards in this example you can see a few things:

1. The card in the middle is the Jack of Clubs. The Jack of Clubs represents the person who consults the cards; it seems that the Gentleman does almost everything to achieve his goals; but he will only be successful if he uses his abilities and intelligence purposefully, makes promises and thus skillfully seduces others. Note here that this card only uses the large image and the actual core meaning of the card to describe the person.

2. Directly to his left is the Queen of Clubs, a woman of good company, kind & generous. Note the smaller picture on the left side of the Querent (a woman holding a fan). This means the Gentleman seems to meet a woman who is carefree and enjoys the pleasure, and from whom he can expect an advantage because of her generosity.

3. The second card to his left, is the King of Clubs, an experienced man who can give wise advice. This means that the Querent must deal with business matters that may require a long journey (remember Jason's story, to which this card belongs). The second small picture on the left (two groups of rocks and a pigeon that must pass the rocks) also means that

the Gentleman should be careful and generally take precautions, because success is still doubtful.

4. The first card to the right of the Querent is the 10 of Clubs which promises success in an uncertain, risky situation/ in an uncertain matter. Now, if you look at the small picture pointing to the right side of the middle card (a branch of a vine with several grapes, above which is the talisman of Mars), you can see that the Querent has a powerful enemy, which is an obstacle to his business affairs. And all the ambitions and desires of the enemy focused on this one business, the enemy can be a rival or rather a competitor.

NOTE Based on the original instructions of the Grand Jeu, here is already given this additional note for interpretation: Remember, the picture contains the image of the Mars talisman, and this said: *"Third Fatality. Great courage that will make you risk your life to take an enemy a degree of strength. The talisman of Mars makes you invulnerable."* For now, however, you can put this information aside, because this will be part of a later chapter in this book.

5. Now you see the 9 of Clubs – this card is very good for the Querent because it predicts success for him (see page 53 in the interpretation section. 9 of Clubs). The Querent might be a merchant/ a businessman, because he has a card of commerce to his left (the side that tells you, for example, more about the habits and life circumstances of the person). He is not married, because he has no card to his left that would be a sign of marriage. He is not rich because he has no card to his left that stands for wealth. There is nothing extremely unfavorable to the Querent in all these cards. And even the smaller picture of the 9 of Clubs, which points to the right of the middle card (a merchant), and which refers directly to the Querent, thus indicates success and profit.

6. As a final message you can say that the Gentleman will succeed in what he desires, but not without experiencing

difficulties, and even at the peak of its success, certain events can still damage its interests or jeopardize its success.

In the explanation just given, you may have noticed that among the smaller images used for the interpretation, only the two pointing to the right were used, and the two pointing to the left side of the card representing the Querent. This is because only these pictures are directly related to the Main Character. The other pictures have nothing to do with the Main Character, and therefore they can go unnoticed.

Third Rule Now imagine another situation: You have a male client, and the card of the female Main Character appears at the same time in the five cards drawn, so this is proof that the Querent, is particularly interested in someone; this one person is represented by the opposing Person Card. In this case, it will not be difficult to interpret the cards according to the previous rules to see what the Querent wants to know.

Fourth Rule If one of the intentions of the Querent is to learn more about the thoughts or fate of another person, the small pictures that are not related to the card in the middle (in this case the other person) and were unimportant before, now relate to the person who consults the cards, so to speak with the actual Querent.

NOTE If you do this reading to find out the thoughts of another person; be it what they think about yourself or about another person, the only difference is that the card or position represent the Main Character (a person card or the card in the middle) represents the person you are asking for, not yourself.

Example (to imitate)

This example is intended to make this more understandable and transparent for you: Imagine a Lady will come to you to ask the cards and she tells you what she wants to know:

"I would like to become clear about the intentions of a young man, who, according to his words, seems very interested in in a relationship with me. I want to know what to hope for, what can I expect?"

You shuffle the cards for the Lady, cut them, put them face down on the table and take the first five cards (always explain to your client what you will do and always allow your opponent to ask questions).

The following cards have been drawn:

7 of Clubs — 10 of Diamonds — Jack of Diamonds — 6 of Hearts — 2 of Hearts

1. The card in the middle is the Jack of Diamonds (Odysseus in disguise). It indicates that the way the person presents himself to the Lady does not correspond to the way the person is, or that the said words do not correspond to the person's true intentions: the person's thought is hidden. The person seems to be dishonest, lying, or at least not telling everything, the person is "disguised". Note here that only the big picture and the actual main meaning of the card for the person is used.

2. The first card on the left, Karo 10, (Jason & Pelias) states that the man seems to be responsible for and works for a trading company and the card gives an indication that he will leave the company.

3. The second card on the left, the 7 of Clubs (Pan), is an important sign of seduction. Therefore, the actions of the young man in whom the Lady is interested are not profound or even serious intention. He is not rich because there are no cards on the left showing wealth. But he has intelligence and talent; this is evidenced by the small picture (the architect, the plans of the Argo) to his left. But the second, smaller picture (a worker holding his tools in his hands) explains that he never had the power or opportunity to make a great fortune.

4. He hopes to become rich and wants to achieve this through marriage, which could help him gain a higher position in society. This is explained by the 6 of Hearts (the alchemist looks with satisfaction at the stone turned into gold), which belongs to the theme of marriage. The material turns into gold, which shows wealth and success. Here is the first important small picture to the right side of the card in the middle (the small left picture of the card). An elderly and wealthy woman shown together with a younger man, this picture also underlines the person's intentions.

5. The second card on the right, 2 of Hearts (a group of partridges with a dog), and the small picture pointing to the right side of the middle card (a hermit, a monk) says that the Man is actually very withdrawn and quite disinterested; this Man has honestly no deep thought/no firm or inner intention to be in a marriage/relationship with the Lady.

This was a closer look at the other person's life or thoughts - but now comes the step of looking at the pictures related to the Lady who consults the cards (in this case, these are all small pictures that are not closely connected to the other person's card, to the middle card):

The interpretation of the smaller pictures, which are not directly related to the person being asked for, refers to the person

asking the cards, the actual Querent. Now look at all the small pictures that were not used for the interpretation before. This also applies to the small pictures of the card in the middle. These remaining small pictures tell you something about the Lady. The card in the middle, however, still represents only the person for whom the Lady asked and not the Lady herself - and the small pictures on this card belong to the Lady, because they were not previously in direct contact with the Man, and so you must put them in relation to the Lady.

Now look at what the small pictures on the right tell you about the Lady:

6. The card in the middle, Jack of Diamonds, shows with the small picture (soldiers in a row) that she believes in a superior, commanding force/ power that causes events in life to happen and must be followed, this suggests that the Lady might think that all of this is happening for a reason, a kind of destiny.

7. The second small picture of the card 6 of Hearts (an older man with a young woman) shows the honest and sincere intentions of the Lady, and this is also proved by the following card, 2 of Hearts, which can be interpreted from its core as a card of loyalty.

8. However, the third small picture (a fountain surrounded by green) on that card, 2 of Hearts, is more of a flattery, but it will make them happy, even if only for a certain time.

9. The first small picture you see on the left (Hera on a cloud) shows a kind of protection, which means that the Lady is guided through this situation.

10. The second small picture to the left, 10 of Diamonds (Jason in the forest of Dodona, an oracle) is already an indication that all this might give cause for concern, and this is indicated by the third small picture to the left on the card 7 of

Clubs (a furnace, with fire and sparks) with the message that the one she is interested in will only be a seducer.

NOTE You see, this reading is a way to answer all the questions someone has about another person's thoughts, intentions, or life situation. And remember here, if someone wants to do this reading to experience another person's thoughts, the essential difference is that that the other person is always represented by the original card of the Main Character or by the card in the middle of the spread.

Within the different ways to consult the cards, there are two other situations that you need to know:

Fifth Rule It is also necessary to anticipate the situation in which a card of the Main Character is found among the cards drawn, but this card does not appear as a middle card. Regardless of whether the Main Character's card is placed to the right or left, the way in which it is dealt with, and the explanation remains the same:

For example, if there are one card to the left and three to the right of the Main Character's card and vice versa, the meanings of the cards to the right and left are to be put in context as usual, as previously explained in the examples. This should no longer cause you any difficulties.

However, if the Main Character's card appears as the first card on the left and the Querent has all the other cards on his right, so after the Main Character's card, this is sometimes also a sign of conflict or quarrel with other people or oneself. Also, it can speak of indifference of the person. Indifference to everything that concerns friends, family or people close to the person. It would also mean that this person longs for and desires all that he does not have, and that he may not be satisfied at all with what he is currently given.

On the other hand, if the Main Character's card appears as the first card on the right and all other cards are on the left of the Main character, this is a sign of simplicity, a person full of affection, a sign of stability, loyalty to the family and to those with whom the person is often in contact and around himself.

Sixth Rule If both Main Character cards, both the female and the male main person, appear in the same spread of five cards, it is always the case that the interpretation is to be made as usual. But nevertheless, it is necessary to consider an important message: one of the two Main Character cards, which is placed more on the right, sincerely loves that person who is on the left, and the one placed more on the left side is rather indifferent to everything regarding the person on the right side. The affection shown here would usually be more out of duty or courtesy.

Seventh Rule For some reason, it can sometimes be important to take a closer look at the female and male Main Character. This will only be possible with the complete deck of Oracle Cards. Shuffle the cards again, cut them once and draw up to nine cards in a row. Do this until all the cards are dealt, forming eleven piles, and placing them from left to right.

The 11th pile contains only 4 cards. Now look at the different piles: The first pile, in which one of the Main Character cards is, you take, and it is put by you to the left. The pile with the 4 cards, the 11th pile, is now placed in the middle by you. The pile in which the other card of the Main Character is now placed to the right as a third pile.

All other cards are left aside and are no longer part of this set.

Example (to imitate)

Imagine that the first of the two Main Character cards in the left pile is the female Main Character; to the right of this pile, the

four-card pile (the eleventh pile) is now placed so that it is in the middle, and the pile containing the male Main Character card is placed next to the middle pile. So these three piles should now be in front of you:

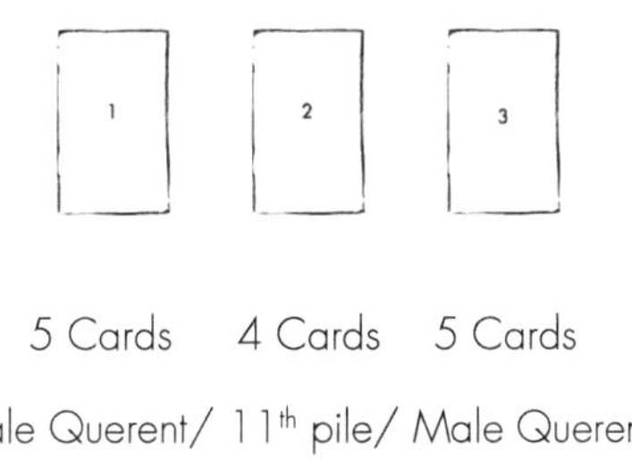

Together this makes a total of 14 cards. Now you put them together and divide them into two parts, since there are two people, now you have two piles with seven cards each. If you now deal the cards from left to right, this results in:

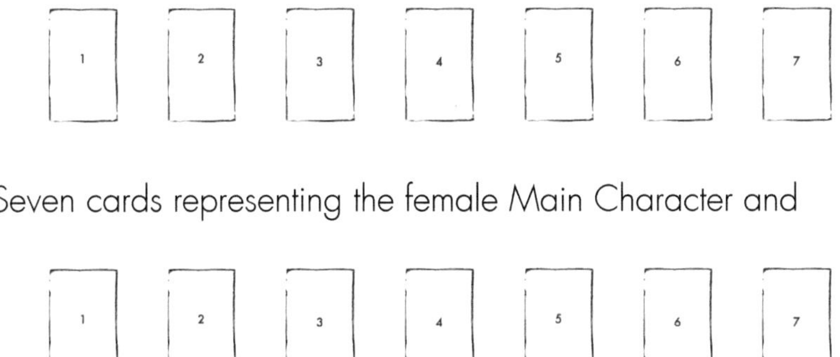

Seven cards representing the female Main Character and

Seven cards representing the male Main Character.

If you now follow the basic rules of the previous steps, you know now and the method of interpretation, it is easy to find out everything you want to know about the two people.

Practice Part & the Modern Tradition

Training with small spreads/the Shortcuts

This now following section in this chapter is for practice purposes and is not part of the traditional Grand Jeu.

It is always more effective, motivating, and fun to learn a new card system by practicing with the cards and being active. You can already start practicing card reading, even if some of the symbols and characters on the cards have not been explained yet. You get closer to the cards by using them by playing with them - you will build a foundation on which to build, and you will be more easily able to add the further information of the upcoming chapters.

To start practicing cartomancy, you can use a smaller spread, a shortcut. This type of spread is always with fewer cards, and this will help you get familiar with the cards and the different starting situations. You'll get a sense, a sense of certainty about which picture to choose for your interpretation - this will teach you how the cards interact with each other.

To practice, you can use different types of small spreads:

- Three Cards (Ancient or Modern Tradition)
- Three Cards (including Main Character Card)
- Five Card Spread (including Main Character Card)

At this point, while practicing, it is not important that you make the right interpretation or the true prediction. It's - as I said - about getting a feel for how the cards interact with each other and what matters in the first step of Grand Jeu.

Example (for practice)

Three cards without a Main Character Card

Start your exercise with a three-card spread in Ancient or Modern Tradition (in Modern Tradition, this means that this setting is not mentioned in the original manual and has been handed down from another source).

Take three cards from the pile - the original cards are huge - I don't really shuffle them like other cards, you can do it, but I prefer to hold the cards, let the finger go over it and feel like pulling out a particular card. Or I always take the top cards directly, no matter how, take three cards and put them on the table in front of you:

Now you have the cards in front of you - and in this example no Main Character card is drawn, and you now follow the traditional basic rules.

NOTE According to Modern Tradition, you would now interpret the cards from left to right only with the big picture, because there is no Main Character card, In the case of the modern variant, look at the meanings of each card and then try to make a sentence as a final statement with the three meanings. Always put the words of the images in the context of the question. If there is no card of the Main Character, in the Modern Tradition, you just focus on reading the big picture,
(If you would get into a Grand Jeu correctly, you would of course have to take the steps of the basic rules).

Example (for practice)

Three cards including a Main Character Card

In this example, to practice, you take a Main Character card, depending on who consults the cards, a female or male client. Place the card in front of you on the table, then take the deck and draw two more cards and place them around the Main Character card on the left and right. Now look at card number 2, the card to the left of the Main Character: here you now need the small right picture for your interpretation. The small right picture is that of the two small pictures, which touches the Main Character card on the left - At this point you do not have to look at the big picture of the card, but only at the small right picture. Then you look at the card number 3, you look at again only a small picture. Here you need for your interpretation the small left picture on the card, because the left picture is that of the two smaller pictures, which touches the Main Character card on the right side. The big pictures have no meaning.

NOTE If a Main Character card is present in the spread, you must consider: The cards that touch the Main Character must be read with the message of the small pictures. Always depending on which of the small pictures touches the Main Character card. The left side of the Main Character refers to the small right image of the card placed to the left of the person. The right side of the Main Character refers to the small left image of the card placed to the right of the person. A card that touches a Main Character card cannot be read with the big picture.

IMPORTANT The basic rules in this chapter describe the original and real method of interpretation. You connect all the small pictures with the card of the Main Character or the card in the middle.

Here the Modern Tradition differs somewhat in the interpretation: in the case that no Main Character is available, the focus is on the big pictures.

In the case that a Main Character is available, only the nearest small pictures are interpreted.

This should not confuse you. But it is important for you to know a method that comes from the Modern Tradition and is also preferred by some.

This does not have to be wrong, it is only a modern method of interpretation, and it helps you in practice purposes to get used to the meanings of the big pictures faster. But if you want to do the Grand Jeu for someone, always choose the original method, please.

Example (for practice)

Five cards spread (including Main Character Card)

In this example, to practice, you take a Main Character card, depending on who consults the cards, a female or male client. Place the card in front of you on the table, then take the deck

and draw four more cards. Place them left and right around the Main Character card as shown in the picture above.

You start with the cards that are directly adjacent to the Main Character (remember: a card that touches the Main Character card must be read with a small picture; the big picture is ignored). So here you would read the small right picture of card number two and the small left picture of card number three - because it is the small picture, which touches the Main Character card and thus have an influence on the person and their situation.

After you have made your interpretation of the two small pictures of card number two and three, you now go to the cards four and five. According to the traditional basic rules, you will now only use the small pictures for your interpretation.

Here the Modern Tradition differs somewhat in the interpretation: Modernity says that card number four and five, do not touch the Main Character card, therefore you now use in Modern Tradition the meanings of the big pictures. After you have made your interpretation of the two bigger pictures, you close your reading with a final statement in which you connect all messages of the cards (of course always in the context of the question).

NOTE In a spread with more than three cards, you may use the meanings of the big picture in the Modern Tradition for the interpretation of the cards that do not touch the Main Character card, and only for the interpretation of the cards adjacent to the Main Character card you must look at the small picture.

With the conclusion of this chapter, you now know the different possibilities of an interpretation of the small spreads. One of them is the Method of 1845, the way the cards were read. This is a real step back in time.

And with the practice part you can get used to the cards by experimenting, if you like, with the variant of the Modern Tradition.

Remember that the second variant is good for practice, but if you want to use the Grand Jeu Lenormand in a serious, professional, and authentic way for you or others, then you should always follow the seven basic rules and the upcoming rules for fortune telling with the Grand Lenormand Cards.

NOTE You may have noticed and remembered a small sentence in the example of the reading on page 261 that said:

"... This is explained by the 6 of Hearts (the alchemist looks with satisfaction at the stone turned into gold), which belongs to the theme of marriage..."

The 6 of Hearts is part of the theme of marriage, the next chapter will reveal all the secrets about the themes of the Grand Jeu Lenormand.

CHAPTER III

The Division of the Grand Jeu Lenormand

The Themes of the Grand Lenormand Cards

Coup de Cinq Cartes sur les Cinq Parties

The spread of Five Cards in Five Groups

Past, Present & Future

(based on the zodiac signs)

The Themes of the Grand Jeu de Mlle Le Normand

As you can read in the original manual of the Grand Jeu de Mlle Le Normand, the cards are divided into different groups. The groups have different content and are subject to different topics. Each of the groups often tells their own story in an order of cards that does not correspond to the order of the playing card symbols. The order given to you by the groups is the original order of the Grand Lenormand Cards. It is the best way to learn the cards based on the groups they belong to, so you will later recognize each card faster and understand the meaning more easily, instead of just learning the cards in the order of the playing cards. And you will also see how several cards relate to each other and explain themselves. This will help you understand the cards even better. For the future interpretation with these cards, it is necessary to understand the structure and the true nature of each card, otherwise you will lose yourself on the way through the world of the Gand Lenormand cards.

The deck is divided into 6 different groups of cards. These groups have a main theme, such as work, trade, love, relationships, and that will have an impact on any spread & interpretation.

NOTE I always say 6 groups because I find the cards of the Main Characters very important and therefore see them as an own group. In the original manual you can read about 5 groups, because the Main Character cards do not belong to a group.

I "Les Consultantes"

The Main Characters

The Gentleman The Lady

This group is very easy to keep in mind, it is the group of Main Characters - the two cards of the Main Characters. Here you will find the card of the Lady & the Gentleman, representing a person, the Querent. These cards can be selected for placement, or you can make them appear randomly if the cards so wish. If one of these cards is selected for a placement, you start here with your interpretation. If the card was not selected before and one of these cards appears, it is especially important because it has a great influence on the current situation, and you then interpret this, and the other cards based on the rules mentioned above.

II "La Conquête de la Toison d'Or"

The Conquest of the Golden Fleece

The Conquest of the Golden Fleece is a group of five cards, the first ancient legend the cards speak of.
These cards all together represent the subject of trade, work, business, and profession.

These are the 5 cards of the group (according to the storyline):

10 of Diamonds   King of Clubs   Ace of Clubs

9 of Diamonds.   4 of Diamonds

These five cards tell the story of Jason and his conquest of the Golden Fleece. Usually, the story ends with the card Ace of Clubs, but in the original manual it is mentioned that you can add the 9 of Clubs after the Ace as the last card, since Hercules was part of Jason's companions. But it remained only with this mention, because as you can see with the Ace of Clubs, the actual task of Jason is over and completed, so the card 9 of Clubs seems to be a bit out of place. And so, the original instructions of the card 9 of Clubs only gave this double feature by name: it stands for both the trade and for a zodiac sign. Nevertheless, the card was only assigned to the group of the zodiac. All cards in the "Golden Fleece" group have a certain effect on a reading: In a spread with more cards, it may be that many cards come from this group. The reading will therefore have a more commercial, trade-related touch, because you already know that these cards represent the subject of trade, work, business, and profession. And as mentioned earlier, if several of these cards appear in a spread or on certain positions, this can already be seen as an indication that the concern is very business-related, professional nature or more material and sober character and less emotional.

III "La Guerre de Troie" ou „Le Droit du Fort su le Faible"

The Trojan War or The Victory of the Strong over the Weak

The next ancient story takes you back to the time of the Trojan War. The Trojan War is a well-known chapter of ancient history and mythology, so it also had to take place in this game. This group was also called by Mlle Lenormand "The victory of the strong over the weak" and symbolizes situations of private life, challenges, social problems - it is important to know that there is only one positive card in this group; the others are to be seen as worse and less favorable cards.

These are the 9 cards of the group (according to the storyline):

Queen of Diamonds 2 of Spades 10 of Clubs 6 of Clubs

5 of Clubs Jack of Diamonds 9 of Spades

6 of Spades 8 of Spades

Now you visit the alchemist's workplace, his laboratory and learn more about:

IV "La Science Hermetique" ou "La Mariage di Beya et Gabertin"

The Hermetic Science or The Marriage of Beya & Gabertin

Due to the chemical experiment of the alchemist, this group of cards is also called the search for the "Philosopher's Stone".

There are seven cards in this group, and you can easily recognize them, because the scene of the big picture is always the laboratory/kitchen of the alchemist who works and researches with passion. These cards are examples of all love and relationship situations in our lives, so this group of cards is the one that leads you into the topic of personal relationships. These cards usually represent our connections and interactions with others, our friendships, our marriage, and our (love) relationships. In his experiment, the alchemist goes through different levels/stages in which his materials interact and react differently with each other - these reflect the different stages of the relationship or coexistence; for example, from tender bonds of love to a firm bond of marriage. And you can therefore imagine that it could be a bit more emotional when these cards appear.

These are the 7 cards of this group (according to the storyline):

7 of Spades

3 of Clubs

4 of Clubs

8 of Clubs

7 of Hearts

10 of Hearts

6 of Hearts

V "Les Événements Imprévus"

The Unforeseen Events

The cards of "unforeseen events" speak of different life situations and different events in life. They show everyday aspects and situations of life. They can be seen as cards that respond to a kind of fateful events and situations; the destiny that is given to us and that we must face. These cards also talk about social life and social problems. We know many of these happenings that happen by accident, and these cards are about those challenges of everyday life. This card group comes close to the group that tells the story of the Trojan War, but it is listed as a separate group because here the different cards are not connected by an ancient historical story. Each card appears independently of the others in this group; there is no continuous storyline. Each card has its own, independent story.

These are the 19 cards of that group:

Taken from the Suit of Clubs:

2 of Clubs Jack of Clubs Queen of Clubs

Taken from the Suit of Hearts:

Ace of Hearts 3 of Hearts 8 of Hearts
2 of Hearts 5 of Hearts King of Hearts

Taken from the Suit of Diamonds:

Ace of Diamonds 6 of Diamonds King of Diamonds
2 of Diamonds 7 of Diamonds

Taken from the Suit of Spades:

3 of Spades. 10 of Spades King of Spades
4 of Spades. Queen of Spades

VI "Zodiac" ou "L'Ordre du Temps"

The Zodiac Signs or the Order of Time, the Determination of Time

The last group of cards represents the zodiac signs - they are designed to give an indication of the time or time of an event, depending on the position and appearance in a spread (in the old tradition, they also gave conclusions & indications of upcoming diseases). Of course, if the cards are not related to the calculation of time, they have their core meaning, which is explained by the stories of the pictures and symbols - just like the other cards. These cards are, regardless of the zodiac sign, comparable to the card group "The unforeseen events", because even these cards (except as already mentioned the 9 of Clubs) are not through a coherent story like the Trojan War", the conquest of the Golden Fleece" or the wedding of Beya & Gabertin" connected. Each card can be considered independent of each other - they only have in common that they symbolize a zodiac sign and the only order they follow that is the zodiac.

These are the 12 cards of this group (in the order of the zodiac signs):

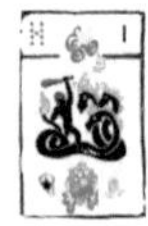

Jack of Hearts   3 of Diamonds   9 of Hearts

Ace of Spades   9 of Clubs   Queen of Hearts

Jack of Spades. 5 of Spades 8 of Diamonds

5 of Diamonds. 7 of Clubs 4 of Hearts

A gender is assigned to each of the 12 zodiac signs:

Jack of Hearts	Aries	masculine
Ace of Spades	Taurus	feminine
3 of Diamonds	Gemini	masculine
9 of Clubs	Cancer	feminine
9 of Hearts	Leo	masculine
Queen of Hearts	Virgo	feminine
Jack of Spades	Libra	masculine
5 of Diamonds	Scorpio	feminine
5 of Spades	Sagittarius	masculine
7 of Clubs	Capricorn	feminine
8 of Diamond	Aquarius	masculine
4 of Hearts	Pisces	feminine

NOTE An important reminder for you is to learn the meanings of the cards always according to the different groups, because they have a storyline that you can follow to understand the cards so easier. Because based on the meanings of the old story that you get told by the cards, you can connect the cards faster with each other. When learning, please do not stick to the order of the playing cards, but always to the order of the groups and stories, so the Grand Lenormand Cards show up without confusion. It is also important to say that you do not need to be or become an expert in mythology to interpret the cards. In chapter I you were told all the stories, so you can always look up. It is only important to transfer the message of the stories to the life situations and put them in context. If you know what is happening from the pictures on the card, you will no doubt understand what the card is trying to tell you.

Coup de Cinq Cartes sur les Cinq Parties.

The Five Card Spread of the Five Groups.

(based on the groups into which the Grand Jeu de Mlle Le Normand is divided)

As you know by now, in the Grand Lenormand there are groups that relate to personal life situations or to the topics of life. There are five theme groups (the sixth is for me the one with the two Main Character cards).

In the case that a life situation is unclear, or a person has questions about what will happen in life, there is the spread of "Five cards of the Five Groups", which is based on the different card groups of the Grand Lenormand, and this will now be the next step in the Grand Jeu.

It is important to keep track of the names and positions of the five decks in this spread and not to confuse them, so the following picture should help you to remember which pile, which group is in which position:

The 5 piles/ the 5 groups

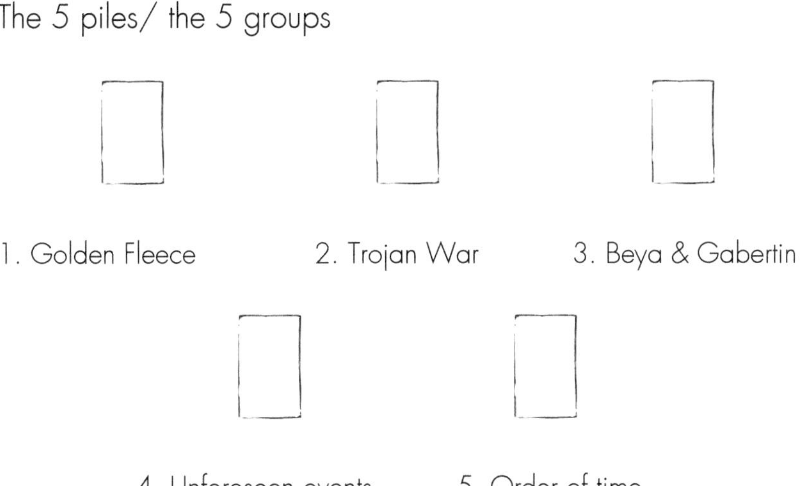

Before you start with this spread of the card and the layout, it is according to old tradition important to prepare the layout in a special way - this always makes this all so mysterious, but that is the beauty of the cartomancy.

There is a special way of handing out the cards; tradition says that you must always follow this rule, otherwise the oracle will not speak properly or clearly, or it will hide something from you. It's simple - even if it might seem complicated at first glance, but it's simple:

Shuffle, cut the cards and take away the top card for the male Querent and the bottom card for the female Querent. Always take both cards, whether the person is male or female - you must always take both cards from the deck. These two cards are placed aside as a reserve, and later serve as additional information about the topic or event that interests the person consulting the cards the most.

Now we continue with the layout of the other cards:

1. Count the cards from 1, 2, 3… up to twelve and place the 12th card on the first pile/position.

Now count 1, 2, 3… this time only up to ten and place this card on the 2nd pile.

Again, count to ten and put the card on the 3rd pile.

Again, count to ten please and put the card on the 4th pile.

And once again count to ten and put the card on the 5th pile.

Now you should have five piles with one card each.

You'll have to do these four more times, but it will change a little each time. Follow the instructions here to follow the next steps:

2. Count the cards again, but this time it will be different: please only count to eleven and put the 11th card on the first pile.

Now count until card number nine and put it on the 2nd pile.

Count to nine again and put the card on the 3rd pile.

Count to nine again and put the card on the 4th pile.

and count to nine again and put this card on the 5th pile.

Now you have five piles with two cards each.

3. Repeat the process, but now with this difference:

Please count to ten first and put this 10th card on the 1st pile.

Now count to eight and place the eighth card on the 2nd pile.

Count to eight again and put this card on the 3rd pile.

Count to eight again and put this card on the 4th pile.

Now count to eight again and put the card on the 5th pile.

Now you should have five piles with three cards each.

4. In the fourth step, you must first count to nine and place this card on the 1st pile.

Then please count to seven and place this card on the 2nd pile.

Now count to seven again and place the card on the 3rd pile.

Count to seven again and put this card on the 4th pile.

If you count to seven again, you can place the card on the 5th pile.

Now you have five piles with four cards each.

5. (last step) Now you must first count to eight and place this card on the 1st pile.

Please count to six and place the 6th card on the 2nd pile.

Count to six and put this card on the 3rd pile.

Count to six again and place the card on the 4th pile.

And finally count to six again and put the last card on the 5th pile.

Now you have five piles with five cards each.

You realize that you have done everything right when you have no cards in your hands after each step because the cards are counted. It's math, and it's calculated to always work, so after each round you've made, there should be no cards left in your

hand. The remaining cards, which are not part of the spread can be put aside until further notice.

Now that you have laid out the cards, you can follow the next step:

The five piles of five cards can now be turned over, one card at a time, and should be laid from left (position of the first card) to right (position of the last card), starting with the first pile of five cards.

Now you look closely to see if among the five cards of each stack you can find cards of the type that belong thematically and by classification to the group after which the pile is named (for example: check if you see a card from the series "Golden Fleece" in the pile that belongs to the story of the Golden Fleece).

But if there is no card of the series "the Golden Fleece" in the first pile representing the profession & trade, it is because there will be no professional action, no professional topic, no event in this matter for the Querent.

And if there is no card of the "Trojan War" in the second pile, which represents the "victory of the strong over the weak", then it means that in the current and coming situation, the Querent must not be afraid of deception and injustice.

If there is no "Hermetic Sciences" card in the third pile that represents the "Mariage du Beya et Gabertin" /Marriage & Relationships, it means there will be no relationship problems.

And if the fourth pile, the "Unforeseen Events", contains none of the different cards belonging to this group, it tells the Querent that nothing unforeseen will happen in future.

If there are no cards of the "zodiac signs" in the fifth pile indicating the "order of time", this is because the Querent currently has no important phase of life to go through or that it is not an event, that causes the Querent to stop or even rethink their journey. In addition, if this type of card is missing here, it is also a sign that the hint of the cards is missing to determine the time of an event based on a zodiac sign.

NOTE Here it is important for you to know that in the pile "Order of Time", the first card placed determines the time of the event of the first pile/ group of the entire spread, the pile of work life, the second card determines the time of the events, through the pile of the Trojan War" are shown, the third placed card in the pile of "Order of Time" determines the time of the events of the third group (that of the relationships); and the fourth card reveals the time of the events in the pile of "Unforeseen Events", so the events of the fourth pile. The fifth card of the pile "Order of Time" always refers to the Querent himself. It is very important to remember and know that only the cards showing a zodiac sign have a function/meaning in the last pile, others are meaningless at this point and can be ignored. To determine the time, you should know that there are different time periods which relate to each sign of the zodiac.

To determine the time, you need to know that there are different periods that refer to the zodiac signs.

Past, Present & Future

(indicated by the zodiac signs)

These periods generally apply in advance:

1. Aquarius & Pisces - past
2. Pisces & Aries - recent past
3. Aries & Taurus - present/ present
4. Gemini & Cancer - present/ near future
5. Leo & Virgo - distant time/ distant future
6. Libra & Scorpio: far time/ far future
7. Sagittarius & Capricorn - very distant time in the future, uncertain time

See the timescale here:

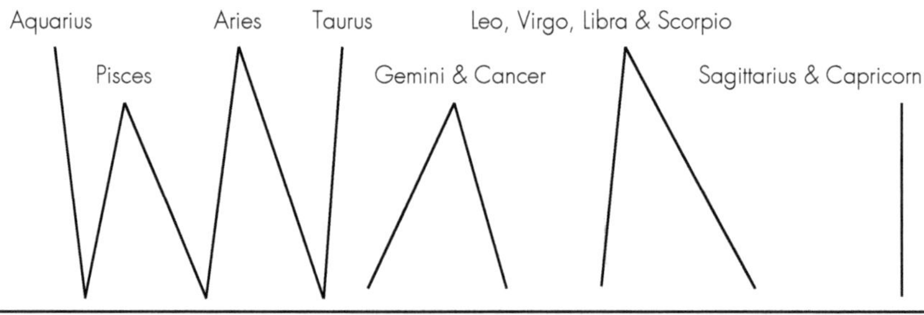

You can use these periods if you want general information about an event or situation. Sometimes, for example, in the past there is an event that is still the cause of the problems or current situation of the Querent. With the sign of Aquarius, you get the hint that something happened in the past, which is partly the reason that some things are exactly as they are now.

NOTE As known from contemporary witnesses, it is said that Mlle. Lenormand had a passion for mathematics, horoscopes and calculating and playing with numbers - and so it was always a pleasure for her to explore the methods and circumstances to be able to calculate the time of upcoming events even more accurately.

Thus, each zodiac sign is also assigned a numerical value - this number will later be important for a more accurate calculation of time.

The individual numerical value of the zodiac signs:

Aries	3	Leo	15	Sagittarius	27
Taurus	6	Virgo	18	Capricorn	30
Gemini	9	Libra	21	Aquarius	33
Cancer	12	Scorpio	24	Pisces	36

Therefore, if a zodiac sign determines the time of an event alone, you can see from the numerical value that the time in which the event occurs always in relation to 3, 6, 9, etc. stands.

For example, if the timing of an event in work life or wedding is influenced by the zodiac sign of Gemini, this event takes place at a time that is twice as far in the future as it would be influenced by the sign of Aries. (Aries has the value of 3 and Gemini has the value of 9; this means that the Gemini has with

9 twice the value of the Aries: 3 + (2 x 3) = 9). But if this event is determined, for example, by Cancer or Leo, then takes place 3 times or 4 times later in the future on the time scale, as if the event would be determined by the zodiac sign Aries.

For the timescale of the future, you can always refer to the age of the Querent and/ or the average life expectancy that we generally have. And so, you will be able to easily calculate the time of the event with some practice and experience in the future.

Example (to imitate)

Imagine that a person wants to be clear about a life situation, and you use the method of Five Cards in the Five Groups, which was explained in this chapter. You have laid out the cards as before and set aside two cards as a reserve.

1. The first pile does not contain a work card, so it is not useful, and will not be important for your interpretation.

2. The second pile contains only one card of the "Trojan War", and this card does not reveal anything the Querent is associated with, so it does not indicate anything important – just more general information, no warning, nothing bad. The card stands out, but you don't have to go deeper.

3. The third pile does not contain a card that is like the theme of relationship or marriage, so it is not important for your interpretation.

4. The fourth pile is the only pile containing important cards related to the theme: a card is part of the Trojan War (Queen of Diamonds), and the four other cards all belong to the "Unforeseen Events" group.

Queen of Diamonds 3 of Hearts 2 of Clubs

King of Spades King of Hearts

The card in the middle is the 3 of Hearts. Due to the position of the card next to the King of Spades, the right small picture (the bailiff and the sealed letter) is to be interpreted in such a way that the Querent seems to be a poor young man, who may have financial worries or debts and is simply trapped by this situation / in chains.

The second card on the left, the Queen of Diamonds, indicates an unpleasant acquaintance the Querent made (it is the card that represents a bad person). And because of the small picture on the right of this cards (Paris hands over the apple to Aphrodite) it can be said that this young man is in this situation because he has close contact with a person of malicious intentions. This person is jealous because he sees that someone else is put above himself, so this person tried to harm the young man and harmed him in an act of revenge.

But the Querent is an honest man. This is proved by the interpretation of the first card to his right, the King of Hearts, and by the small left image of this card (the Book of the Laws of Solomon): A young man has a clear and good mind and spirit; he must follow the advice and teachings of his own experience and perhaps even the advice of a wise man to whom he is inclined and to whom he looks up positively.

The second card to his right, 2 of Clubs, with the small picture on the left (a rock on which a bird sits), can be interpreted in such a way that the Querent will get out of this embarrassment,

the bad influence of this person. Later he will again be regarded as a good person and gain fame and wealth in his own way, if only if he henceforth concentrates on his talents and his spirit and no longer on the wrong persons.

In the following you should now look at the card that was put away at the beginning of the reading. The first reserved card is for the male Querent. It turns out in this example that this card is the 6 of Clubs:

The Querent is warned by this card of problems, conflicts, and disagreements. But he should continue straight on the actual path; turning back now would lead to failure. He must overcome the situation because he cannot step back and undo things.

Now look in the last, the fifth pile. Here the fourth card in the pile "Order of Time" (it stands for the time of events of the fourth pile in the spread) is randomly the zodiac sign Gemini, the sign Gemini represents the number/ the value 9.

It is the card that determines the event/time at which the Querent will experience a change in the situation.

Comparative chart of life with years

Explanation of the chart

The ancient philosophers divided life into 12 periods, each lasting 5 years, beginning from the age of 15 years. Each of these periods is under the influence of a zodiac sign. Just like the lunar year that the philosophers used, which here consists of 360 days, it is divided into 12 parts of 30 days each. Within the 30 days always belong to three periods of 10 days.

Zodiac Sign	Number of years under the influence of the zodiac sign	The order of the zodiac signs	Value of each Zodiac Sign in relation to a year
	from/to		Days/ Decade (ten days)
Aries	15 – 20	1	30 / 3
Taurus	20 – 25	2	60 / 6
Gemini	25 – 30	3	90 / 9
Cancer	30 – 35	4	120 / 12
Leo	35 – 40	5	150 / 15
Virgo	40 – 45	6	180 / 18
Libra	45 – 50	7	210 / 21
Scorpio	50 – 55	8	240 / 24
Sagittarius	55 – 60	9	270 / 27
Capricorn	60 – 65	10	300 / 30
Aquarius	65 – 70	11	330 / 30
Pisces	70 – 75	12	360 / 36

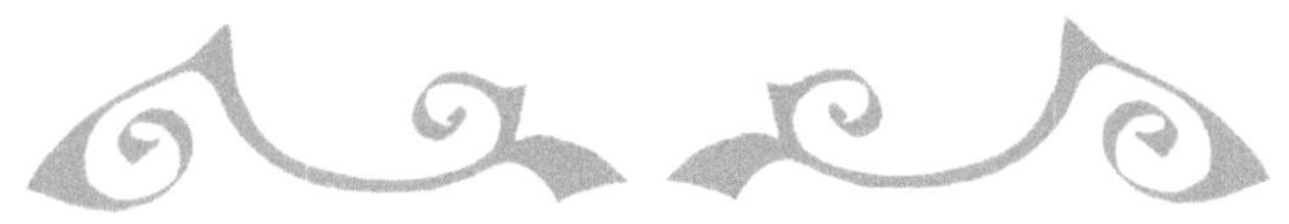

Example (for recalculation)

This is how you calculate the time of the event according to this chart:

1. Suppose the Querent is 26 years, 6 months, and 15 days old; he is, therefore, as can be seen from the chart in the sign of Gemini, begins with the age of 25 and ends at the age of 30.

2. It is now necessary to calculate the time that the Querent had to remain under this sign according to his age: if one subtracts 26 years, 6 months and 15 days from 30 years, the result is: 3 years, 5 months, and 15 days. The Querent must therefore remain under the influence of the zodiac sign of Gemini for another 3 years, 5 months and 15 days.

3. Then you must split the 3 years, 5 months, and 15 days into 12 parts. To simplify this classification, you should convert the entire time into days:

Starting with the years: 3 years are 3 times 360 days (remember that the year of the ancient philosophers was 360 days long), which results in 1080 days.

Now look at the chart to convert the months: It is to see that 5 months give 150 days. These must therefore be added to the 1080 days, which results in 1230 days, to this sum the remaining 15 days must now be added, resulting in a total of 1245 days.

Divide these 1245 days by 12 and this division results:

1245: 12 = 103,75

The result is 103 days, with a remainder of 0,75. You can always neglect the rest, as the rest is not significant. It is also not rounded.

4. After that, the 103 days should be multiplied by the number of the position of the zodiac sign associated with the event: in the example, this is the zodiac sign Gemini, whose place in the order is number 3. The calculation is therefore: 103 days x 3 = 309 days or 10 months 9 days.

So, the situation of the young man will be change at this time.

NOTE The original instructions of the Grand Jeu state that the position in the order of the zodiac signs and not the independent value of the zodiac sign should be taken for the last multiplication.

However, there are also sources that calculate with the independent value of the zodiac sign, which in this example would be the value 9 - there are these two different options. And with the second, it makes perfect sense that you need to remember and keep an eye on the overall value of the zodiac sign found in the pile.

It is also said that without a card of the zodiac it is not possible to determine the exact time of an event and you have to resort to another method of timing: It is then possible for you to ask about the age of the Querent and then from this part to follow the steps mentioned; and in the last step it is only necessary to take the sign of the zodiac, which, due to the age of the Querent, still exerts influence on him, which is very easy for you to see in the chart.

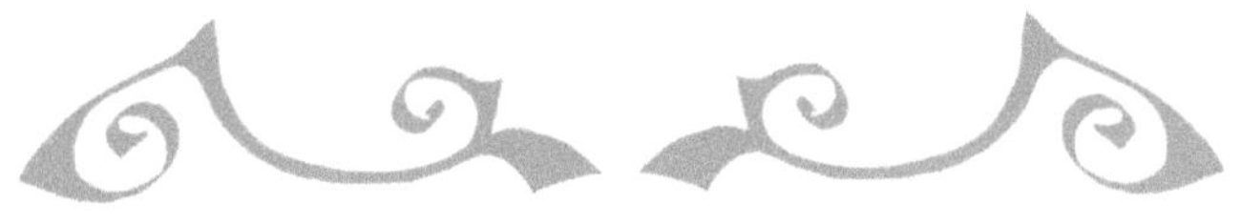

CHAPTER IV

Coup de Cinq Cartes sur les Cinq Parties

The Five Card Spread of the Five Groups.

Additional Spreads

The Spread of the Fifteen Cards

The Spread of the Nine Cards

(additional information – example)

Coup de Cinq Cartes sur les Cinq Parties.

The Five Card Spread of the Five Groups.

The Additional Spreads of 15 & 9 Cards (as a kind of proof)

Fortune Telling with the Grand Lenormand cards is subject without exception to certain rules, which are always better and easier to understand if you explain them with concrete examples. This chapter explains an example of an additional step to be taken when using the spread "five cards in five groups".

NOTE During each reading, you must adhere to the seven basic rules mentioned at the beginning and the statements you make within the various steps of the Grand Jeu should be made carefully and, if necessary, explain and justify these statements.

In the instruction from the year 1845 another example taken from the life of the Mlle. Lenormand became for a better understanding of the spread of the five groups.
For this example, you need this few historical background information for a better understanding:

There were many important and extraordinary forecasts from Mlle. Lenormand, some of which are also written down in one or the other biography of this famous fortune teller. A famous story was about a prophecy she made at a young age, even before her great career, during her time in a monastery. Mlle. Lenormand was in a Benedictine monastery when the abbess was deposed for misconduct; this led to many rumors spreading in the monastery and even outside of these walls. It was said that Mlle. Lenormand had secretly questioned the oracle regarding this lady. This prediction was made known through narratives, and revealed the consequences of this impeachment and whether the abbess would be reinstated or replaced.

Example (to imitate)

You start by shuffling and cutting the cards, as explained in the second chapter, and proceed as explained to see how the Querent's situation is represented and whether some events are highlighted by the cards.

The following seven cards are:

9 of Spades — King of Spades — 3 of Spades — Querent — Ace of Spades — 5 of Spades — Ace of Diamonds

To the left of the center is the 3 of Spades (the Moirai), the second card is the King of Spades (Menes), the third card is the spades 9 (Helena, who hides her despair, in the company of her maids). On the right, the first card is the Ace of Spades (Zeus turns into a bull to kidnap Europa), the second card is 5 of Spades (the death of the centaur Chiron) and the third card is the Ace of Diamonds (Harpocrates).

After you have looked at these six cards, in the middle of which the Querent, in this example the abbess, is located (she is represented by the card of the female Main Character and thus appears to you of great importance) you can interpret the cards as follows:

The first card to her left, the Moirai (the card with the strongest influence on the Querent), indicates death; she thinks of death. Death overshadows her; but to say that the Lady herself would be threatened with death, she would have to have a card like the 8 of Spades on the right. So, it is obvious that the card of the Moirai announces the death/end of her position, her loss, her downfall; and what this proves is the fact that the Moirai are preceded by the card of Menes presiding over the negotiations, a card that also represents law, rigor, justice, decision, or judgment. The third card on the left, Helena, shows the desperation of the Querent. There is also a thought of remorse in this card, the Lady is "fallen", she knows about her defeat, the severity of the law, justice has hit her.

The three cards on the right now indicate the cause of the loss, and these cards also indicate the thoughts: You see on the map Ace of Spades, Zeus and Europa, a scene that indicates an ambiguous behavior. On the second card you see the death of the centaur Chiron, which indicates weakness and negligence in pursuing obligations and thus shows a culprit, a self-inflicted. And the third card, Harpocrates, the card of the messenger & the messages, and its left small picture with Argus, which here refers to the Main Character, shows the indiscretion.

The last of the six cards on the left, 9 of Spades, shows the despair of the Main Character and the last card on the right, Ace of Diamonds, shows an indiscreet messenger or confidant. With all this information, there is no doubt that the removal of the Lady was caused by the indiscretion of a confidant.

With the following method, the proof, you can see if and what to confirm, refute or add from this first preview:

The Spread of the Fifteen Cards

You shuffle all the cards again, and after you shuffle the cards, cut them once and draw fifteen random cards from the deck. Now these fifteen cards are laid out from left to right in the order in which they were drawn. The first card on position one, the second card on position two..., etc., (see the picture).

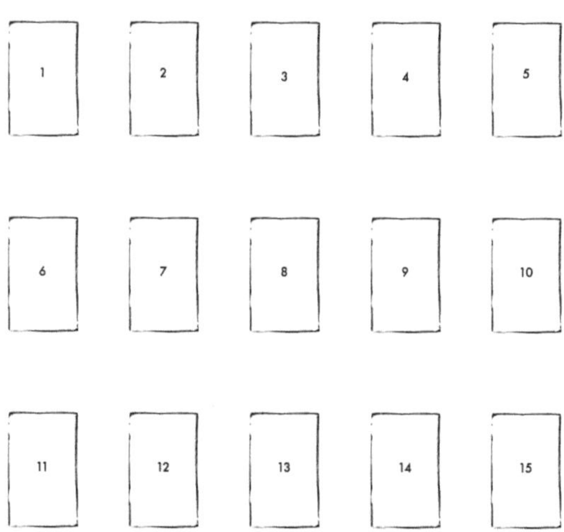

Each of the fifteen positions occupied by a card is assigned a certain meaning, which is then set in relation to the meaning of the card that is in the corresponding position after the layout of the cards.

The **1st position** describes a peaceful person, a self-employed person or someone who follows a paid profession or generally an employment, someone who has a fixed income, could be also a pensioner. And the card on this position describes or is related to a person. If this is a good card, it predicts ease and tranquility.

The **2nd position** means loss of wealth, a bad lifestyle, disorderly living conditions. The position shows where loss and disorder are.

The **3rd position** means happiness, health, security, protection. The position shows where joy and security are.

The **4th position** is inauspicious for lovers, unbound persons. It is only good for officials, doctors and artists, and people who have the ambition to achieve something.

The **5th position** means that a person does not keep their promises or promises more than they can really keep. The position that shows areas where unreliability can be expected.

The **6th position** describes situations where a start does not go well; a bad start to business or a bad start to some undertakings, which is caused by the carelessness of the person involved.

The **7th position** indicates that someone, through the support of a person, often a woman, gets what he wants, or expects messages that will be good or bad depending on the card.

The **8th position** stands for a marriage or a relationship that causes difficulties, but also difficult living conditions in general.

The **9th position** describes a deception, a theft, something is taken, be it the idea of something or, indeed, an object. If the card 5 of Diamonds lay here, it would be a theft by a servant, a theft in the domestic, private area; the card Ace of Diamonds, on the other hand, would indicate damage due to indiscreet behavior; and the 10 of Spades would be a theft, that would greatly affect personal destiny.

The **10th position** is good for trials and benefits everyone raised with dignity and decency.

The **11th position** stands for a change of location, change of residence, a movement, a change in general and it shows where inconsistency is.

The **12th position** means getting good news and things, showing success, successful ventures, or success at work.

The **13th position** is only good for villains and traitors, because they do not mind the bad that it promises, but for a person who unfortunately finds himself in this position, although he has good intentions and behaves well, this position will still be a loss (e.g., of money or job).

The **14th position** means unforeseen illness or injury.

The **15th position** means happy marriage, travel, joy.

If you use the cards & method of the proof often, you will soon know the basic meanings of the fifteen positions, but since this alone is not helpful for explaining this method, the following example is a support, to help you understand these steps.

Example (for explanation & to imitate)

You have prepared the spread and now see that the Main Character's card is not part of your fifteen cards and that among these fifteen cards there is only one card of the six cards that have previously surrounded the middle card (the Main Character).

The 9 of Spades (Helena) is the card that reappears. Since almost no card reappears here and the card of the Main Character is missing, your first interpretation alone could be a bit vague and does not seem to belong to the person alone.

Take a closer look at this for more information:

The first of your fifteen cards is 8 of Hearts (the eagle and the toad). This card means that a person is free from anyone who does damage to him, this card is peaceful happiness. A real connection between the meaning of the card and the meaning of the position can only be established if one can say that an honest and peaceful person, regardless of his status or wealth, has become happy only through this, because he got rid of someone who hurt him.

The second card, 7 of Hearts, (the alchemist who adds the solvent) indicates a visit or receipt of a message. This card is in second place, the position of loss of wealth and bad living. The interpretation could be that a person who is thoughtless and behaves badly, due to his own misconduct, receives a message or a visit with the message that there are consequences in the form of immediate punishment. This leads to the loss of something or even the loss of the economic existence of the person.

The third card is the King of Diamonds (Cadmus & Minerva) and the third position it occupies represents luck, ease, and conviction. These are opposites that cannot be easily reconciled. There is also no simple explanation, as the card represents a serious man full of wisdom and reason. Here you have to look a little behind the facade and pay close attention to the context, because there are some cases where this card can be explained in this position: A young man, for example, who simple origins, without possessions, but still very vain, because he has a good reputation, wants to win the attention or favor of others by deliberately showing himself to be serious & helpful and convincingly arguing to gain the desired respect.

The fourth card, 2 of Diamonds, (A child on a goat) and the fourth position it occupies, are unfortunately not promising for people in love. If the Main character is a married person, no explanation will be necessary here, as the person is already

officially bound. It is then necessary to look more closely at the map if it is a young girl or a young single woman. She must be afraid to make a mistake of inattention. This would lead, for example, to an unwanted pregnancy that would make her despair. If it were a young man, he would find himself in an unwanted, unfavorable situation because of his thoughtless behavior.

The fifth card is the 9 of Spades (Helena). Of all the cards that have just been explained, this is the only card that really interests you in this example, as this card has already appeared before. In the scene of the big picture Helena hides her despair, this card is a card that shows not only despair but also remorse. The fifth position this card occupies can only be interpreted in such a way that the person does not keep his promises. The Lady for whom you interpret the cards will therefore feel remorse because she has not kept her promises.

You can stop here with this reading, because in this example there is no other card that would be useful for you, because it is not a card among the others that had already appeared. And you walked the path to the card, 9 of Spades, which was there before.

NOTE If no cards were to be included again, these cards would only be everyday events, business relationships, private situations or the cards may even be of minimal or less important importance.

The Spread of Nine Cards

After the spread of these fifteen cards there is the next step. You shuffle all the cards again, cut them once and this time take nine cards from the deck and place them in 3 x 3 cards (see picture).

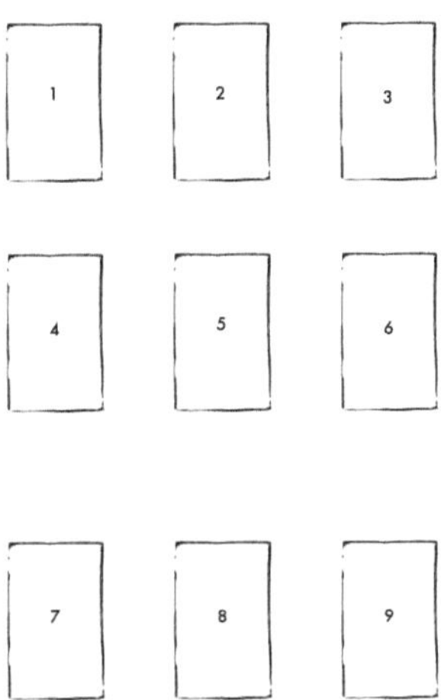

These nine cards may show signs of very important and significant events in some spreads, but it should be noted that an event always begins with the first card and is completed and explained by the third, sixth and ninth card:

The cards 1, 3, 6 and 9 are important within these nine cards. So, important within these 9 cards, will be the cards No. 1, 3, 6 and 9.

Example (for explanation & to imitate)

This time, among these nine cards, only one of the six cards that previously surrounded the Main Character is found. It is the 3 of Spades (the Moirai), but the Main Character's card is still not included in the cards drawn.

In this example, you have these cards drawn:

9 of Diamonds 3 of Hearts 10 of Diamonds

Jack of Clubs 4 of Spades 7 of Hearts

2 of Spades 5 of Clubs 3 of Spades

The first card is the 9 of Diamonds (the Argo); the second card is the 3 of Hearts (the Cynocephaly); the third card is the 10 of Diamonds (Jason & Pelias); the fourth card is the Jack of Clubs (Hypomennes & Atalanta); the fifth card is the 4 of Spades (Semele & Hera); the sixth card is the 7 of Hearts (the Alchemist & the solvent); the seventh card is the 2 of Spades (Menelaus & Calchas); the eighth card is the 5 of Clubs (Paris & Helena); and the ninth card is the 3 of Spades (the Moirai).

The first card, 9 of Diamonds (the Argo with the Argonauts embarking on the journey to Colchis), indicates a departure, but the third card, 10 of Diamonds (Jason & Pelias), theoretically shows nothing that can follow the departure (referring to the core meaning or plot of ancient history). And as for the meaning of the card in terms of "insidious advice", there is hereby a meaning that would be interesting, but to follow this approach seriously, this card should be chronologically in front of the departure card.

The sixth card, 7 of Hearts (the alchemist who adds the solvent), according to the card, announces something to be added: for example, a visit. This card could also be a companion, which for your interpretation would mean that the departure would be not only from one person, but from several people.

The ninth card, 3 of Spades (the Moirai), the only card in this spread that is one of all the cards that previously accompanied the Main Character's card.

Therefore, it is also the only card that should primarily interest you because it should give an important hint, and yet, placed there, it unfortunately has no satisfactory meaning, because the card means loss, fate, destiny, inevitable. And it would be better, this card would precede the card, the event of departure, farewell. The information that gives you this reading therefore seems to speak less in favor for the Main Character when it comes to whether they will be reintegrated into their position, because the cards rather confirm that their employment really ends, and they will be replaced in their position.

Summary: interpretation of the 9 cards

The first card, 9 of Diamonds, indicates a departure, and can also mean a journey or a change.

The third card, 10 of Diamonds, shows that the Querent received insidious advice.

The sixth card, 7 of Hearts, which represented the message and the visit - that is, the harbinger of the event, and its consequence, the loss of the workplace represented by the ninth card, 3 of Spades, in the form of "death".

You can now see the direct relationship between these cards. The last card means "death", the end of the Main Character's employment.

It is obvious that this proof shows you that the prognosis indicates the removal of the nun.

This removal is a deprivation of their duties and is due to the insidious advice of another person and contact with persons who were contrary to the rules and laws of the church. Always in the background with the intention of loss; the indiscretion that caused this loss was previously also seen in the cards.

NOTE In order to play the Grand Jeu Lenormand true to its original rules, it is important and essential to use this part, which has just been declared as a spread of the fifteen and nine cards.

After you have carefully memorized all the information, you can now move on to the part of the Five Groups spread, which was explained as previously on pages 282 - 287.

...more in the **example**

The cards are dealt.

You start with the first pile (Profession, Work & Trade), and it does not need to be examined, because there you will neither find the card of the Main Character nor one of the six cards that were present with the Main Character at the beginning, and there is also no card from the group "Conquest of the Golden Fleece" in this pile.

You cannot find the Main Character card or any of the six cards in the "Right of the Strong over the Weak" pile.

But the pile contains a card that belongs to the story of the "Trojan War", so this pile must be viewed and interpreted by you.

It contains the following cards:

Ace of Clubs 8 of Diamonds 8 of Hearts

5 of Hearts Jack of Diamonds

The first card is the Ace of Clubs (Jason and the Golden Fleece), the second card is the 5 of Hearts (the audience with the king) and the third card is the 8 of Diamonds (Ganymede), the fourth card is the Jack of Diamonds (Odysseus in disguise), and the fifth card is the 8 of Hearts (the eagle that removes a toad).

In this example, the card representing a person is now the 8 of Diamonds, the card of the Ganymede since it is the card in the middle and there is no direct Main Character card.
This card shows a safe position and the first card on the left, the 5 of Hearts (the audience with the king), shows a person in

a powerful position, and it is the card with the greatest effect on the Main Character. The second card on the left, the Ace of Clubs (Jason and the Golden Fleece), announces the full success.

The first card on the right, the Jack of Diamonds, (Odysseus), shows a wise person, a useful discovery or insight that the Main Character is thinking about, and the second card on the right, the 8 of Hearts (the eagle with the toad), indicates a secret joy, a relief to, loss of, or arising distance from a person who was harmful.

Now, this safe working atmosphere, this strong character and personality, this full success, and on the other hand, this smart character, this smart personality, and the loss of a harmful person, does all this apply to your Main Character, the Lady? No, probably not; but that may be true of another person, perhaps a person who wants to replace them, or who will then stand in their place.

Now we come to the next pile, "Beya & Gabertin", in which the Main Character's card is located, and which is composed as follows:

8 of Clubs 6 of Diamonds 7 of Spades

Person Card Ace of Hearts

The first card is the 8 of Clubs (the alchemist with two test tubes or the wedding of "Beya & Gabertin"). The second card shows the Lady herself and the third card is the 6 of Diamonds (the crocodile & the Ichneumon), the fourth card is the Ace of Hearts (Danaos and his daughters), and the fifth card is represented by the 7 of Spades (the alchemist begins his experiment).

You should first look at the position of the Lady's card, with the 8 of Clubs to her left. The 8 of Clubs is the marriage card, the first card on the left is the card with the most influence on the person.

NOTE If the card 8 of Clubs is found within the "Beya & Gabertin" pile, the Marriage pile, the card always displays a definitive marriage or the term of an important connection, regardless of its position or sequence of cards within that pile.

To the right of the Lady is the 6 of Diamonds, a traitor she thinks about, and some thoughts also belong to family matters, represented by the Ace of Hearts, and the last card, 7 of Spades, is about her relationship.

With this first overview, there are initially some difficulties in connecting all the facts these cards reveal together, but go through it step by step:

The Lady is "married", bound, because she has the card of marriage to the left of her. The 8 of Clubs is the card with the greatest effect on the Lady and there is another card in this pile associated with the theme of marriage, the 7 of Spades.

But remember, you still have a reserve card from the beginning of your spread, which always has its place in the Main Character's pile (page 283).

In this example, this reserve card is the Jack of Spades (the man with the scales), which represents justice and at the same time a warning to the Main Character.

So, the cards give you the information that the Lady is "married", which is indicated by the left card and the small picture. The small picture shows " two materials that do not bond, the hard and the volatile, remain separated from each

other", but this means that there is disagreement in their "marriage".

However, since the nun had to take a vow for her religious path and conclude a contract with a spiritual association, the card 8 of Clubs, the marriage card, for this association, stands. But this vow was broken, which is evidenced by the small picture of the card 8 of Clubs with the disagreement, so the facts about the Main Character are proved and the reserve card, the Jack of Spades, warns the Main Character that their fall is safe, justified and without return. This warning is all the safer and more serious to take, as it is pronounced by a serious figure, the Jack of Spades.

The card on the right, the 6 of Diamonds, explains what the Lady thinks. The card suggests that she remembers that her irreversible fate was caused by a traitor, and the small picture that signifies disunity and refers to the Main Character further proves this interpretation.

The Lady will also retire to a less respected family, which she does not belong to, which can be seen through the small left picture on the card Ace of Hearts (the incense burner). This family is of low social standing, less educated, because it is described by the card 7 of Spades, which represents the simple and ordinary.

Now we move on to the pile of "unforeseen events", which consists of these cards:

2 of Spades King of Spades Queen of Clubs
King of Hearts 10 of Diamonds

The first card is the 2 of Spades, the second card is the King of Hearts, the third card is the King of Spades, the fourth is the 10 of Diamonds and the fifth card is represented by the Queen of Clubs.

You will see that the Main Character is represented by the King of Spades (Menes), which is also the card of legal processes. The Lady is plagued by bad thoughts, a bad conscience, and she goes from counseling to counseling to figure out what to do.

The first card to her left is the King of Hearts, a symbol of wisdom that should lead her back to calmer thoughts and recommend her to find harmony & peace with the religion she must always respect.

And the second card on the left, the 2 of Spades, tells the Lady that what she wants to do is to her disadvantage. She should accept this useful advice, but the next card on the right, the 10 of Diamonds, stands for a harmful advice that impresses her more and with which she conforms more, because the last card on the right, the Queen of Clubs, indicates lightness, negligence, a pleasurable, worldly life. Also, on the suppression and forgetting of everything that from the Lady's point of view brings the end of her own worries. She wants to forget as soon as possible and enjoy life again.

Now look at the "Order of Time" pile, which consists of these cards:

10 of Spades 4 of Spades Queen of Hearts

3 of Diamonds 10 of Clubs

The first card is 10 of Spades (Laverna), the second card is 3 of Diamonds (Castor & Pollux), the third card is 4 of Spades (Semele & Hera), the fourth card is 10 of Clubs (Odysseus and Diomedes) and the fifth card is represented by the Queen of Hearts (Astraea).

NOTE As already explained, only the cards representing a zodiac sign have a function in this pile.

Only the second and fifth cards represent a zodiac sign in this example. The second card, the card of Gemini, which is assigned to the events of the pile number two "the right of the strong over the weak", indicates that not immediately when the complaints about the Lady were made was decided that the Lady would be replaced, but that this decision was only taken within a period of three to nine months.

The fifth card, the card of the Virgo, which does not correspond to any other pile, but is in direct contact with the Main Character, shows that she has received the warnings from the monastery itself and was convinced that she and her position would be replaced in a period of nine to eighteen months.

To calculate the correct or even more accurate time, you would have to know the age of the Querent, the Lady.

SUMMARY (step by step, so far)

For a traditional spread with the Grand Lenormand Cards, the following sequence of action is to follow so far:

1. Starting with the first spread (page 255), it says that you first shuffle, cut and deal the cards (including the reserve cards), then you look at whether the card of the Main Character is to be found, and you begin to describe them by the cards, on the left and on the right.

Also note the variations if the Main Character's card appears at one or the other end of the card row and does not have two or three cards on one of its sides; then you can only describe the person by the cards, which are adjacent on one side or the other.

Remember the cards of this spread, they can give you an interesting insight into the life of the person: This is especially the case when these cards reappear in the next steps, when shuffling, cutting, and laying (regardless of whether these are just one or more of these cards).

2. In the second step, the spread with the fifteen cards, however, you should make sure that you always lay out all the cards drawn face up, the second card next to the first - from left to right and the third card next to the other two and so on, until the fifteen cards are taken from the deck. So, you can immediately see in the fifteen face-up cards whether the cards that previously accompanied the Main Character are present. And if there are any, you can immediately see how many of them are part of the spread again and what positions they take.

Explanation

Suppose that two of the fifteen cards were part of the cards of the initial spread and the cards are now in the first and fifth positions.

(The explanation of the two positions, the first and fifth, you can look up on page 301).

Now compare the type of card with the position it occupies. You will surely recognize the important message of the new appearance of the cards.

If no cards are repeated, these first cards would only be everyday events, business relationships, private situations or the cards can even be of minimal or less important importance.

In this case, you must always put the fifteen cards drawn in context to the meaning of the positions in which they are and interpret them to reveal interesting facts about the Main Character.

3. After you shuffled and drew the cards a third time, you draw nine cards and put them all face up in front of you, from left to right, 3 by 3 (page 305). You will immediately see whether one or more cards can be found repeatedly under the nine cards. How important these are to the Main Character, and how they relate to the person, you will learn when you look at the way the nine cards are interpreted (starting page 305).

If the cards that reappeared include the cards of the Main Characters, this means that the person is more closely connected to the events or a person, depending on which Main Character card is in play.

4. These preliminary steps also include the next step: the "Five cards in Five Groups" spread (as explained on page 282).

With the first pile you can see if the Querent is in an employment, a company, or a business, what profession or income the person has and whether the economic life is good or bad. It can also be seen whether the Querent's concern is of a professional nature. All of this happens when one or more of the five cards from the "Golden Fleece" series are in the pile.

In the second pile you can always see if the Main Character in life or the situation has been wronged. This is the case if one or more of the cards from the series of the "Trojan War" is present.

In the third pile you can see whether there is or will be a wedding or binding relationship for the Main Character. This is the case when one or more of the seven cards of the "Hermetic Science"/ "The Wedding of Beya & Gabertin" is present in it.

From the fourth pile, you can see the information whether the Querent is facing an unforeseen event and if so, which one it will be, this is the case, if one or more of the nineteen different cards from the series of "unforeseen events" is in this pile.

And with the fifth pile, you can determine when an event detected in the previous four pile will occur. But remember, you can only calculate at what time the event will occur if the corresponding card in this pile is one of the twelve cards representing a zodiac sign (on page 280).

NOTE It should always be noted that during the entire game, the Main Character must be described depending on their position, next to a card or between two cards, according to the big and small picture, as explained starting on page 255.

Now you know the first and important steps of fortune telling with the Grand Lenormand Cards, but it's not over yet. It only begins, because the following chapters of the book contain

further steps to fortune telling with the Grand Lenormand Cards. This will await you now:

The next significant step will be the "Great Spread of the 48 Cards". This is explained to you in all its details and serves to give you further important hints about what the person who consults the cards must expect in the future.

In addition, you will learn about the spread of the flower oracle "The Aphorisms of Flowers". The characteristic of the flowers is to indicate where the good or bad deeds of the Main Character have led and will still lead.

Followed by the "Voices of the Animals", which show you different facets of the character of the Querent or persons involved. Here you can check if the good or bad actions attributed to the Main Character by the oracle can indeed be applied to them or how they influence the complete situation.

Finally, the "Achievements" show the general outcome.

PART II

Complete Explanation of the Cards Astro – Mythological - Hermetic

The Great Spread of 48

of Mlle. Lenormand

1845

The Aphorism of Flowers

The Voices of the Animals

and the Achievements

2 BONUS Chapter

CHAPTER V
The Great Spread of 48

The Great Spread of 48 (Cards)

The 34 Special Cards

The Signs of the Zodiac

The Misfortunes of Life

The Colored Stars

The Alchemist's Masterpiece

The Great Spread of 48

(The Grand Lenormand "Grand Tableau (GT)"

This spread, the most extensive step in divination with the Grand Lenormand Cards, is called "The Spread of 48". For this method you use all cards: Four always remain in one position from the beginning and the remaining cards you use again and again in four steps and through each of these steps, you make a total of twelve piles of four cards each, 48 positions and for each position of the card there are 48 different explanations in each round. Hence the name of this spread.
The two cards of the Main Character are part of the spread but are never counted numerically.

You build the piles in the order shown in the following illustration.

The row in the middle represents the four cardinal points, North, East, South & West:

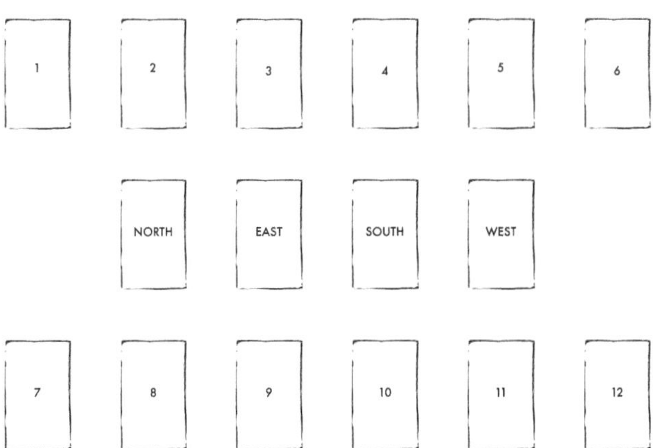

Step 1

The cards are laid out by you as follows:

After you have shuffled the cards and cut them once, simply take the first card, the top card, and place it face down in the position that represents the North.

The next card is placed in position number one, the next card in position number two and so on until the thirteenth card is placed, it takes position number twelve.

The second distribution of the cards takes place in the same way and in the same order as the first, but this time you place the next card of the deck (the fourteenth) in the place that represents the East. The fifteenth card is placed on the card that already covers position number one, the sixteenth on position number two and the same until the twenty-sixth card is dealt out, it takes position number twelve.

The third distribution of the cards is the same as the previous two: You first place the twenty-seventh card on the position representing the direction South, and the twenty-eighth on the two cards already in position number one, the twenty-ninth card you place in position number two and so on until the thirty-ninth card is discarded by you, it takes the position number twelve.

Finally, the fourth distribution of the cards ends with you placing the fortieth card on the position representing the direction West, the forty-first you place on the deck of cards on position number one, the forty-second card you put on the pile in position number two and so on, until the fiftieth card that the pile in position number twelve completed, is filed.

Once you have completed the process correctly, two cards remain in your hand. And as soon as you later see that one of the Main Character's cards is under the cards laid out, you add one of the two cards in your hand to this Main Character card and there is only one card left in your hand:

As soon as one Main Character card is among the cards laid out, only one card remains in your hand; if, on the contrary, both Main Character cards are among the other cards, two cards must remain in your hand.

(You will see where the Main Character cards are after turning the cards over later in the second step).

However, it is very likely that both Main Character cards will be in one of the twelve piles and in a position of the four cardinal points. In this case, as mentioned, you add the one or two remaining cards to the pile (or position) with the Main Character card.

However, if one or both cards of the Main Character are in your hand, these cards must also be added to the spread. If this happens, you place both cards on the first pile.

Step 2

Once you have completed the first step, turn all the cards over, one pile at a time. And this time you place the four cards from the first to the twelfth pile in rows (as shown in the following illustration). This means that instead of the twelve piles of four cards each, there are now 48 positions with one card each.

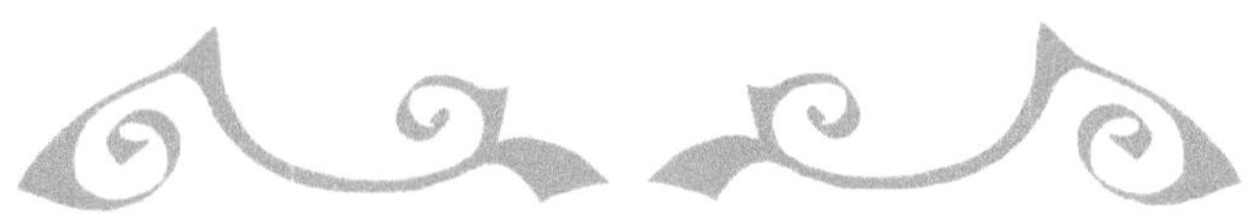

Layout

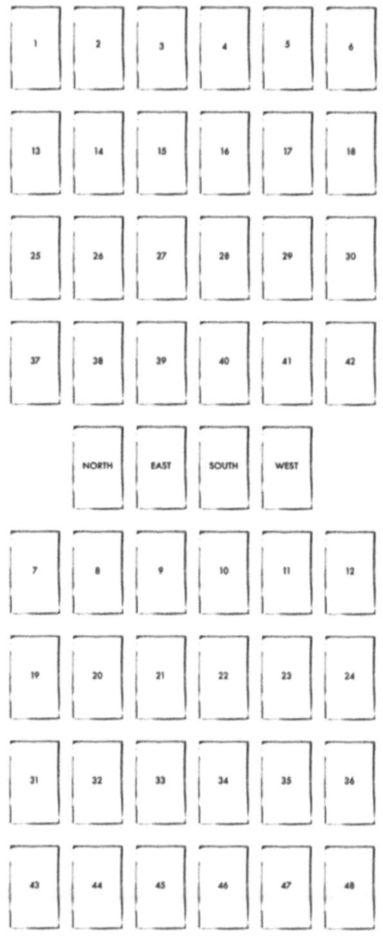
1
2
3
4
5
6
13
14
15
16
17
18
25
26
27
28
29
30
37
38
39
40
41
42
NORTH
EAST
SOUTH
WEST
7
8
9
10
11
12
19
20
21
22
23
24
31
32
33
34
35
36
43
44
45
46
47
48

NOTE Before the cards were turned over, card number one was in the first pile, face down the bottom card, and now when the cards are turned over, that card is back on top; this card is again considered as card number one, and you put her back in position number one. You place the card that follows the card number one in the same row on the position number thirteen (see the number of the positions in the illustration; position thirteen is because of the distribution of the cards in the first step, the card took this position). Place the next card on position number twenty-five and the fourth on position number thirty-seven. (Always keep an eye on the example illustration and remember that the position numbers refer to the order in which the cards were dealt in the first step and the positions of the cardinal direction are not numbered and were not counted).

When splitting the second pile, proceed in the same way, put the top card on position number two after turning over, put the next card on position number fourteen, the next card in position number twenty-six and the fourth card in position number thirty-eight. Do the same if you reveal the cards of the remaining piles (numbers three, four, five, six to twelve).

The cards of the four cardinal points always remain firmly in the same place. (The original instruction does not talk about the cardinal points in detail).
When all the cards are face up, you will now be able to see all the Main Character cards, and you will now know where to add one or all the two cards that were left in your hand.

(The position that a Main Character card holds requires another card, and therefore this pile of cards will contain more cards).

This card layout places the forty-eight cards in their respective positions. If you have a large enough table, this is easy to do. However, if you don't have a lot of space, it is also possible to

arrange the cards so that you only see the top cards and then always take a pile to interpret the cards. This always depends on how much space you have available and what is easier or more convenient for you to implement.

Each of the 48 positions is assigned a fixed meaning, the interpretation of the cards takes place in several rounds and during the rounds also the meaning of the positions varies. You can find them in the following table (which will be explained later with an example):

Explanation of the Positions

The meanings of the positions for the first round

First row

Position 1 what to expect in life
Position 13 business, professional trouble
Position 25 concern, anxiety
Position 37 intentions, personal wishes

Second row

Position 2 undertakings, transactions, a change
Position 14 treacherous advice
Position 26 rivalry, enemies
Position 38 hope, satisfaction

Third row

Position 3 brothers and sisters, siblings
Position 15 respect, trust, wisdom
Position 27 fraud, deception, theft
Position 39 property, wealth, abundance

Fourth row

Position 4 passion, temptation
Position 16 hard work
Position 28 high position, elite
Position 40 close relatives

Fifth row

Position 5 disagreement
Position 17 meeting, encounter
Position 29 preparations for departure
Position 41 parents, father, and mother

Sixth row

Position 6 thoughts, dreams
Position 18 association, union
Position 30 dignity and humiliation
Position 42 friend, affair

Seventh row

Position 7 children
Position 19 illness, pregnancy
Position 31 priest, nun
Position 43 defeat, downfall

Eighth row

Position 8 boredom, grief
Position 20 inheritance,
Position 32 legitimate offence
Position 44 arrest, conviction

Ninth row

Position 9 infertility
Position 21 revenge
Position 33 joy
Position 45 invention, genius

Tenth row

Position 10 recognition, reward
Position 22 intrigues
Position 34 unexpected event
Position 46 acquisition, purchase, takeover

Eleventh row

Position 11 protection
Position 23 artists
Position 35 birth
Position 47 separation

Twelfth row

Position 12 marriage proposal, application
Position 24 new acquaintance
Position 36 stranger, unknown
Position 48 jealousy

The meanings of the positions for the second round

First row

Position 1 start, beginning
Position 13 positive welcome, good forecast
Position 25 renewal of something, restart
Position 37 madness

Second row

Position 2 rules, structure, order, economy
Position 14 trade, commerce
Position 26 correspondence
Position 38 bad company

Third row

Position 3 friendship, agreement
Position 15 bondage, captivity
Position 27 cunning
Position 39 loneliness

Fourth row

Position 4 uncle or aunt
Position 16 attempt
Position 28 precarious situation, uncertain life situation
Position 40 authority, office

Fifth row

Position 5 children's condition
Position 17 punishment
Position 29 escape
Position 41 duty, loyalty

Sixth row

Position 6 despair
Position 18 conspiracy
Position 30 move, change
Position 42 conquest, success

Seventh row

Position 7 celibacy, abstinence
Position 19 insulation
Position 31 prestigious, famous
Position 43 fear, anxiety

Eighth row

Position 8 courage
Position 20 message, news
Position 32 suspicion
Position 44 malaise, discomfort, aversion

Ninth row

Position 9 liveliness, enthusiasm
Position 21 chance, opportunity, possibility
Position 33 generosity
Position 45 actor, drama

Tenth row

Position 10 success
Position 22 game
Position 34 clarification, enlightenment, clarity
Position 46 debauchery, riot

Eleventh row

Position 11 good friends
Position 23 deception
Position 35 vague hopes
Position 47 betrayal

Twelfth row

Position 12 contact
Position 24 give commands, order
Position 36 travel, journey
Position 48 surprise

The meanings of the positions for the third round

First row

Position 1 inclination, preference
Position 13 complete ruin
Position 25 cheerfulness
Position 37 trap

Second row

Position 2 duel, confrontation
Position 14 weakness, negligence
Position 26 domestic care
Position 38 relief, rescue

Third row

Position 3 visit
Position 15 Field work, heavy work, bone job
Position 27 skillful, political, diplomatic
Position 39 generosity

Fourth row

Position 4 boldness, impudence
Position 16 obligation
Position 28 result, outcome of a situation
Position 40 promise

Fifth row

Position 5 unfair to weak persons
Position 17 applause, encouragement
Position 29 ridiculous, foolishness
Position 41 luck, Fortune

Sixth row

Position 6 theater (situational)
Position 18 change of residence
Position 30 industry
Position 42 insult, attack on honor

Seventh row

Position 7 lawyer
Position 19 crime
Position 31 success
Position 43 report, legal proceeding

Eighth row

Position 8 discovery, revelation
Position 20 age
Position 32 constancy
Position 44 harmful mental burden

Ninth row

Position 9 travel at sea/ travel by water
Position 21 average
Position 33 inconsistency
Position 45 take precautions

Tenth row

Position 10 useful advice
Position 22 stupidity
Position 34 careless action
Position 46 wedding, banquet, festive occasion

Eleventh row

Position 11 possessing sovereignty, superiority
Position 23 fearless
Position 35 somewhat overshadowed, a disaster threatens
Position 47 happy meeting, happy encounter

Twelfth row

Position 12 waste
Position 24 amorous adventure
Position 36 prison
Position 48 indiscretion

The meanings of the positions for the fourth round

First row

Position 1 perfect happiness
Position 13 bad result, bad outcome
Position 25 dark hours in life
Position 37 luxury and misery

Second row

Position 2 decency in private life/ decent origin
Position 14 unknown, unrecognized genius
Position 26 court, trial
Position 38 protector, protection

Third row

Position 3 poverty
Position 15 forced, arranged connection
Position 27 cheerfulness, lightheartedness
Position 39 forget the sorrow

Fourth row

Position 4 unexpected gain, treasure/ unexpected joy
Position 16 hard-won assets
Position 28 lovers, lover, sweetheart
Position 40 harmful behavior, action

Fifth row

Position 5 will, last will
Position 17 hypocrites, heretics
Position 29 return
Position 41 late remorse

Sixth row

Position. 6 extramarital union, "wild marriage"
Position 18 long journey
Position 30 trustworthy work
Position 42 uncertainty

Seventh row

Position 7 triumph
Position 19 endless discord
Position 31 freedom
Position 43 predetermined, foreseeable end

Eighth row

Position 8 honorable age
Position 20 reward of endurance
Position 32 united persons
Position 44 clergy

Ninth row

Position 9 good role model, idol
Position 21 campaign
Position 33 envy
Position 45 worldview, character

Tenth row

Position 10 hidden rage
Position 22 legacy or gift
Position 34 high sovereignty, unrestricted, freedom
Position 46 courage and endurance

Eleventh row

Position 11 malicious joy
Position 23 important information and notes
Position 35 vocation
Position 47 predestination

Twelfth row

Position 12 on a high scale, exaggeration
Position 24 triumph over yourself
Position 36 compulsory loans, mortgage
Position 48 fraud, theft

The cards distributed are now assigned to the 48 positions with one card each and based on these positions the interpretation of the cards is performed in the following steps:

1. You look for the meaning of the position (see table) where the Main Character's card is located. You remember and interpret the cards that appear here with the Main Character.

2. However, if the Querent is more concerned with a topic than with another person, look for the position that has to do with that concern and look at which card is in that position.

3. If you have gained information about the Main Character from the previous course of the Grand Jeu, that is, the previous spreads, and have given you some cards information that you may question in more detail, you should follow these cards in all rounds of the "Great Spread of 48" to deepen the previous hints.

4. You look at these important cards in their positions to see how the meaning of the position relates to the respective meaning of the card. (For those familiar with the 36 Lenormand Fortune Telling Cards, a parallel might be drawn here to the technique of the houses in the GT, the method of reading all 36 cards.)

You do not have to look at positions and cards that are not important.

5. Remember the cards and positions that were important in the first round.

Example (based on some cards)

To help you understand this better, here is a brief overview of how a type of connection or relationship between cards and positions can exist:

On the one hand, the theme of the position combines with the meaning of the card, which is in that position, and on the other hand, cards and position also connect directly with each other, if they both cover the same theme, stand for the same. This is always preferable in the interpretation.

The 10 of Diamonds, which refers to a false advice, combines all positions with treacherous advice, deception and deceit and is also directly related to all positions that describe the same topic.

The Queen of Diamonds connects all positions with discord, confusion, disagreement, jealousy, or revenge and is also in direct contact with all positions that describe the same topic.

The King of Hearts connects all positions with reason, wisdom and he represents knowledge. When this card points to a father, mother, or person, it takes the values of that card as a characteristic.

The 2 of Diamonds connects all positions with the topic of pregnancy, marriage, or children. But if this card appears in a position of misconduct, it means, for example, that this kind of misconduct will lead to pregnancy.

The Ace of Hearts connects any position with family affairs or the family itself. But if the card refers, for example, to a position of inconvenience or to both wealth and mediocrity, luxury, or thrift or to a change of residence, these cards indicate that that

the Querent's family has one of these attributes. The position then describes the family.

And if, for example, the Ace of Hearts is in the position of flight, gloating, sorrow, joy, or other things that probably cannot be related to an entire family such as business inconvenience, in this case, this is to be understood more as an indication that the main person does not have his own or closer family.

The 4 of Diamonds connects all positions with the topic of rescue, protection, or help.

The 9 of Diamonds connects all positions with a journey, a change of location or a movement, such as a return, a departure. Also, this card shows changes in the topic described by the respective location where the card is located.

The 7 of Diamonds which indicates punishment and misfortune of all kinds, is always easy to interpret, no matter what position the card takes.

The 3 of Spades, for example, associate a position with illness, infirmity, in which case you must take good care of your health.

The 2 of Clubs connects the topic of the position with happiness, success and, for example, material values.

The 10 of Spades states a theft, loss within the scope of the topic of the respective position and is also directly related to all positions that describe the same topic.

The Jack of Clubs connects all positions with success through intelligence and skill and is also directly connected to all positions that describe the same topic.

The 2 of Hearts connects all positions with righteousness, selflessness and loyalty or friendship.

The 6 of Diamonds shows misconduct, debauchery, disunity, strife, vice within the theme represented by the position on which the card is located. In the tradition of Grand Jeu cartomancy, this card showed terrible crimes that almost endangered life; the original manual even spoke here of crime up to murder.

The 3 of Hearts connects each position with genius, fame, prestige, success, achievements. However, if this card is in a position that indicates grief, pain, deception, or disappointment, it is caused by the actions or behavior of a very intelligent person.
But if the same card is in the position of mediocrity, weakness, stupidity, the positive value of this card is diminished, or it is an indication that the mind is not really used.

The Queen of Spades connects all positions with the theme of widowhood, abandonment and the consequences that can accompany it, such as grief, isolation or consolation, inheritance, but also a recurring joy after a great loss; the reversal of fate, which is often addressed by this card.

The King of Spades connects all positions with the law, the police, court proceedings, prison or also with the flight from these topics, and finally also with everything that has to do with civil or criminal proceedings.

These examples should be enough to make the method of interpreting the positions more understandable. You must always follow these steps in the rounds of the "Great Spread of 48".

NOTE If a card is perfectly related to the meaning of a position and thus corresponds to both the sense of the position and the card itself, the card and position are in direct connection to each other, and in this case, this meaning is to be put directly in connection with the Main Character and considered as particularly important and is always preferred to the other.

Step 3

After the first round, in which you have made all the steps mentioned, you shuffle the cards again, cut them once and then distribute them in a second round in the same way as before in the first round.

Then you first look at the position where the Main Character is and the cards that are now with the Main Character card.

After that, it is important to look at the position that relates to the problem, another person, the topic, or the concern of the Main Character.

And next, look again at the cards and their positions that are important for the Main Character:

You repeatedly look at the cards that were important in the previous first round and that you remembered. You see where they appear, what position they are in and what this means.

Finally, you perform the third and fourth rounds in the same way. So, you carefully examine the same cards, adding always the cards appearing new with the Main Character, again and again in their details and can thus recognize their statements clearly and without doubt.

NOTE The positions of the cardinal points become important only if there is a Main Character card and the position is therefore assigned a new card. Only then will this card of the cardinal direction be of importance and can be followed in the coming rounds: that is, on which positions it appears in the further rounds and what does this mean. If there is a previous important card appearing on the cardinal points, during the rounds, it will contain a message for the Querent.

Example (to understanding)

Let's say the Main Character's card or another card with a theme that interests your client is in position number eighteen. This position refers in its basic meaning to an association (see table for the definition of the position in the first round, page 326 - 328). And in the second and third round, the card is in position with the theme of structure, rules, economy, work or similar. These topics, these positions now attribute these characteristics to the association or classify the association in this sense.

And if this card in the fourth round refers to the position of wealth, or something similar, the meaning of this position would predict a logical purpose and sense of union, of the association, or even show what the logical consequence, the consequences of this connection will be. The connection is based on a solid structure, there is an economic purpose and work will be there.

But if in the second and third rounds the same card takes the position of inequality, disagreement, waste, or similar meanings and in the fourth round the card is in the position of poverty or similar meaning, this shows that poverty will be the logical consequence, the consequences of inaction, or disagreement within this association.

However, if this card appears in the position of a will, inheritance, or unexpected happiness, it is not to be interpreted as a logical consequence of an action: it is not real consequences of the previous own influence or own action, but it is rather the effect of luck or chance, or an influence of external circumstances.

NOTE The rounds tell stories by combining the statements of each round into an overall statement.

An important event is not always immediately recognizable in the first round. It is possible that only in the second round a card can show an event that is not a direct consequence of an event of the first round. Or sometimes it is to be recognized only in the third or fourth round through a card a natural consequence of an event from the first round.

Because despite some incidents or deviations that prevent things from moving on, things often go on without knowing or realizing. Thus, the event is no less associated with the Main Character.

The same applies to a position that you must follow if you have recognized that it was occupied with an important card in the first round. Just as you look at where the cards fall in the rounds, you should also look at the course of the positions in the further rounds, for example which cards always fall to position eighteen and what does this tell you within each round.

The 34 Special Cards within the Spread of 48

Now all that remains is to talk about some special cards - thirty-four in number - which have their additional function: they influence the position in which they are located, and thus give additional useful hints for the interpretation of the future.

The twelve Zodiac Signs

Each position containing a card representing a zodiac sign assumes the gender indicated by this sign. Among other things, this will be helpful when it comes to recognizing whether a male or female person is involved in a situation or could play an important role. For example, if a male zodiac sign falls on the position of the friends, it will be a male friend and not a female friend.

When one of the cards representing a zodiac sign is in the position of disease, grief, suffering, the position assumes the type of diseases represented by this zodiac sign.

Represented by the following cards (special card number 1 to 12):

Card 1, the Jack of Hearts, represents the sign of Aries, and therefore takes on the male gender and has the quality of indicating diseases of the head and ailments that appear on the face.

Card 2, the Ace of Spades, represents the sign of Taurus, and thus takes on the female gender and has the quality of showing sore throats and those that occur in the mouth.

Card 3, the 3 of Diamonds, represents the sign of Gemini, and thus takes on the male gender and has the quality of indicating illnesses caused by moods and infirmities, as well as those arising in the arms.

Card 4, the 9 of the Clubs, represents the sign of Cancer, and thus takes on the female gender and has the quality of indicating lung and chest diseases.

Card 5, the 9 of Hearts, represents the sign of Leo, and thus takes on the male gender and has the property of indicating heart, stomach, and back pain.

Card 6, the Queen of Hearts, represents the sign of Virgo, and thus assumes the female gender, and it indicates flank diseases and side pain.

Card 7, the Jack of Spades, represents the sign of Libra, and takes the male gender and has the quality of indicating stomach and kidney pain.

Card 8, the 5 of Diamonds, represents the sign of Scorpio, and therefore assumes the female gender and indicates the diseases of the lower abdomen and the bladder.

Card 9, the 5 of Spades, represents the sign of Sagittarius, and thus takes on the male gender and refers to rheumatic pain and thigh pain.

Card 10, the 7 of Clubs, represents the sign of Capricorn, and therefore takes on the female gender and indicates knee pain.

Card 11, the 8 of Diamonds, represents the sign of Aquarius, and therefore takes on the male gender and refers to pain in the legs.

Card 12, the 4 of Hearts, represents the sign of Pisces, and therefore assumes the female gender and indicates foot pain.

The Seven Fatalities of Life

In the Grand Lenormand you will find some cards with a small symbol of a planet - these seven cards are all part of the group "The Trojan War" - that group of cards that represent social problems and difficulties. This is why Miss Lenormand called these cards the "Seven Misfortunes of Life". In the original manual, they are called the "Seven Fatalities of Life".

Each planet symbol on these cards also represents a talisman of the same name, which is associated with an effect.

NOTE Each position that contains a card indicating one of the seven misfortunes of the "Fatalités de la Vie" shows an inevitable event. The talisman indicated on the card should be used for protection in the case of an unavoidable event. For this it was necessary to make and wear the appropriate talisman. Since it was often very expensive and difficult at that time to get natural materials, which according to tradition were necessary to produce the talisman, many people, especially those of the common people, decided to paint the symbol on clothing, fabric, or paper, and then carry it by itself. Some also drew the symbol of the planet directly on their own skin so that it was particularly close to the body and soul. At that time, this protection was considered excellent to avert the catastrophic event that could threaten oneself.

A misfortune shown by such a card was initially seen as inevitable, but this rule has exceptions that will be explained later. An event that was shown by such a card was only inevitable if in the following rounds the card or the position where it was previously, the event itself, is not covered by a card with a "colored star". Because a card with a colored star would change the misfortune for the better or worse (the explanation of the stars is made after this section),

These seven misfortunes are represented by the following cards (special card numbers 13 to 19):

Card 13, the Jack of Diamonds, represents the first misfortune and the first talisman. It prevents the success of a business unless the Querent discovers what is necessary to do to overcome the obstacles.

The Jack of Diamonds is the Talisman of Mercury, and it was a true help in financial difficulties.

Card 14, the 9 of Spades, represents the second misfortune and the second talisman. This misfortune indicates that the person may fall into dishonor if they do not use the strength and prudence that are necessary to protect themself from this situation or from deceitful behavior.

The 9 of Spades is the Talisman of Venus, and it is a kind of cure in a time of real disappointment and feeling guilty, or bad consciousness.

Card 15, the 10 of Clubs, represents the third misfortune and the third talisman, and it indicates that there is a dangerous enemy around; it is important to prevent oneself from harm and hurt by skillfully outsmarting the enemy and by avoiding what the enemy could abuse.

The 10 of Clubs is the Talisman of Mars, and it was useful in a struggle against a dangerous enemy or opposition (today we would say in a conflict with someone).

Card 16, the 2 of Spades, the fourth misfortune, and the fourth talisman; it indicates that the Querent is threatened with losing the friendship and affection of a loved one and laments and quarrels because the situation will be fatal. In this case, it is best to take the advice of an enlightened, honest, and experienced person and to behave according to the advice this person will have given.

The 2 of Spades is the Talisman of Saturn, and the power of this talisman is useful during times of hurtful loss.

Card 17, the 6 of Spades, the fifth misfortune, and the fifth talisman. It is talking about a bad surprise. The Querent will be surprised by an event that brings some difficulties and devastation into his life and into his soul; that situation can even cause the Querent's failure if he does not act carefully.

The 6 of Spades is the Talisman of Jupiter. It was useful in threatening or dangerous situations that were created by others or outside influences.

Card 18, the 8 of Spades, the sixth misfortune, and the sixth talisman, it indicates that if the Querent does not listen to the advice of life experience or does not treat others with moderation and prudence, ambitious recklessness leads to pain, loss, and loneliness.

The 8 of Spades is the Talisman of the Moon. It is helpful in a time of depression or a desperate situation.

Card 19, the 6 of Clubs, the seventh misfortune, and the seventh talisman. It indicates that there is a risk of loss of money, an incident, or a risk of theft. This misfortune is to be avoided by not giving confidence to anyone or by giving it only to those people whose behavior and morals are well known to the Querent.

The 6th of Clubs is the Talisman of the Sun. It helps in situations of deceit, abuse of trust, and if there is a risk of loss.

REMINDER It was said that an event shown by such a card became inevitable only if, in the following rounds, the card or the position in which it is located, that is, the event itself, is not covered by a card with a "colored star" that would change the misfortune for the better or worse.

The explanation of these colored stars is now in the next section.

The Colored Stars

There are eight cards that carry special stars (not to be confused with the star constellations in the sky of the cards). They are called the cards of the colored stars. These eight stars represent planets of different colors (on each of these cards you can see a special star near or somewhere in the part of the star constellations, the sky of the card; on cards without star constellations the colored star can be seen elsewhere, often in the place of the playing card insert, there it is replaced by the star).

This star has an influence, especially regarding the cards of the "seven misfortunes" described above. If one or more of these cards appear along with a "misfortune of life", this will affect this event, this misfortune of life. If there is no card with a "misfortune of life" in the spread at an important position, but a card with such a colored star appears, this star card affects the situation of the Main Character in general.

The stars will give important clues to a situation, such as whether it is good or bad, with hope or without. You can imagine that the dark color of a star darkens the situation, just like a bright or a colorful star brightens it and makes it more pleasant. A game of light and shadow.

NOTE Any position containing a card with a colored star is therefore subject to the effect indicated by this star card. The star influences the value and character of the position.

These are the colors represented by the eight stars on the following cards (special cards number 20 to 27):

Card 20, the King of Clubs, the first star, planet Saturn, is dark in color and announces that the event (the misfortune of life or the current situation) is very serious.

Card 21, the 5 of Hearts, the second star, planet Jupiter, is colored blue and indicates that the situation seems to get better, that the situation seems to improve in the future.

Card 22, the 5 of Clubs, the third star, planet Mars, is red color and announces that the situation is unpleasant, scary, or creepy.

Card 23, the Ace of Clubs, the fourth star, the Sun, is saffron in color and indicates revival of glory, success, and wealth for the Querent.

Card 24, the Queen of Clubs, the fifth star, planet Venus, is colored green, and indicates only temporary inconvenience.

Card 25, the Ace of Diamonds, the sixth star, planet Mercury, is multicolored, and indicates that the event will benefit the person if the person is discreet.

Card 26, the 4 of Spades, the seventh star, the Moon, is white and indicates events without a solid foundation and that something will fade away on its own with time.

Card 27, the 8 of Hearts, the eighth star, a Nebula, indicates in its origins the death of a child, or in modern card reading, a hint that a new start, a (new) project, will come to fail. Something "died before real life was possible".

The Alchemist's Masterpiece

(or the seven steps of successful work)

These seven cards represent the hermetic science or fusion, connection of materials by the action of fire. These are the seven cards that show you as a scene the laboratory of the alchemist. The different degrees of mixing, the different working steps of the alchemist are to be equated with the different stages and forms of the approaches, encounters, connections, and relationships between two people.

Represented by the following cards (special cards number 28 to 34):

Card 28, the 7 of Spades, the first step, the first act of the alchemist, describes the separate, not yet interconnected raw material in its simplicity. The beginning of everything: When this card appears in a position that stands for success, lovers, and love or similar (themes that point towards interpersonal connections), it indicates an honest, sincere, and carefree friendship. If the card is in a position that represents a marriage, a marriage proposal, a relationship, or something similar, this indicates a marriage of two people with low attraction (the raw materials in the experiment are not connected).

Card 29, the 3 of Clubs, the second step, the second action of the alchemist, describes the material after a long time of work, and it finally begins to dissolve. When this card appears in a position for success, love, or similar, it indicates that the Main Character will encounter a wise, serious person who will prefer the secure and serious lifestyle and will be like a role model for the Main Character. If it is a position that indicates a marriage, relationship, or similar, the card announces that the Main Character will marry a respected person with wealth and orderly economic circumstances.

Card 30, 4 of Clubs, the third step, the third act of the alchemist, describes the material during the process of dissolution; if this card appears in a position that represents success, love or similar, this card indicates an approach of two persons of short duration, without honesty, without faith or trust and without advantage - the connection dissolves, so to speak. If it is a position that points to marriage, relationship, or similar, the card indicates fickle feelings, misconduct, arbitrariness, disagreement.

Card 31, the 8 of Clubs, the fourth step, the fourth action of the alchemist, describes the mixing, fusion of the solid with the volatile material. It is the card that is called the "wedding of Beya and Gabertin". If this card is in a position that represents success, love, or similar, it indicates that the Main Character will have a relationship (for example, be married or live in a solid, stable partnership). If this is the case, you must also look closely at this card of marriage in the previous or subsequent piles & positions to learn what kind of luck or misfortune will result from this relationship/ marriage. If the same card is in the position of a union, marriage or similar, then a wedding will take place and you will recognize based on the following positions on which this card of the wedding is located, what the Main Character must expect from and in this marriage.

Card 32, the 10 of Hearts, the fifth step, the alchemist's fifth act, describes the material that has now become solid, and its surface begins to fade; when this card takes a position that represents success, lovers or similar, it points to a chaste, faithful, sincere, and lasting love. If the same card is in a position indicating a marriage, proposal, wedding, or similar, this card stands for a simple marriage, with fewer assets, but instead for a happy coexistence.

Card 33, the 7 of Hearts, the sixth step, the sixth act of the alchemist during his work, describes how the alchemist adds liquid to the stone. This card shows the visits, encounters of all kinds of people and their messages, including what comes and goes in life; if the card is in a position that represents success, love or similar, it means that the Main Character receives a "visit", a message of this kind is received: if it is a position of marriage or similar, for example, the Querent receives a marriage proposal or will soon enter into a relationship. If this card is in a different position, it means that the "visit", encounter, or message the Main Character receives is of the kind represented by the position on which the card is placed.

Card 34, the 6 of Hearts, the seventh and final card of the alchemist's work, describes the material in its perfection. If this card is in the position of success, of lovers or similar, this card predicts a special and promising connection, the great happiness, the almost perfect relationship. And that someone makes a big profit in his life. If the card is in a position that represents a relationship, a marriage or something similar, it is proof of a rich and well-off marriage in the future.

This card also ends the 34 special cards.

Based on these various explanations, you can now see that in the "Great Spread of the 48", these thirty-four cards can always have a special function and are therefore the subject of a special study. Taking a closer look at these cards is unavoidable, as it unlocks other secrets within the reading that are important and remain hidden if you don't look for them.

The cards produce messages that influence the interpretation of the other cards and thus contribute to the complete understanding of the message of all cards.

CHAPTER VI

The Aphorisms of the Flowers

The Flower Oracle

Dictionaire Emblématique

The Aphorisms of the Flowers

The Flower Oracle

The aphorism of the flowers is the next step in the Grand Jeu and is explained to you here, as it was described in the original instructions for use of the Grand Lenormand.

Again, it should be mentioned here that by ancient writings and traditions it was known that the clients of Mlle. Lenormand, among other things, should first name her those flowers that were preferred by them for their beauty and scent.

In this chapter you can now expect:

- The explanation of the flower oracle
- The spread
- Examples
- The emblematic dictionary (The different flowers, their value, and the signification of the flowers)

Floriography (the language of flowers) is a means of secret communication with the help of a flower arrangement. For thousands of years flowers have been assigned meanings, and in traditional cultures in Europe, Asia, and Africa the form of floriography is practiced. Plants and flowers are used as symbols, especially for lovers and other very personal, secret messages that only initiates should reveal themselves.

Different flowers, plants and specific flower arrangements were combined to send the encrypted message to the recipient. This encrypted form of communication allowed the sender to express feelings that could not or could not be expressed loudly in society.

Many people often exchanged small "talking bouquets" or wore them as a visible fashion accessory to send a message.

To this day, in our modern society, we have flowers with certain meanings, just like in my country. The most well-known form of floriography still goes hand in hand with the rose and its various colors: red, for example, is a sign of love, the yellow rose is the one you give in friendship and the white one when someone has died, or you express a farewell.

And the flowers also speak in the Grand Jeu de Mlle Lenormand. In this step in which you now learn the message to read the hidden messages of the wisdom of the flowers and thus to be able to reveal further secrets of the future.

The Grand Lenormand cards are very famous for this unique Oracle of Flowers and even though it is only a small part of the Grand Jeu, it is an important & popular part of the game.

NOTE Unfortunately, the flowers are too often used as independent oracles or even the message of the flowers on the card is simply attached to the other interpretations of the card without having done the spread of the flowers, but this is not correct and not in the sense of the old tradition. Thus, the oracle will be falsified, and it will give false information. Likewise, it is not tradition to classify the flower oracle as Victorian.

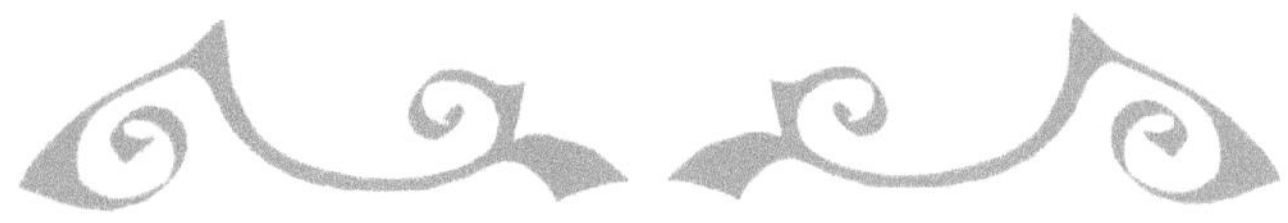

The Flower Oracle

To understand the wise words of the flowers, it is always necessary to make this spread of 25 cards. The cards are randomly selected by you and placed on the table, in the form described in the picture below (page 357).

NOTE The numbers in this first figure do not represent the order in which the cards are placed; the order of the placement of the cards is of course explained in the next steps. The numbers you see in this image are the numbers that are important for the later interpretation of the cards and flowers. They correspond to a basic position of the respective column, and they correspond during the spread to a position of a flower, which arises due to the respective value of the respective flower. The positions of the cards have numbers, and the numbers correspond to the number/value of the flower. Each flower has a value between one and twenty.

You can see from this illustration that twenty of the twenty-five cards form four columns - two are horizontal and the other two are vertical.

On the five positions (A – E) in the middle column are placed the cards that contain the actual prophecy, the advice of the flowers; they focus on the words/message passed on by the flowers. The flowers on the cards in these positions tell the Querent what to expect. This can give a positive or a negative prediction about the upcoming events.

GRAND JEU Lenormand

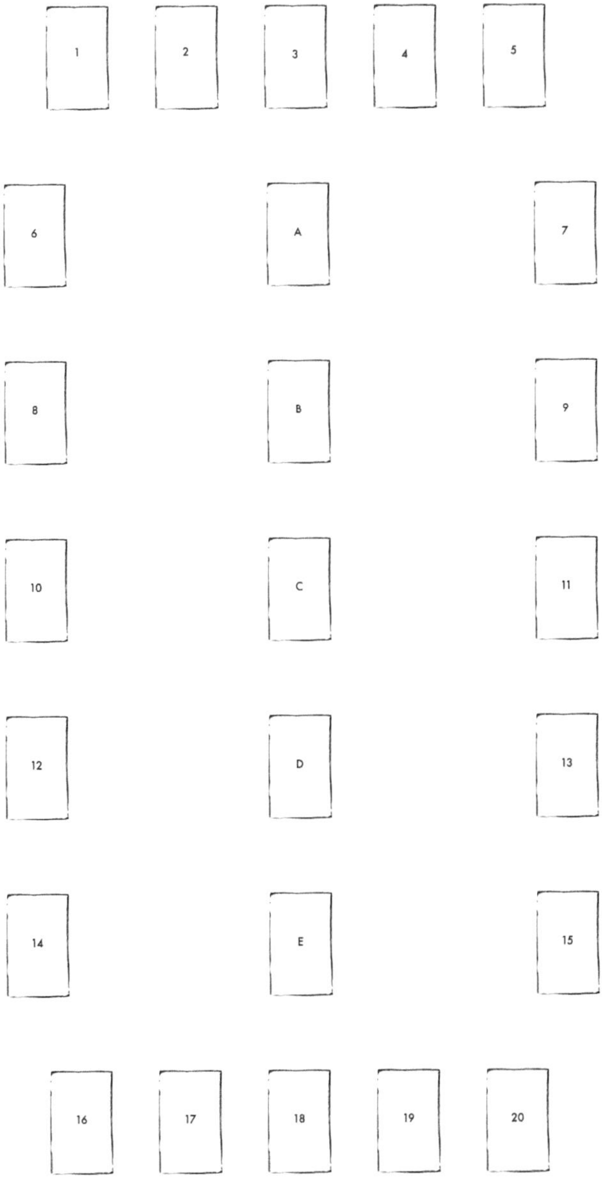

1	2	3	4	5

6	A	7
8	B	9
10	C	11
12	D	13
14	E	15

16	17	18	19	20

There can always be different situations in which the Querent is interested or expressed by these cards.

The important positions in the middle column

Along with the messages in this middle column, you will always receive important information about the Querent. It can be said that the row in the middle represents the Main Character (and his future) in general.

Nevertheless, the five positions are based on the following meanings:

1. The first position shows the Main Character in relation to himself or anything that concerns the Querent personally or is in any way related to him. This is the information about the person himself: husband, wife, children, health, reputation, worries, joys.

2. The second position refers to the social position/reputation of the Main Character, his status, his professional life. This position is related to the way of life so far or what the Question has already achieved. This position provides information about the status, professional life, commitment and diligence in professional matters, here is also shown the source of income of the Main Character, the financial status.

3. The third position of this column shows information about the family and/or friends, especially closer ones, of the Main Character: the family, relatives in general, either in person or by marriage or firm partnership.

4. The fourth position refers to persons who are superior to the Main Character, persons on whom the Querent is or may be dependent. Also, people for whom the Querent is most concerned despite a personal distance or with whom he maintains good contact. For it is people who trust the Main Character, be it an acquaintance or the employer; someone to whom one owes credit for a service or help; those whom one should treat with respect. In short, all the people who deserve the appreciation and trust of someone.

Such a connection could be, for example, a worker, an employee who is dependent on his boss. Such connections can be seen here: the professional or more distant social environment.

5. The fifth position shows the events that cannot be predicted. The Grand Lenormand often speaks of the "unforeseen events" and thus it is not surprising that this term also is mentioned here.

All this, which has not yet happened, and which will unexpectedly occur in the future of the Main Character.

The positions of the four outer columns

Now the explanation of the important meanings of the four outer rows/ columns.

1. The top column, which consists of positions 1 to 5, usually says more about what the Main Character appreciates, honors, adores; here information about the person for whom the Querent has the greatest respect and trust can be seen. Often it is a person who is in some way preferred or represents an important or related person in the life of the Main Character.

2. The left column with the positions 6, 8, 10, 12, 14 shows the opinion, the attitude, the thoughts of the Querent regarding justice, morality. This row of cards concerns the habits of the Main Character and areas of private and social life.

3. The right column with positions 7, 9, 11, 13, 15 reveals more about the temperament, the feelings, the emotional life, and the desires of the Main Character.

4. The bottom column with positions 16 to 20 represents the things that the Main Character disapproves of, despises, and rejects, neglects – "figuratively speaking also tramples underfoot".

NOTE It should always be remembered later that the card that is in the first position of each of the four columns - whatever its meaning - will always correspond to the first position of the middle column (the personal column of the Main Character). Each card in the second position of a column is therefore always associated with the second position of the middle column. The same applies to the cards in third, fourth and fifth positions, which are then always connected to the third, fourth and fifth positions of the middle column.

The Spread

Now it's time to start the spread. You shuffle the cards, cut them once, and place them face down (now take the illustration on page 357 again as a guide to see how the cards are placed):

The first card is placed in the first place, followed by the second, third, fourth and fifth card (now the top column with positions 1 to 5 is complete).

Place the sixth card in position 6. The seventh card must now be placed at the first position in the middle column, which represents the Querent himself.

The eighth card is placed in position 7 and the ninth card in position 8.

Now place the card number 10 at the second position of the middle column, which represents the current state of the Querent.

The eleventh card is placed in position 9 and the twelfth card is placed in position 10.

The thirteenth card is placed in the middle column at the place representing the family of the Querent.

The fourteenth card is placed in position 11 and the fifteenth card is placed in position 12.

The sixteenth card is placed in the position of the middle column representing the environment of the Querent.

The seventeenth card is placed in position 13 and the eighteenth card is placed in position 14.

The nineteenth card is placed in the position of the middle column, the unforeseen events.

The twentieth card is placed in position 15. Thus, the two outer and middle columns are complete.

The twenty-first card is placed in position 16 and the twenty-second card is placed in position 17.

The twenty-third card is placed in position 18.

The twenty-fourth card is placed in position 19 and the twenty-fifth card is placed in position 20.

Now the bottom column is complete and all 25 cards you need for the spread are placed in their positions.

SHORTCUT In simple terms, you can see it in this illustration: the numbers here refer to the order of the distribution of the cards; according to the original instructions, the distribution was written down as explained above.

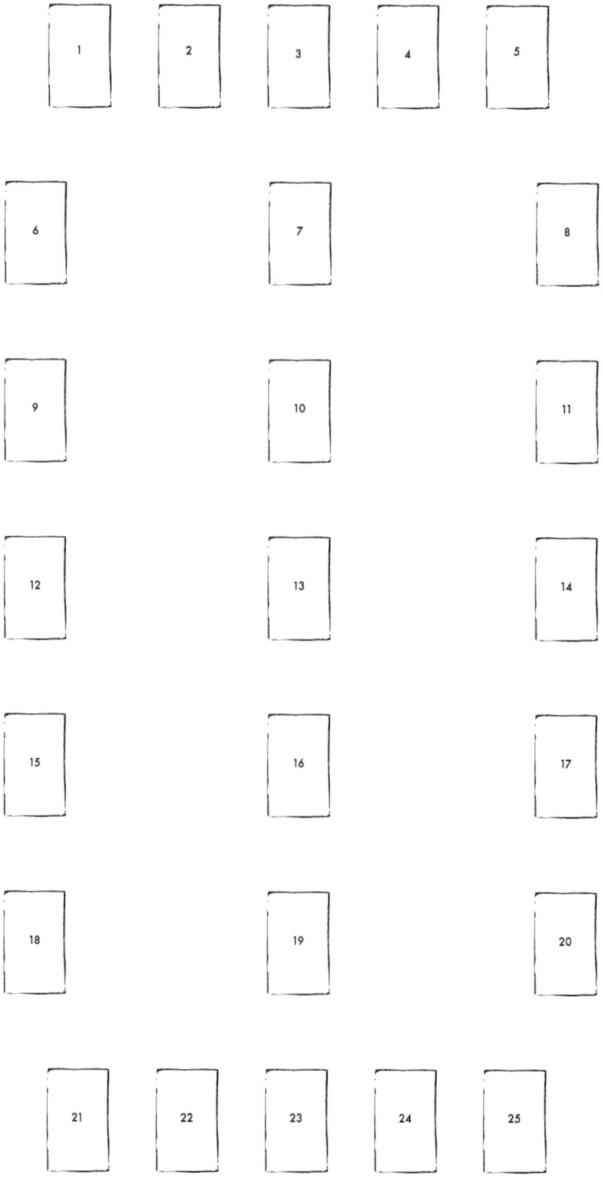

1
2
3
4
5
6
7
8
9
10
11
12
13
14
15
16
17
18
19
20
21
22
23
24
25

Now the oracle starts:

The original instruction describes that after the distribution of the cards, the Querent should be asked which flower is his favorite flower: the most beautiful flower and which is preferred by the Querent because of its fragrance; Just as Mlle. Lenormand once practiced, if she did the Grand Jeu for someone (provided that the person had knowledge of the flora, but in the times of Mlle Lenormand this was often the case).

With this information about the Main Character, you now look in the emblematic dictionary of flowers (it is added to this chapter) after the corresponding value of the respective flower.

To avoid this difficult step, as knowledge of flowers, their names and scents is rare nowadays, it is also possible to shuffle the remaining cards and let the Querent draw two of them. Look in the dictionary which flowers are on the cards and let the Querent select one of the three flowers from the first card to get the value of the first, the beautiful flower, and let the Querent choose one of the three flowers from the second card to get the value of the second, the well-scented flower.

NOTE The choice of beauty and fragrance is important and must be made accordingly, because for the interpretation of the Flower Oracle, two important things must be observed later: the flower, which is selected for its beauty, in tradition, it is rather referred to as a more "meaningless" choice, because beauty is transient and lies on the surface, and the flower chosen for the fragrance is considered in tradition as a more serious and meaningful choice. Because the scent comes from the inside. Now you can start to do the flowers' oracle.

The Aphorism of Flowers

Example

Suppose the Lady, who was part of the previous examples, now in this step of the oracle loves the Hyacinth, whose number is 19, because of its beauty, and prefers the Peony, whose number is 7 because of its fragrance.

Now look in the first figure (page 357) where the position 19 is. The number 19 is located at the fourth position of a column (the lower one) and thus also corresponds to the fourth position of the middle column, the row that represent the Main Character.

Now you must turn all the cards that are placed in the fourth place of each column.

In our example, these cards are:

The card in position 4 of the upper column is the 10 of Diamonds.

The card number 12, which is in the fourth place in the left column, is the 5 of Spades.

The card in position 13 in the right column, is the Queen of Clubs.

And the card at position 19 in the lower column, is the 2 of Hearts.

Now you must interpret these four cards and associate them with the Querent:

With the card 10 of Diamonds, you get the information that the lady thinks of a wise but not very sincere person, this person gives the Lady insidious advice and does not act in her interests to make her happy

The card of the left column, 5 of Spades, which also describes the Lady's emotions, tells you that she is neglecting her duties; it is therefore for you a proof that the woman's private life is in a kind of disorder and without a certain routine, and that she's in personal conflicts about her lack of discernment about the people she's with. are attributable.

The card of the right column, the Queen of Clubs, indicates that, however, she loves the ease of life and that her thoughts & priorities are more dedicated to entertainment and the joys of cultural life.

The bottom card, 2 of Hearts, reaffirms to you that the Lady's lack of discernment is the reason for rejecting a wise person who might advise her well and be a great help in her situation.

Now take a closer look at the card at the fourth position of the middle column, 7 of Diamonds, whose "aphorism of flowers" is the message of terrible setbacks. The event cannot be prevented, so the Lady will have to deal with setbacks in this situation in the future.

Now you look for the second flower:

The flower of the Lady's second choice was of a value of 7. The number 7 occupies the first position of a column, thus closely related to the first card of the middle column, the row that represents the Lady herself.

Now you must turn all the cards that are in the first position of a column. These cards are the 9 of Diamonds - the first card of the upper column; the 9 of Clubs - the first card of the left

column; the 4 of Diamonds - the first card of the right column; and the Queen of Spades - the first card of the lower column.

You see in this example contradiction and a struggle that now refers to the Lady herself, because everything is related to the first position of the middle column. This seems to be serious and necessary, and it is again the 9 of Diamonds, which indicates a departure.

The card of the left column, 9 of Clubs, shows the unrest, the fight.

The card on the right column, 4 of Diamonds, (position of thoughts, wishes) indicates that she still hopes to be protected or not to be alone in all this.

The bottom card, the Queen of Spades, (the position stands for those who are rejected), describes the widowhood and can only show the position of the Lady.

She is broken, she has experienced a loss, she is "a widow", the meaning broken is an indication that she "broke the bond to religion, her spiritual connection that she had" - her relationship is broken. She cannot accept fate and is more likely to force herself to be satisfied with her departure, the loss and not to identify with the situation of a "sad widow", widowhood is here a symbol of the loss of a position. She flees and is more concerned with pursuing her own interests, and yet she hopes to be protected on her way, but she refuses to question all the causes that have brought her into this situation, and she refuses to learn from the consequences. She refuses to take her fate into her own hands.

The "Aphorism of Flowers" of the card 5 of Diamonds (this is the first card at the first position of the middle column) says:

"This card is an important lesson for ruthless people who will never reach their goal."

This sentence confirms the Lady's struggle with herself and the contradiction of her ideas and thoughts.

Remember the note at the beginning regarding the meaningless and meaningful decisions.

This example explains it well: The Lady attaches little importance to the rules of life and coexistence, which she should consider binding and important; and for her fate she makes negative experiences because of this attitude.

NOTE For your interpretation of the cards, it is important to know that the cards in the four outer columns are always interpreted only by the big picture of the card and not with the small picture and not with the interpretation of the flowers. The cards in the middle column, the column representing the Main Character, are those cards that pass on the message of the flowers. This is the aphorism of flowers. When it comes to the Main Character and not to another person, everything else on these cards is of no importance.

The Aphorism of Flowers

Example

As before, the cards are shuffled, cut, and laid out as described. After that, it is always necessary to determine the value of the flowers selected by the Querent to start the oracle, then to learn what the aphorism of flowers is.

In this example, a Lady admires the Violet, which has a value of 16, and prefers the scent of the Bellflowers, which have a value of 5.

The No. 16 is the first position of a column, and this means that all cards in this spread refer to the first position of the middle column The first position of the middle column will reveal the aphorism of flowers.

After you have turned over all the cards that occupy a position in the first place, you can read the cards.

These cards are part of this example: The 5 of Hearts is at the top of the top column. This card in the top column indicates that an unknown/stranger in a high position has caught the Lady's attention, and that nothing and no one means as much to her as this person.

The Main Character's card is in the first position of the left column.

NOTE If a Main Character's card is part of the spread, for example, this is a sure proof that the Main Character has a great influence on the situation. Sometimes it is understood as a sign of ambition and courage in a positive sense. The opposite can be a kind of weakness or less ambition, depending on the other cards that are part of the spread, and on the context.

The 9 of Diamonds is in the first position of the right column and indicates that the Lady is thinking of a journey that she will undertake soon.

The 8 of Clubs is located at the first position of the lower column. This card in the last column indicates that the Lady was probably proposed to, but inwardly she feels absolutely to want to reject it. She seems emotionally averse to a wedding, at least in connection with that person.

Now you turn the first card of the middle column over, it is the King of Clubs. The flowers on this card have a message that I should consider useful and encouraging:

"The business/project you are about to do is a happiness; there is wealth and honor, but only by following the advice of a wise man will you be so successful."

Then you look at the cards of the second flower, which had a value of 5, so now all cards that are in the fifth position of all columns are important:

The 3 of Hearts is located at the fifth position of the left column. The King of Hearts is at the fifth position of the right column, and in the last column you see the Queen of Hearts.

From these cards you can see that an intelligent, rich man or possibly a great artist is very close to the Lady - this one person is represented at this moment by the card 6 of Hearts. she seems to love him, and a marriage for her might be safe.

With the card of the right column, the King of Hearts, a person is represented, and it is confirmed by this card that the Lady in her situation still feels to ask the wise gentleman advice; already once in the cards was seen how a gentleman stands in the interest of the Lady, in the cards' interpretation, which was made before.

However, the card in the bottom column shows an action that proves that the Lady often does not take things so seriously or is not always honest or correct. Unworthily she rejects "the card to be a praiseworthy woman", the values of the Queen of Hearts. She refuses to be a good woman.

The fifth card of the middle column, the 4 of Clubs, now reveals the message of the flowers: The Lady is warned by

these words that her decision has nothing to do with her true character if she continues with it.

NOTE This second message of flowers is very important, because it corresponds to the serious choice of the flower, and in terms of what has not yet happened, the warning of flowers is an important and serious sentence for the future.

There is a very sensitive nuance that should not be underestimated by you as a fortune teller & card reader.

Always remember that the choice of a flower is called a more "meaningless" choice because of its beauty, and the choice because of the fragrance is a "meaningful" choice - so never underestimate the second message, no matter what the previous one was.

The message of the second flowers made you rethink your first interpretation of the cards. In this one you recognized for the Lady an upcoming wedding. And here in this statement of cards this marriage has not yet been concluded. This proves that the announced marriage is either delayed or even cancelled after the proposal.

It is even more likely that the Querent wants it to be like that, because it corresponds to the message of the meaningful choice of the flower; the feeling against marriage, against the status of wife and the message of the flowers, which says clearly that the decision would not correspond to her true character, which was already indicated in the first interpretation, in which she did not really feel connected to a wedding. It is also a probable forecast because it refers to the unforeseen events in the future, regarding the position of the card in the middle column.

NOTE And if, in general, a situation described in each of the four cards is also described by the card in the middle column, it is proof that the prediction will be confirmed and will take place unhindered.

Continue with the example

There is also another emotional contradiction in the Lady's situation. A sign that the Querent is being held back not only by herself, but also by the card of the left column, 3 of Hearts. The card shows that she seems to love another person or that she is at least very connected to someone in her heart. But she still wants to seize the opportunity to be part of high society. This seduces her; but her need for freedom and the loss of it, which she may regret, causes her to consult a friend before making a final decision. Hoping to feel calmer and better.

The message of the flowers says that the decision to marry the man will not coincide in any way with her character and feeling. This tells you that the Lady already has an inkling that her happiness/life will not feel complete.

These two aphorisms are intended to serve as an example and make it understandable how the flowers reveal something. The flowers give clues about what the Main Character needs to take a closer look at in life or in their interest to become clearer about a situation.

NOTE Remember, life situations and these interests always mean what is shown in the middle column (In this case, you can look at the cards of the middle column to get more information about the subject areas, far from the message of the flowers).

1. All in relation to the person who consults the cards, their wife, husband, children, health, reputation, worries, joys.

2. Everything related to the personal situation, social standing, employment, work, good or bad leadership of the Querent whether in his own company or in employment.

3. Everything related to the family, the relatives in general, be it personal or by marriage, and the devoted or closest friends.

4. All in relation to the environment of the Main Character and its superior persons, including those who give the Querent the opportunity to earn a living, as well as those who trust the Main Character and those who to whom someone owes thanks for the services rendered. People who have earned mutual appreciation and trust, but also those to whom you owe something in general.

5. And everything in relation to the unforeseen events in life is to be understood by everything that the Querent cannot foresee, what has not yet happened to him, but will happen in the future.

Example (to explain how a card in the five positions has different statements and can be interpreted).

Let's say your client has chosen a flower for its beauty, and the card in the top column that comes out is the 6 of Diamonds "Deceit".

This would indicate that the Querent feels an affection for someone who, unfortunately, is a cheater, a dishonest person. The Querent may not know the person for what he is and is deceived by appearances.

If the same card, the 6 of Diamonds, is in the left row, this indicates that the Querent is connected to a dishonest person but is aware of it. There is nothing hidden here.

NOTE sometimes the card placed in this column may even apply to the Main Character; this is often the case if the card in the next column, the right column, turns out to be a negative one.

But if the same card, the 6 of Diamonds, is placed in the right column, it indicates that the Main Character himself is involved in (hidden) affairs with a fraudulent or traitorous person; but in this case it may be, that the Querent still does not know the malicious character of the other person and thus could also be a victim.

For the card, 6 of Diamonds, in the lower column there are two possible interpretations:

If the card, the 6 of Diamonds, is in the bottom column, you could also say that the Main Character rejects the deception and such bad, immoral behavior, despises that it detests this vice and such persons. Also, the card in this position may mean that the Main Person recognizes a betrayal but does not want to admit it and cannot accept or believe it. The person does not admit that he/she has been cheated.

This dual view can be the same for many other cards, positive or negative cards. It is always necessary to look closer and make the decision of the final interpretation based on the context. Also, the experience with the cards will be helpful to you gradually.

When the card, 6 of Diamonds, appears in the first position of the middle column that is directly connected to the Main Character, it turns out that it is really a bad card and describes the person as such a bad person.

If the 6 of Diamonds appears in the position of the middle column, which represents the state and living conditions of the

Main Character, this would be proof that the person had serious and legitimate reasons to fear an event, that would have a negative impact on his current life circumstances or on his social status.

If the card, 6 of Diamonds, is in the position of family or friends, it indicates that those close to the Main Character are desperate and affected by what happens to the person. In the worst case, however, this card would also indicate a betrayal or a dishonest person within the family or circle of friends.

The same card would indicate in the position of the Main Character's environment and the superiors that the Querent ignored advice or instructions of others, which should have been followed. This behavior was wrong and would have negative consequences.

If the 6 of Diamonds is in the position of the unforeseen events, it is important for the Main Character to know that in due course of time it will not be able to see certain results as they are and will be deceived. All events must therefore first be evaluated by the Main Character in a neutral way and viewed with caution, because it is a deceptive time that the Main Character is about to face.

Dictionaire Emblématique

Dictionary of the Flowers

(The flowers, their value & the sentence of the flowers)

The Suit of Clubs

King of Clubs

- Leadwort 1
- Large Basil 5
- Poppy 18

"The business/project you are about to do is a happiness; there is wealth and honor, but only by following the advice of a wise man will you be so successful."

Queen of Clubs

- Fruit Pistil and Pollen 15
- Honeysuckle 5
- Monthly Rose 13

"You will eagerly seek someone's company/ contact with someone; decisions are difficult. Warning: You are threatened with anger through attachment."

Jack of Clubs

- Feather Carnation 20
- Pimpernel 12
- Moon Flower Seed 14

"However, your situation is now, only after much effort and by using your mind and being smart, you will be able to achieve your goal."

10 of Clubs

- Pineapple 5
- Spirobassia 6
- Tobacco Plant 20

"At this moment or in this situation, courage and presence of mind are required."

9 of Clubs

- Liverwort 12
- Christmas Rose (Hellebore) 20
- Red Clover 13

"This card predicts multiple disasters in the midst of a certain success: you will learn at your expense that happiness is not always constant."

8 of Clubs

- Fruit Pistil and Pollen 15

"Surely from the very first moment of your marriage, relationship or connection, you will know what you need to do to maintain happiness. But make sure you don't lack these qualities and make sure you always do what you have to do."

7 of Clubs

- Chestnut Tree 4
- Weeping Willow 8
- Chinese Rose 7

"This card promises great honor, success and glory to those with ambition, discipline and (some) talent.""

6 of Clubs

- Yew 7
- Sumac 13
- Geraniums 15

"Unfortunately, nothing will develop as you hope and desire; the one who loves himself most will only reach his goal at the expense of the other."

5 of Clubs

- Fruit Pistil and Pollen 15
- Bedstraw 16
- Linden Blossom 3

"The deed / the plans you think of are cowardly, you will only feel shame and remorse; do not hurry now when there is still time. Don't make the wrong move."

4 of Clubs

- Red Levkoye 13
- Ice Plants 7
- Cocoa Blossom 4

"You will be warned by this card that your decision does not is your character."

3 of Clubs

- White Lilac 15
- Weeping Willow 8
- Saponaria 10

"This card is perfectly good, soon there will be joyful times."

2 of Clubs

- Oats 18
- Zedrach Tree 16
- Carnation 19

"The comforts or talents of yourself will enable you to make considerable or great fortune."

Ace of Clubs

- Gelatinous Tremor Mushroom 11
- Daisy 3
- Bellflower 5

"This card shows the full success; but you will have to fight against someone who is disgraceful to you, and if you are not careful and if you do not try to stay away from it, your success is in danger."

The Suit of Hearts

King of Hearts

- Lily of the Valley 5
- Mallow 19
- Cherry Tree Branch 14

"This card assures the Main Character of unexpected happiness, but only if it follows the behavior and advice of a good and honest person."

Queen of Hearts

- Cistus 8
- Poppy 18
- Lilac 20

"This card shows the conflict of a young person either following a frivolous society or being with people full of wisdom."

Jack of Hearts

- Fuchsias 7
- Duckweed 6
- Weed 19

"There is fear and confidence in this card; a person may well lose the heart of their love; they will know how to recognize their rival; someone will have everything else in abundance but will hardly get the love of the other. "

10 of Hearts

- Violet 16
- Lilac 20
- May Rose 14

"There are two major difficulties in finding the person you are looking for: pleasantries of the mother and daughter (after all, it is necessary to satisfy the family and the loved ones when you are together with the right person). "

9 of Hearts

- White Lilac 15
- Arum 14
- Strawflower, Everlasting Flower 7

"This card is the symbol of true merit and strength; in no case can it be a negative card. There is always a positive impact that this card has on the situation."

8 of Hearts

- Daphne 9
- Orchid 15

"This card shows the distance, departure or loss of a person who has harmed you in the past."

7 of Hearts

- Dahlia 6
- Morning Glory 1
- Snowdrop 20

"This card is very important: it contains the message that you need to stay in control and stay focused and that you should handle messages you will receive - whether good or bad - discreetly."

6 of Hearts

- Ivy 4
- Rose 14
- Sage 4

"This card predicts unexpected and strange moments, situations that require unexpected actions, but which create success and wealth. A young person (a woman according to the original instructions) will find what he needs."

5 of Hearts

- Germer 4
- Icelandic Moss 19
- Sorrel 8

In the original instruction, the sentence reads: "Be careful who you trust and what you represent; anyone who represents the interests of his king, people, country and even religion threatens to be betrayed by the one to whom he is faithful." - If you too strongly represent the interests of the wrong person and too little protect your own interests, you will be betrayed by another person."

4 of Hearts

- Safflower 9
- Pondweed 6
- Papyrus 1

"The card is to be understood as a warning: unfortunately, this card foretells someone of seemingly endless torment and deep regret."

3 of Hearts

- Elderberry 12
- Cyprus Grass 1
- Laurel 2

"This card foretells a brilliant person's opportunity to shine in the near future, and if enemies are nearby, they will soon be gone."

2 of Hearts

- Bladderwrack 17
- Violet 16
- Hyacinth 19

"This card favors the good and honest man; but woe to him if his great position makes him forget justice: for then this map predicts a terrible downfall for him. "

Ace of Hearts

- Boxwood 11
- Banana Tree 8
- Bud of a Rose 14

"If you do not able to recognize who are the people you spend time with, you will make mistakes that will harm yourself in future."

The Suit of Diamonds

King of Diamonds

- Orange Tree with Blossoms and Fruits 14
- Water Lily 14
- Delphinium 6

"You will receive gifts or services that are exactly what you need right now."

Queen of Diamonds

- Black Nettle 16
- Stinky Cranesbill Geranium 15
- Cattail 14

"This card is an evil card, telling of envy and revenge rooted in pure malice and resentment."

Jack of Diamonds

- Foxglove 16
- Balsam Herb 19
- Bell Vine 2

"This card shows the triumph of tactics and skill, supported by some kind of powerful protection."

10 of Diamonds

- Borage Flower 3
- Red Carnation 14
- Tulip 17

"Some claims are made out of bad intent; however, if you listen to wise and honest advice, you can still succeed."

9 of Diamonds

- Safflower 9
- Morning Glory 1
- Conifer 6

"Only with care, attention and courage will you overcome the challenges of a difficult journey."

8 of Diamonds

- Chrysanthemum 12
- Gladiolus 14
- Silphium Plant 19

"Only with your talents and your physical benefits will you manage to change your position and thus improve the situation."

7 of Diamonds

- St. John's Wort 19
- Soap tree 17
- Hellebore 14

"Woe to those who cannot take this card away (on which this card falls): it announces misery or the most terrible setbacks."

6 of Diamonds

- Rhododendron 12
- Wild Strawberry 12
- Heather 20

"If you are not completely corrupt and if you have a good character and decency, then distance yourself from the wrong people you spend time with, because their life is notorious / without honor."

5 of Diamonds

- Clover 19
- Levkoje 13
- Paronychia 5

"This card is an important lesson for ruthless people who will never reach their goal."

4 of Diamonds

- Nettle 4
- Moss 16
- Judas Tree 11

"Do not be discouraged by difficulties: soon you will reach the goal of your desires."

3 of Diamonds

- Ivy 7
- Lilac 20
- Rosemary 14

"Your painful memories will remain for a long time: this card is the symbol of suffering."

2 of Diamonds

- Gentian 19
- Light Violet 3
- Buttercup 15

"While you are just waiting for the bright future to come and you are still hoping, you will bitterly cry for a faded happiness that you have not recognized."

Ace of Diamonds

- Reed 13
- Purple Loosestrife 15
- A Rose 14

"This card shows the need to warn you of the indiscretion of the people around you."

The Suit of Spades

King of Spades

- Tulip 17
- Cedar Tree 16
- Tubular Flower 20

"If this card is surrounded by a majority of positive cards, the terrible fears described by the card will pass in a short time."

Queen of Spades

- Asparagus 6
- Fern 3
- Acacia 18

"The pain implied by this card will hardly be extinguished; however, one must not lose faith in better times, for the help of this attitude is the only effective in these circumstances."

Jack of Spades

- Veronica 19
- Red Levkoye 13
- Evergreen 1

"This card is good for anyone who has suffered injustice, as it indicates that there will be help and protection at some point."

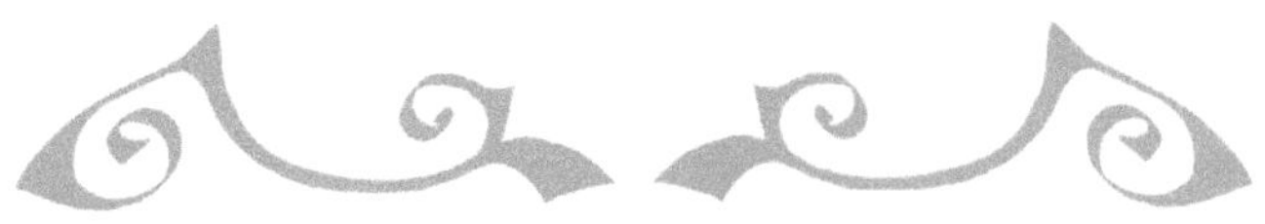

10 of Spades

- Saxifrage 6
- Barberry 5
- Gutty Tree (Ficus) 19

"Fix everything: your house, your life... Bring order to your affairs, and through the perseverance, discipline, and consistency that you put into your actions, you will be able to track down the "thief" who haunts you."

9 of Spades

- Fireweed 6
- Centifoil (Rose) 9
- Cornflowers 20

"After a time of suffering and terrible uncertainty about the fate that awaits you when repentance has tormented your mind, your soul will eventually be recovered and healed."

8 of Spades

- Wild Orchid 9
- Rapeseed 1
- Thistle 10

"This is a sad card for both the strong and the weak: whoever triumphs today will soon be defeated."

7 of Spades

- Oats 13
- Peony 7
- Dog Rose 11

"This card indicates a strong connection; a true promise and it is the traditional sign of the marriage proposal."

6 of Spades

- Shrub 1
- Poppy 18
- Conifer 6

"This card is a warning: you may become the victim of malicious act. Only the Jupiter Talisman, which the card recommends possessing, can prevent this loss."

5 of Spades

- Yellow Carnation 2
- Raspberry 2
- Calamus 3

"This card, when it appears together with other positive cards in the spread, indicates a kind of special success and prestige - it was once the sign of the respected men of science, the writers, the scholars and the doctors."

4 of Spades

- Common Reed 10
- Sunflower 16
- Cotton 12

"This is a symbol of traps that are placed on you, there are people and situations that you cannot mistrust enough."

3 of Spades

- Sedge 1
- Milkweed 11
- Laurel 2

"The person being tracked by this card (who comes in contact with this card) must be careful with the situations in life."

2 of Spades

- Houseleek 13
- Currant 4
- Blackberry 14

"A thunderstorm is rising; you could be a victim if you're not careful."

Ace of Spades

- Paronychia 5
- Wild Garlic 7
- Peas 11

"This map, which represents bad passions, predicts a situation with a potentially disastrous outcome."

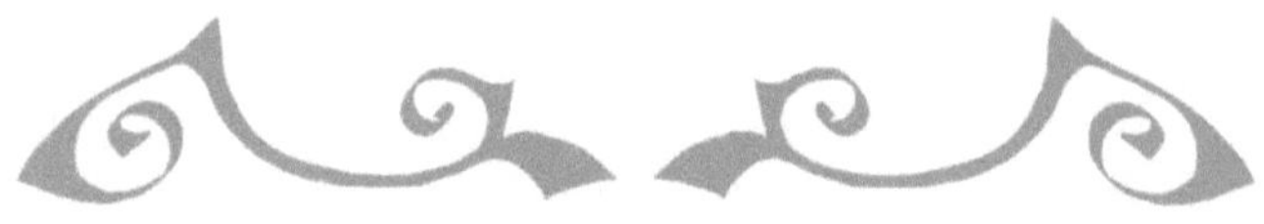

CHAPTER VII

The Voices of the Animals

(to add the Aphorisms of the Flowers)

The Oracle of the Animals

The Chart of the Animals, Reptiles, Insects, and Birds

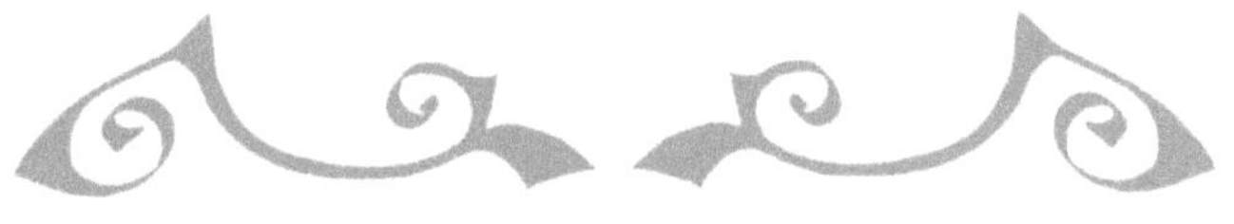

The Voices of the Animals

The Oracle of the Animals or an additional Exercise to the Aphorisms of Flowers.

It's no secret that Mlle. Lenormand was very fond to draw conclusions about a person's personality from the fact of a person's favorite animal and because of the fact which animal was less preferred by a person. Thus, this part of the Grand Jeu again forms a demonstrable bridge to the methods and life of Mlle Lenormand.

For this spread you need twenty-six piles of cards or positions representing twenty-six different personalities and which are also related to various animals, reptiles, insects, or birds.

You shuffle the cards, cut them once and place them one by one in twenty-six positions, starting from card 1 to card 26.

You must repeat this step until all cards are dealt and the last card remaining in your hand is intended to be placed later in the position where the Main Character's card will be located.

NOTE always depending on the situation that at least the card of one of the Main Characters must be left in the game. If both cards of the Main Characters are needed, two cards remain in your hand after the distribution: one would be for the pile with the card of the Querent and the other for the pile of the other Main Character card.

The following figure shows the arrangement of the cards, followed by the explanation of the individual positions.

NOTE This time you can also give a different form to the arrangement of the cards, the example is not binding. This time you are free to decide how you want to position the cards. According to the original instructions, the cards were laid out in

three rows: in two rows of 9 cards each and in a row of 8 cards.

My arrangement of the cards

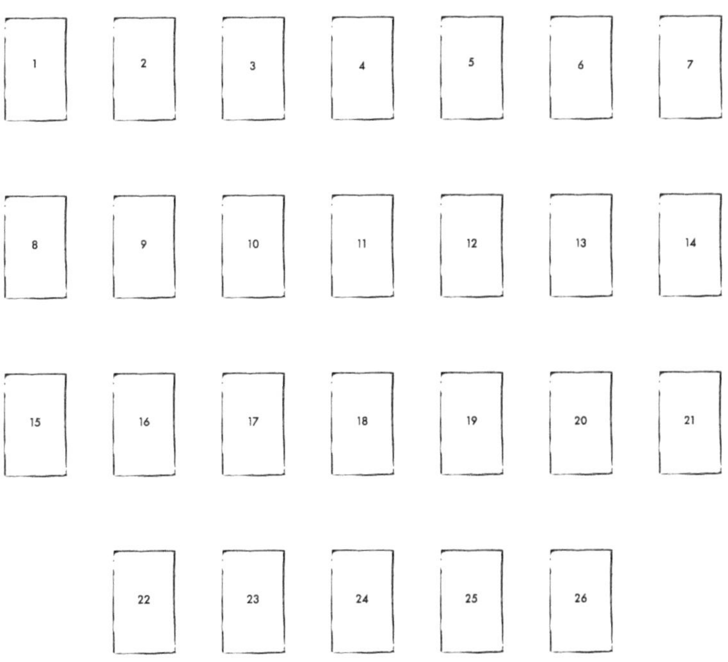

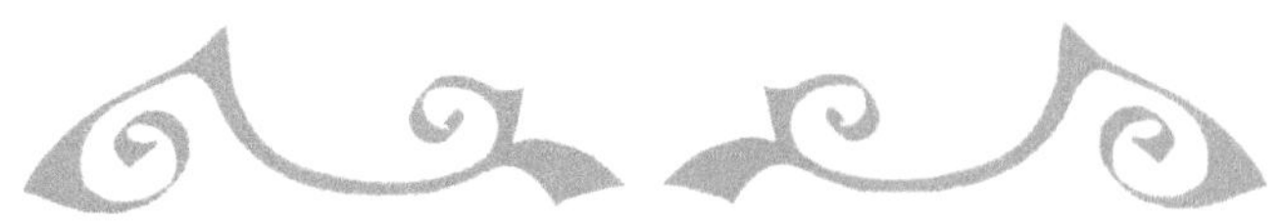

Explanation of the 26 positions and "personalities"

1. The Curious One A curious character, persistent, insatiable, always ready to haggle for the price; for this person, even minimal expenses are always too much, especially for bad or used things. This person is less generous and does not always give a person what he is rightfully entitled to but takes great care that he himself gets what he is entitled to. If it is money, he holds it back and only pays it at the last moment, also he only gives it back in parts. He keeps it for his own benefit; this person never lacks the money for his own interests, these always have priority; And if the person passes the responsibility over himself to others, he is skillful in setting "traps" to convince themselves of their loyalty.

2. The Indecisive One An indecisive character, vague, concerned, neat, even strict with himself and with little knowledge of others or life itself. Such a person is often afraid to expose himself, but always asks everyone for advice, while he should rather implement the plans on its own. This person starts with something, then in the middle of it is stopped, dissatisfied with what has been achieved so far, and thus it is preferred to live with less or to be satisfied with less, rather than to get involved in something new or to stay consistent with something. After all, this person is more likely to be urged to do something, and although he will start over, he will never finish. But gentleness dominates this person; this person often isolates himself and hides to see no one.

3. The Moody One This person is of irritable, quick-tempered, capricious character. This person takes the most innocent and harmless things and twists them into evil. This person cannot speak without hurting or shocking the people around them with statements; never does this person agree with the needs, opinions, or statements of others. Their views are often heretical to others. This person is often very superstitious and tends to believe in supernatural powers and beings; for example, if the person had a bad dream, it is a sign that people will talk badly about them, that others will steal peace, will endanger their reputation and reliability.

4. The Cunning One This person pretends to be noble, but is also cunning, and quickly connects with other people. A great ease of expression characterizes this personality. This person has the talent to convince but is driven by self-interest. This person is persistent, he only becomes sociable with those people he needs. He is keen, flatters with skill, knows how to hide his feelings when it is necessary. He is interested in many things and that gives him great knowledge. This person will always do other people's business with success but also for his own benefit.

5. The Selfish One This person is skillful and compassionate to all. This person likes to praise himself but talks a lot about the bad qualities of other people. Also, this person quickly praises others a lot, at least when they get to know these people, but then this person quickly takes care of their own interests again. This person is committed and makes a lot of effort, but only when it is noticed and seen by others, otherwise the person is rather reserved, apathetic, unapproachable, and very meticulous. If a person is without worry and without suspicion, this personality tends to be negative and fraudulent or not sincere.

6. The Derogatory One This person is very elegant, often with feminine features or more feminine. In addition, this person is characterized by certain negative peculiarities: without style, no eye for aesthetics, without decency. This person does not do anything that he believes does not strengthen his reputation; he speaks emphatically and complacently about the services he has rendered, and he also speaks in this way about his relationships. This person despises those of higher rank, in higher positions and jobs, and is known to make fun of people to whom he feels superior. In a word, this person does without a guilty conscience everything you can expect from someone with a lack of empathy and decency.

7. The Excessive One A dark character, silent, threatening, and when angry, he shows himself mean and sometimes even brutal. He hates work and duties, prefers to live the moments of pleasure full of debauchery and excess. He knows no limits and thus exposes himself to everything, even situations that lead to litigation, he accepts, regardless of the law and the measure. Everything just to satisfy one's own needs; in a word, it violates all rules, be it those of men or even the spiritual world.

8. The Good – Natured One This personality shows a lot of kindness, tenderness, and has sympathies for almost everything and everyone. Love for family, parental, and caring feelings are important. The education and attitude are pious and meek, this person always acts with wisdom and healthy discernment; he knows how to show himself selflessly, to put his own interests behind and to renounce his own advantage to everyone who surrounds him, to please. This person is faithful and devoted, and their attachment or attachment is sincere and lasting.

9. The Sober One A person of a sober, peaceful, chaste, liberal, and good nature; but sometimes he shows an aggressive, angry, violent side. Especially when you contradict this person or when he is mocked, he rebels and is reluctant to be restrained. If this person is deeply offended, he becomes vindictive and fights for own rights until to the end.

10. The One without Empathy When this person is inactive, he is very lost in thought, absent, without composure: in the eyes of this person or in his movements one recognizes something wild, uncontrolled. Also, something false, not authentic. But when this character gives in to his inclinations, he appears cool, impudent, slanderous. For the most shameful deeds, this character feels no guilty or moral conscience. The original instruction was very extreme in the words and describes that person as bloodthirsty, cruel, barbaric, his character leads him to ruin, to murder.

11. The Narcissistic One A busy person, active, laborious, but full of vanity and self-love. This person has an extreme desire to shine in front of others and to stand out. But since the person basically has no ability, it inevitably follows that he makes great mistakes in all his actions and in all his undertakings. Their excess of self-love and the high opinion they have of their own person do not allow them to accept the true reasons why one or the other is assigned to them. Since this person is doing better than he really is, much is perceived as wrong. She rejects the advice to act only according to her own abilities and not to lean too far out of the window. Others are often forced to turn away from this person because of stupidity and ridiculous vanity and pride.

12. The Self – Righteous One A hard, cold heart, which hides indifference and selfishness under the appearance of devotion or benevolence towards its fellowmen and only does good to brag about it. Secretly, however, that character is saddened that he does not seem better. Compliments and good words are spoken, but only rejection and sometimes only contempt for the other person is felt. If someone tells of an unfortunate event that happened to a righteous family or person and nearly ruined it, that person is not touched. Sometimes this person even says that these people are likely to have caused fate itself and deserved it because of their behavior.

13. The Sneaky One A self-righteous and deceitful person, no one recognizes the intentions of their actions or the meaning of their words. This person has the gift to hide the true feelings and intentions and to direct them according to the circumstances. When this person enrages someone, they ask him in an affective, artificial way how he is doing and whether he is satisfied with his situation. This person shows himself with hypocritical interest, to build up a bond with that person, while he, however, acts in the background against the other person to sometimes cause loss and failure of the other person. Here a person is shown who is jealous and if he wishes to have something, he knows exactly what the price is and is willing to

pay it. This person also knows how to make others do something that leads to the success of their plans.

14. The Loving One A gentle person, spiritual, kind and cordial, the face shows the expression of goodness that is in the heart. This person's expressions and conversations are graceful, humorous, charming, familiar, and respectful at the same time. The person is sensitive in their dealings with others, quickly recognizes what someone needs, and this person is always ready to move forward. Their grace and lightness can be traced back to a good education and to an environment and dealing with honest people.

15. The Determined One A noble character with a serious and thoughtful side. Most of the time he is engaged in the planning and elaboration of a project, or the execution of such. If this person pursues a great goal, he does everything for it, examines his project, and lets his environment know as if he wants to be understood and admired by the people who listened to him. He's looking for confirmation. But after a firm decision, sometimes one or the other thought of fear arises, so this person stops for a moment and hesitates; a dark cloud overshadows his zeal and drive. But then he continues with all his courage, his fearlessness, and the ambition. This person has everything he needs to succeed, he overcomes challenges, he overcomes all obstacles, and he only stops after a downfall, total failure, realistic hopelessness, or a complete triumph.

16. The Virtuous One A cute person, delicate & fine. The kindness is exemplary, this character is harmless and simple, modest, discreet, and loyal, not at all negative. This person obeys without resistance and never deviates from the duties. The face is an expression of serenity and expresses gentleness and goodwill. If you ask this person for a favor, he is always ready to follow up on this request. This person is friendly and cheerful with each other. Inside this person is a true bond with himself and thus this bond is also possible with others.

17. The Impolite One An inconsistent character, taken by himself, without realizing that he can be unpleasant, tiring, or annoying to others. This person does not behave in public, does not hesitate to say what should not be said; simply falls into the mouth of the people with whom he speaks. In a conversation that is about a topic that doesn't interest him, but the others, he still wants to have all the attention. An impatient person who knows his rudeness, but he still does not stop for example, he wakes up those who are asleep only because he is already awake, or he remains uninvited with others. An „unwanted son".

18. The Sarcastic One A sometimes unpleasant, snappy, sarcastic person. Although he has all the characteristics of a good joker and humor, jokes from time to time, but behaves rather immature. When he smiles mischievously, it's a sign that he's about to tell a joke, often a sarcastic one. Nevertheless, this person shows a noble disposition and distributes himself to be kind or to appear to others as kind. However, this person never complains to others about their own worries or problems.

19. The Suspicious One A suspicious, lazy, jealous, defiant person, but still with a tender, passionate side. This person loves to lose himself in remote places. Sometimes he prefers a tête à tête with someone, but he also likes to be alone. This person forgets himself in poetic reveries and other daydreams, this character loves sentimental & philosophical conversations. Unfortunately, his gaze often expresses laziness, doubt, and uncertainty. This person's life mostly goes on without much drive or ambition, and without thinking about making a name for himself or creating a secure future.

20. The Unconcentrated One This person likes to talk about one and then about the other. And he quickly forgets, because she seems unfocused, for example, goes into a room and looks for an object he needs, leaves the room again, but without having found what he was looking for or without taking it, because he could not really remember, what he wanted. But then he claims to be sure that the object was not there; he

knows the forgetfulness. Talk to friends about something and often interrupt himself to talk about something else. This person also prefers to apologize if they must ask something repeatedly instead of concentrating properly. This person quickly gives up on what he is doing.

21. The Modest One This person has a positive character, but often acts recklessly, but in moderation. This person is sober mind, lives on little, is neither kind nor gallant, and deals only with useful things or subjects or sciences, such as mathematics, architecture, mechanics. This person loves to build or create something. This person wants to improve the world. With an attentive and inquisitive mind, he is given the talent to create something, and one always recognizes the care, the exact method and symmetry in everything he does.

22. The Ordinary One This character has an ordinary taste, is ordinary in his manners, without structure. He does not worry about himself: lives unhealthily, eats too much unhealthy food, enjoys the carelessness in life and the loose company. This person does not think about the future and acts with ambiguous morality. This person seems insensitive, and a little hateful; he is of low intelligence, ungrateful, and without regard for the people he can do without.

23. The Unfaithful One This person makes you wonder, because as thoughtless and fickle it is, so, combative, selfish, and skillfully seductive it can also be. Tyrannical towards the inferior and prone to infidelity. This person loves to be lavish, loves the pleasures and encounters, provided they are only in good company and entertaining. Gatherings where people drink and eat in excess and without embarrassment and celebrate in exuberance. Every celebration, whether as a guest or host, enriches this person with grace, freedom, and good taste. This person likes nothing serious, binding. A moody person who, if he likes, suddenly gives himself very friendly, polite, and gallant and then also does what is required of him.

24. The Artistic One A cheerful, open-minded person, a bit suggestive and he skillfully seduces with his manners and language. He knows how to act correctly and to articulate himself, this person loves nothing more than his own freedom. The life of this person takes place with the pleasure and arts, such as music, poetry, and theater. This character has lightness and grace; but by abusing these advantages, he is mostly fickle, regardless of the damage he sometimes causes. Once a no or a limit is reached for that person or they no longer love someone, crying or begging no longer affects them.

25. The Simple One A sometimes unfortunately incompetent person, slowly, without any imagination or fantasy. There is only what you say to him or what he sees, a person without malice, without will, who is not impertinent, not bold. He lacks wisdom and strength; he is more docile. However, if you want to lead them too much, they become stubborn, and if you contradict their simple principles, they forget themselves: this person overcomes all obstacles in extreme cases, and nothing can restrain them.

26. The Heroic One This character is diligent at work and willingly obeys everyone, while others often exploit this weakness too much. Despite vanity and a lot of self-love, this person is nevertheless susceptible to dependencies. This person loves cultural life; entertainment, music, luxury, large meetings, and events, especially when he can show and prove his strength, skill, and self. In challenges and precarious situations, this person enjoys his own courage. Such a person strives to gain fame, to win the votes of his contemporaries and to earn the honor of posterity. Here, too, the original instruction in the description became very pathetic: "Fiery and fearless, this person would sacrifice himself if it were necessary to better demonstrate the dedication and zeal in fulfilling the duties that he had assumed."

This was the explanation of the twenty-six personalities. In addition to these personalities, there is also a list of animals that are relevant for this spread (page 389). All animals that are part of the Grand Jeu are assigned in this table a number, a numerical value from 1 to 26. And each number of the twenty-six positions (personalities) that have just been explained always corresponds to the same number of an animal: the personality that is explained under position 1 therefore stands for each animal with the number 1 according to the table.

Example

If the Querent does like the horse and does not like the hippo, you can see from the chart of animals that the horse has the number 26, and the hippo has the number 22. Concentrated on this choice of the Querent, you first distribute the cards as mentioned at the beginning of the chapter.

Once this step has been completed, you must turn over the cards in position 26 and the cards in position 22 and, among other things, find the pile in which the Main Character's card is present. Add the remaining card to the Main Character's card.

Based on the position on which the Main Character is, you now judge whether the personality and the characteristics attributed to it can correspond to the Querent at all. This results not only from the position of the Main Character, but also from whether the cards that are also here have a direct connection to this position; if it were not the case, the Querent very likely to be approached in a vague manner or the description could even refer to someone else who is or will be important in the Querent's situation.

Then you examine the pile of the animal that the Main Character prefers, which adds another attribute to the Querent's actual personality or may complement it. This results if the cards that appear here are in a meaningful or direct connection with the previous interpretation of the Main Character.

If the cards are also significantly better or worse in their value and the statement than the statements of the cards of the pile of the Main Character, this is also an indication of the environment of the person. Namely, that the person frequents rather good or rather bad people.

For example, if the cards that are in the preferred animal's pile are more positive in their statement than those of the cards of the Main Character, then the cards indicate that the person frequents people, that are in some way better than the Main Character himself.

And the cards also tell you if these people have an influence on the Main Character: are good, supporting, and loyal, and how they relate to the Main Character in general.

If the cards were worse, that would not be the case: A good influence would not be given, the persons would not act in the interest of the Main Character and would not feel connected or loyal to the Querent.

The animal that the Querent does not like and the cards in its position either confirms the statement of the cards in the first two positions or refutes or relativizes them, by not describing the Querent (because this animal is not preferred by the Querent). This animal therefore also has an important function.

Example (only for explanation)

Initially, it was stated that the animal that the Querent likes is the horse (26) and he unfortunately does not like the hippo (22) very much.

And the position of the Main Character's card in this example is number 23, the position of tyranny and infidelity.
Suppose the cards here point to nothing that refutes the previous interpretation; they point only to strength and grandeur; this can mean nothing but that the Querent was important to his environment, and by this he could live out his arbitrariness towards others better. As far as his infidelity is concerned, you cannot yet judge who it can happen to, since in this example the Main Character card has both other cards to its left. To see this, the cards must be on the right. Because remember, the cards to the left of the Main Character card give facts about the person himself.

As for the cards of the pile of number 26, the number of the animal he likes, the two cards that appear here are harmless in their effect and do not contradict the statement regarding the character of the Querent. You can add the statement of the Main Character's cards and you will see that the Querent has a brave character and that he knows how to make himself useful in important situations. About his environment, that he has, one can say that this is not superior to him, he dominates it and exerts his pressure on it; in this example the cards reveal that the environment is mostly male gender.

The cards of pile number 22, the unloved animal's pile, which indicates a rather ordinary character, can have little to do with the Querent. So that you can assume that the cards speak against him, therefore not represent him:

The first of these cards is also the Queen of Clubs, the card of the Hesperides. A hint that this is now about a Lady in his environment.

The second card, the 4 of Clubs, which perhaps reflects a little of the character of the hippo, as the card in the scene of the big picture represents the ordinary raw material. This can therefore be a slight resemblance to the Querent's intellect

without taking away his superiority or his false pride, which you have previously recognized in his cards.
The Main Character in position number 23 dominates this spread, as many interpretations apply to him and describe him in many ways. That he has a charming, witty, and graceful lover can now be seen from the card of the Hesperides, the Queen of Clubs, but she too, unfortunately, has a proud nature, which is indicated by the card 4 of Clubs. But through the cards of the unloved animal, which do not speak for the Querent, and a female person becomes part of the spread, the person to whom he is unfaithful is shown here. This also closes the circle to the starting position (position 23) which sometimes indicates infidelity.

The Chart of the Animals, Reptiles, Insects, and Birds

A

agouti	1	albatross	2	alligators	13
alpaca	16	ant	1	antelope	16
anthill	22	antlion	21	arctic fox	5
armadillo	19	aspic	12	aurochs (Ur)	9

B

baboon	7	badger	19	bat	19
beaver	21	bear (white)	10	bear (black)	7
bees	21	billy goat	16	bird of paradise	2
bison	9	bittern	25	blue tit	23

F

G

H

I

J

K. %

L

M

N

O

CHAPTER VIII

The Achievements

(Determination of Success or Failure)

Variant 1

Variant 2

Variant 3

The Achievements

About the determination of success or failure

This step of the Grand Jeu, which is called Achievement, means doing exercises to see if something will have a good or bad outcome, whether a wish will be fulfilled or not. For this exercise, use the letters of the alphabet that appear on each card.

For this exercise 28 cards are needed, which are laid out in four rounds as follows:

1. Remove both Main Character cards from the deck.

2. Shuffle the cards: The tradition says here that you should think of what you hope for when you shuffle the cards and cut them once. If you read the cards for someone else, this person must think of what they hope for.

After this you follow the next steps:

3. Remove the top and bottom cards and put both cards aside.

Now you take every 5th card from the deck and count: 1, 2, 3, 4 and put the 5th card aside. So, you continue, you count 1, 2, 3, 4 and always remove the 5th card.

In this first round, you took 10 cards from the deck, plus the two cards you previously put aside, reducing the deck to forty cards.

4. The second round is almost like the first, but without shuffling or cutting the cards and without removing the top and bottom cards. You simply continue by removing every 5th card from the deck, this time there are eight cards you can put aside.

5. In the third round you must take all cards in the 8th position, always in the same way, count 1, 2, 3, 4, 5, 6, 7 and put the 8th card aside. This results in four more cards, which are taken from you out of the deck.

6. The fourth round is like the third, and you proceed in the same way as in the previous rounds but remove every 7th card this time. This will set aside four cards.

Eventually, 28 cards will be removed from the deck.

Variant 1

You now spread the 28 cards face up and search for the answer to the question by trying to form words with the letters on the cards that fit the context of the question. (It is not about just forming any words, the words must relate to the question, it must be in context with the topic).

If it is not even possible to begin to form words with all the letters that come out, it means that it is impossible to succeed in the subject and failure is imminent.

If you find a complete and meaningful word right away, you can count on success.

However, if you manage to collect a few letters, but only one or a few are missing to form the complete word, it is the message of the cards that the more letters are missing, the more difficult it is to succeed. But success is not excluded.

NOTE In order to see a word as valid, more than half of the letters or most of the letters must be present.

Now you must check which number, which value, the missing letter, or letters correspond to.

You do this by working with the alphabet on the "Wheel of Pythagoras" to determine whether this number is even (positive) or odd (negative).

The Alphabet (The Wheel of Pythagoras)

A 1 B 2 C 4 D 5 E 3 F 8 G 10 H 28 I 15

J 15 K 16 L 21 M 19 N 26 O 8 P 21 Q 27

R11 S 20 T 6 U 9 V 9 X 13 Y 50 Z 70

(odd numbers are unfortunate, even are fortunate).

Then you look for the numbers/ the value of the letters that are already present in your word and are not missing, you add these numbers to see if the result of the addition is even or odd or if the sum corresponds to the value of the missing letter.

Example - Question

Let's say you asked the cards if you would be accepted for the position you applied for.

You will find a word that is missing a letter. And to get two more complete words, one is missing four letters, and the other one is missing two letters. Out of this word you could form three complete words, but each with one, four and two letters are missing.

Now you must look for the missing letters and their corresponding numerical value in the alphabet. There you will find out whether this number is even or odd. If you have more than one letter, add the values of the letters and see if the sum is even or odd.

If you then convert the already existing letters of the word into numbers and add these numbers together, you can see whether the sum is even or odd.

Now you compare this sum of the values of the existing letters with the value of the missing letter or with the value of the sum of the missing letters.

Example

For example, suppose the missing letter is an E, which is assigned the number 3 and is odd.

Now you add up the values of the existing letters:

Suppose the sum is 114 and thus even.

Thus, the sum cannot match the odd number 3. It does not work, and so it emerges that this word is invalid, and it would therefore show failure or that success entails difficulties and is dependent on external circumstances (if this is the only possible word).

But since you have found two more possible words to form in this example, you now look at the missing letters of the second word you found.

This word lacks letters that together have a numerical value of 34 and thus result in an even sum. This sum corresponds to the even sum 114. This would therefore speak for success in the matter and a commitment if it were the only possible word and if there had not been the negative result before. So, this still

indicates that the success is rather questionable, and it is not to be expected with an acceptance.

However, in this example, there is a third possible word that is missing letters; this too must be checked.

The third word is missing two letters, which together form the sum of 14.

The sum 14 is also even and coincides with the even number, 114, the existing letters. These are therefore the words that can be considered valid since the sums agree in their even value. The valid words are opposed only by an invalid one and therefore a success is to be expected in this matter.

Variant 2

Sometimes it is possible to form two contradictory words in the 28 cards drawn, such as yes and no or right and wrong, loyalty and infidelity. Or even if, for example, the question is asked at the cards, who one will marry and in answer two names would be to be formed.
Or someone stands between two persons and is undecided which one is to be preferred - and here both names of the respective persons would be to be formed.
Or sometimes someone wants to know which of two persons is the wiser, or the more lovable person - and here too both names of the respective persons would be to be formed as an answer.
Or someone wants to know who of two people would make oneself the happiest - and in response both names would be to be formed.

In such cases, there is another possible method of proceeding: In these and similar questions and situations, you must shuffle the 28 cards, cut them once and turn over one card after the other. And you will have to take that of the two names or that of the two words as an answer, which comes out first completely or most likely.

But if only a mixture of the letters comes out and nothing stands out to some extent, then this indicates equality and therefore sometimes even speaks against mentioned persons or possibilities, because no special emphasis is given.

Variant 3

This third variant is prepared in the same way as the previous one. Now there are the following situations:

- no word at all can be formed:

If there is no word of meaning in the letters that come out, then, unfortunately, the outcome of the situation will not be successful, and a goal will not be achieved.

- no word can be formed because too many letters are missing:

If too many letters are missing to form a complete word, you must check whether the numbers of the letters belong to the lucky numbers or the unlucky numbers. If all the numbers are even, lucky numbers, then a success is still to be expected in this matter; it only must be tried to overcome any obstacles.

If on the contrary all numbers are odd, unlucky numbers, then this means that unfortunately no success can be expected here.

- a word can be formed:

If it is possible to form almost one word, but it is of a bad nature and the sum of the values is even and thus corresponds to a lucky number, this means a moderate success.

- a word can be formed, and letters are missing:

If it is possible to form almost one word, but it is of a bad nature and the values of the missing letters are even and thus correspond to lucky numbers, this means that the success is attributed to someone else, a stranger.

If the word you were able to form is positive and the missing letters are associated with numbers of misfortunes, the success depends on difficulties or obstacles caused by other people around and not by yourself.

Positive words together with a positive numerical value stand for success, negative words together with negative numerical value stand for failure.

Different numerical values of the missing letters:

However, if the missing letters refer to both, even and odd numbers, you need to convert all existing letters into their numerical value and add them together.

For further calculation of success or failure, add the following additional numbers to this sum:

- the number corresponding to the first letter of the Querent's name.
- the number corresponding to the first letter of the current month.
- the number that refers to the day on which this oracle is asked (see the following table of weekdays).

Chart of weekdays

Monday 22	Tuesday 24	Wednesday 12
Thursday 1	Friday 8	Saturday 15
Sunday 16		

You must divide the sum of all these numbers by 30. Using the "Wheel of Pythagoras" you can now match whether the rest of the division is a lucky or unlucky number, and thus you can then predict what result you must expect. Whether there will be a success or a failure.

Example

You ask a question on a Thursday in September and to complete the word, you are missing letters with the numbers 28, 15 and 19. The values of the letters are both positive and negative.

From the "Wheel of Pythagoras" you can deduce that of the three numbers 28, 15, 19 two numbers belong to the numbers of misfortune and one to the numbers of luck.

If you add up these three numbers, you get the following sum:

28 + 15 + 19 makes a total of 62.

Add the number of the day, Thursday, 1 and the first letter of the month, September, S 20 to this total of 62. In addition, the number of the first letter of the name of the person, in the example we assume this would be an E 3.

This is 62 + 1 + 20 + 3 and makes a total of 86.

Now you divide 86 by 30, and you have the division:

86: 30 is 2 rest 26.

The rest is 26. And you see that the number 26 is classified as a lucky number according to the rules of the "Wheel of Pythagoras", because it is an even number.

This is the proof for you that success will come, that something will happen as desired.

NOTE If, when dividing a number by 30, the remaining number would be zero, then by tradition the rule applies to take the number 30 itself as the remainder.

CONCLUSION It is to be understood that when doing the complete Grand Jeu, an achievement in the last instance determines all events that were interpreted during the previous sessions.

This was the last step of Mlle. Lenormand's Grand Jeu.

CHAPTER IX

BONUS

MODERN TRADITION

The Oracle of the Geomantic Symbols

(The Oracle within the Oracle)

&

The Firmament

(Star Constellations on the Cards)

&

The Alphabet

(The Letters on the Cards)

The Geomatic Symbol

The Oracle within the Oracle

It is proven that Mlle. Lenormand certainly worked with the Geomantic Symbols, so they also found the way to the Grand Lenormand Cards; but the difference is this, that Mlle. Lenormand did not practice this oracle as a part of the Grand Jeu - she considered it a separate oracle and so these figures are also called an independent oracle. This oracle consists of 16 different figures formed by dots. These figures are assigned different meanings and given different Latin names. Normally you could take these cards out, and you could answer your question only with the Geomantic Symbols and their value. In the Grand Jeu 15 figures are represented by a selection of the 52 playing cards, some of them even several times, and the 16. Geomantic figure is represented by the two Main Character cards.

In the Grand Jeu you will find a total of 22 + 2 cards with these symbols, for which Mlle. Lenormand had her own meanings. The meanings are given in this chapter.

The Geomantic Symbols are divided into auspicious, inauspicious, and balancing figures.

According to Modern Tradition, which unfortunately simply mix and combines everything on the cards, whether meaningful or not, the Geomantic Symbols also affect the surrounding cards. The ancient tradition, however, differ completely from this idea.

NOTE If you want to question the Geomantic Symbols as your own oracle, you can do this by, as briefly mentioned before, removing all the cards with Geomantic Symbols from the game (including the two Main Character cards), shuffling them and drawing a few cards (for example, 3). Now you can use these symbols to answer your question by taking a closer look at the symbols. For an interpretation, it is now sufficient to use only the keywords or the meaning of the symbol. Within this oracle, a temporal aspect, the question of time, will also play a significant role. Therefore, I also give you the hints that each symbol gives you in terms of time quality. First and foremost, you can determine how long an influence, atmosphere or situation could have an effect and presence. With this method of determining time, you should look at what kind of symbols appear to you, and you can then try to create an approximate time frame (impact period) with them.

First, I will tell you about the auspicious, then about the balancing and finally about the inauspicious figures and on which card they can be found. In addition, I will explain to you what influence the symbols can have on the card and on the spread according to the Modern Tradition of fortune telling with the Grand Lenormand Cards. Finally, I will give you the time reference.

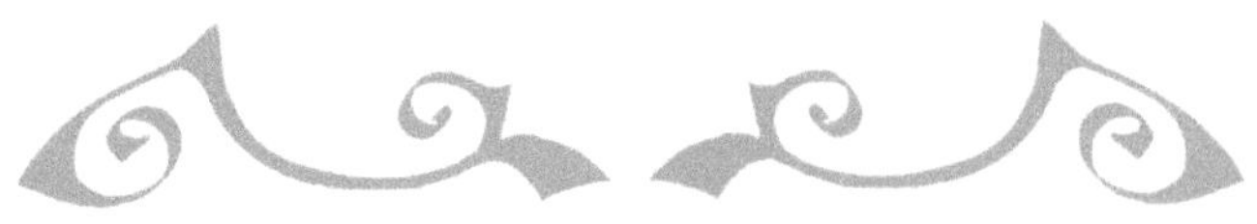

The meanings of the Geomantic Symbols according to Mlle Lenormand

The auspicious figures

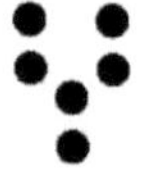

Fortuna Major

Great Luck (only in dangerous situations: carelessness)

The symbol that underlines the luck of this card is considered one of the happiest in the game and is shown on the card, **3 of Hearts**.

Timing: up to 360 days – medium term, uncertain

Caput Draconis

The Dragon Head is shown on the card, **King of Clubs**.

The Man on this card needed a lot of perseverance to succeed due to his mistakes in life.

Timing: up to 180 days - medium time

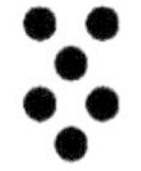

Acquisitio

Change, success at work

The symbol of the profit is shown on the card, **6 of Diamonds**.

Normally, the 6 of Diamonds is a card of deception. The positive geomantic symbol here is an indication that this deception can be prevented by caution. A change from a negative to a positive situation is still possible.

Timing: up to 120 days - shorter time

Laetitia

Joy & Happiness

The symbol of joy is on the card, **7 of Spades**, and on the card **Queen of Spades**.

7 of Spades is one of the most positive cards in the deck, so it's obvious that the symbols confirm this in some way. The Queen of Spades has the messages that there is a recovery from the dark fate and the joy will return to life.

Timing: at least 360 days to 2 lunar years - longer time

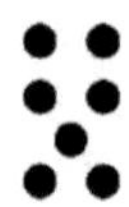

Albus

Maturity/endurance

The symbol is on the card **10 of Diamonds**.

Albus (white) is a sign of the victory of the good - this brings positive influence and success in a reading. And it shows a safe and protected journey.

Timing: many moons, several (lunar) years - longer time/ distant future/ it is not a no

Puella

Happy acquaintance

The symbol of the girl is on the cards, **2 of Hearts**, and **6 of Hearts**.

As a wonderful positive card, the 6 of Hearts indicates happy times and happy encounters. The positive time and the positive togetherness are expressed on the 2 of Hearts by the symbolism of the dog.

Timing: around 21 days – short term

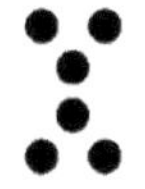

Conjunctio

Connection, marriage, union

The symbol of the connection is on the card, **10 of Spades**.

Normally, the 10 of Spades is a negative card. The symbol of connection is described with the story of the big picture in which Laverna lives together with the wolves, because she did not want and could not stay with the gods in Olympus. She found her home in the forest - so it is a hint, to find your home and that is a connection to yourself and to others, regardless of where you are. This connection, a union is also described by situations where you get back what you lost, some things can return (this is a picture of reunification).

Timing: 30 to 60 days - still considered as a short time

The balancing figures

Fortuna Minor

Relief from great pain

The symbol of small luck is on the cards **10 of Hearts** and **King of Hearts**.

The 10 of Hearts shows a new beginning after the relief of great pain or after suffering. It's an indication that bad times are over and that it's time for a fresh start.

The King of Hearts expresses this with his experience. This means that one can free oneself from pain in life: no suffering is forever, that is what he has learned.

Timing: 1 lunar cycle - depending on the situation also 2

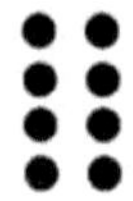

Populus/ Audience & people

Honor & fame

This symbol of the people, the audience, is on the card **Jack of Diamonds**.

Fame is expressed here by the achievement that it was possible to win Achilles for the fight, even if this was just by a trick. This card shows honor and fame especially for artists and professions in the arts.

Timing: 1 lunar cycle - depending on the situation up to 3

Via

Connection, union, painful development

The symbol of the path, the road is on the cards **2 of Diamonds** and **4 of Spades**.

The union is shown here by the intimate act of love of two people with the card 2 of Diamonds and is expressed more negatively in the story told by the 4 of Spades. Both connections create a new path, one positive and another with a painful development. It is therefore under the influence of the Querent which path he will follow.

Timing: 1 lunar cycle - depending on the situation up to 4

The Inauspicious Figures

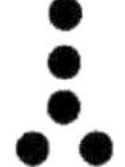

Cauda Draconis

Loss, Heritage

The tail of the dragon is shown on the card **6 of Clubs**.

The card 6 of Clubs shows an uncertain situation, it is still possible to lose what has been achieved. So, this symbol gives a subtle indication that failure is still possible and very likely to happen.

Timing: around 14 days - considered a short time

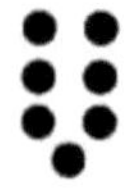

Tristitia

Grief, worries, possible new beginnings

The symbol of sadness and grief is depicted on the card **4 of Clubs**.

The card 4 of Clubs, also shows a relationship that is described rather unhappy. The symbol of sadness tells you more about this negative and sometimes very intense sad aspect of this card.

Timing: at least 360 days to 5 lunar years – very long time/ very distant future

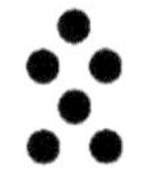

Amissio

Loss

The symbol of loss is on the cards **4 of Diamonds**, **5 of Hearts** and **King of Spades**.

Even if the 4 of Diamonds is a card with support and help, you may lose control of yourself or the situation by accepting this kind of help. From the card of negotiations, the 5 of Hearts, you can see that there is a risk of making a bad deal that can lead to a loss. So sometimes it's important to think over and over. And even the righteous King of Spades, the judge, is represented by the symbol in a more negative way: You must be careful, because if you behave deceitfully, this could be a loss to yourself and not to others.

Timing: a moment - considered as unpredictable – it passes as quickly as it came

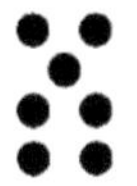

Rubeus

Weakness, violence

The symbol of the red is on the cards **7 of Hearts** and **7 of Diamonds**.

Sometimes we cannot resist weakness. It is exactly like the story of Pandora, which is told with the card 7 of Diamonds: She could not resist, she had to open the vase. A negative symbol, because their act had terrible consequences. The 7 of Hearts shows our weak, unhappy heart when we realize that we cannot have what our heart desires. The troubled times in love and anger at the reality of things that can make aggressive.

Timing: 1 lunar cycle - depending on the situation up to 2 or 3

Puer

Change, movement, twist & turns

The symbol of the boy is on the card **King of Diamonds**.

The King of Diamonds at first glance shows a positive act by helping with the information he gives Minerva, but it is a message about bad upcoming events in Minerva's life. The change that this symbol is therefore often described as negative.

Timing: at least 30 days up to 180 days – shorter time

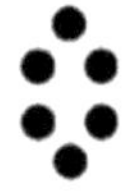

Carcer

trapped, in chains

The figure of the dungeon is on the cards of the **Main Characters**.

Sometimes you are like in chains or "trapped" in a situation or even by your own thoughts or attitudes. This does not mean that everyone is "trapped"; in the Geomantic Oracle the Main Character cards refer to this symbol not to a person. So, if you make an oracle with the geomantic symbol, these two cards do not show the Querent, but rather a state that you will be "trapped" or experience a negative influence or a change for the first time.

Timing: at least 2 to 8 lunar years – very long time/ very distant future/ not now

The Firmament

The Sky of a Grand Lenormand Card

In the past, the stars served people as a kind of map. The stars led you through the night to find your way. And on the other hand, events of the future were already determined with them.

On every classic Grand Lenormand Card, you can see a sky with Stars in the middle at the top. One or more constellations shine down on the other images: like an influence. Some keywords are assigned to each of the constellations. According to Modern Tradition, these keywords can also be part of the interpretation of the card and thus give the card an additional statement. This is not a new core meaning; this only highlights some facets of the card or shows another aspect. Some influences of the Stars may be irritating, especially if you have a negative card in its core meaning and the Stars indicate more positive keywords: This can sometimes be an indication that a loss or misfortune has a positive outcome in the future and a situation is not yet completely lost. Or the Stars tell you with a negative message that, for example, the compliments, that are represented by a positive card, someone may not mean that way.

For the statement of the card, the Stars are not essential, it is not necessary and not in the sense of the true tradition to include the message of the Stars in your interpretation. Like the oracle of Geomantic Symbols, the oracle of the Stars according to the original instructions did not belong to the Grand Jeu of Mlle Lenormand and is not mentioned in it. However, it is known from tradition that Mlle. Lenormand knew how to unravel the future with the Stars and Geomantic Symbols. But if you like, you can use the meanings to refine your prediction. You don't have to know the names of the constellations or focus on them, but they may still be interesting for you to know.

NOTE the only reference to the Stars made in the original instruction is the one to the eight "colored stars", which are shown on eight cards. However, they are not connected to the sky of the cards and are also to be handled differently, you have already read this in Chapter V (The Great Spread of 48, page 320).

The Constellations

The constellations and their meanings are listed here; some appear more often on several cards. And some of them are even still visible in our night sky, but a few others have unfortunately been lost or replaced with time.

The Suit of Clubs

King of Clubs

- Honores Friderici: lucky youth, scientistic skills
- Ursa Major: emotional chaos

Queen of Clubs

- Pleiades: artistic talents, education in arts
- Star Gemma: friendly and lively character
- Lyra: more possibilities
- Cygnus: talent, delayed success

Jack of Clubs

- Capricornus: energy, creativity, endurance
- Perseus: egoism, addiction
- Boötes: discipline

10 of Clubs

- Aquila: rootless, globetrotter
- Monocerus: resist someone with negative touch

9 of Clubs

- Cancer: immoderate ambition
- Hercules: personal success in undertakings & journeys

8 of Clubs

- Auriga: dependent, immature
- Milky Way: grief
- Cetus: temporary separation, short illness

7 of Clubs

- Orion: fake emotions, infidelity, treason
- Ursa Major: emotional chaos
- Capricornus: energy, creativity, endurance

6 of Clubs

- Arcturus: violence
- Perseus: egoism
- Cepheus: arrogance, contempt, pride

5 of Clubs

- Orion: fake emotions, infidelity, treason
- Canes Venatici: Abuse of hospitality
- Psalterium Georgii: desire

4 of Clubs

- Cerberus: addiction, dependency
- Boötes: discipline
- Ursa minor: stinginess
- Scutum: fading beauty

3 of Clubs

- Hyades: inner wealth
- Cassiopeia: soul pain
- Antinous: humility
- Sirius: inner unrest, heaviness

2 of Clubs

- Lepus: lucky love
- Canis Major: positive thoughts, trust
- Piscis Austrinus: cleverness and positive character

Ace of Clubs

- Ophiuchus: wealth through honest work
- Hercules: personal success in undertakings & journeys
- Quadrans Muralis: no support in difficult times

The Suit of Hearts

King of Hearts

- Triangulum: a wise man, a just man

Queen of Hearts

- Andromeda: lack of recognition
- Coma Berenices: inheritance
- Virgo: a beautiful & smart person
- Star Vindemiatrix: shyness, insecurity

Jack of Hearts

- Star Bellatrix: bad company
- Corona Borealis: diplomacy
- Aries: luck, wealth, patron

10 of Hearts

- Star Procyon: early but lucky relationship, connection
- Virgo: a beautiful & smart person

9 of Hearts

- Leo: bravery, honor, wisdom
- Star Regulus: lucky life

8 of Hearts

- Star Aldebaran: help
- Mons Maenalus: waste of money
- Aquarius: wisdom

7 of Hearts

- Sextans: discretion
- Mons Maenalus: waste of money

6 of Hearts

- Aries: luck, wealth, patron
- Caput Draconis: wealth

5 of Hearts

- Corona Australis: treason
- Corona Borealis: diplomacy
- Cepheus: arrogance, contempt, pride

4 of Hearts

- Cygnus: talent, delayed success
- Camelopardalis undemanding
- Pisces: abundance

3 of Hearts

- Pegasus: disparity

2 of Hearts

- Honores Friderici: lucky youth, scientistic skills
- Boötes: discipline
- Capricornus: energy, creativity, endurance

Ace of Hearts

- Milky Way: grief

The Suit of Diamonds

King of Diamonds

- Custos Messium: good character, a lot of talent

Queen of Diamonds

- Draco: malice, deceit
- Cassiopeia: soul pain

Jack of Diamonds

- Lynx: clairvoyance, telepathy
- Centaurus: Provocation, pain, injury

10 of Diamonds

- Leo Minor: good triumphs over evil
- Telescopium: message in delay

9 of Diamonds

- Dolphinus: lonesome, loneliness
- Honores Friderici: lucky youth, scientistic skills
- Cassiopeia: soul pain

8 of Diamonds

- Aquarius: wisdom
- Telescopium: message in delay

7 of Diamonds

- Noctua: trusting the wrong person
- Camelopardalis undemanding
- Eridanus: small (financial) success

6 of Diamonds

- Hydra: the truth is hidden
- Serpens: courage and urge for action
- Caput Medusae: to be attached to a bad person

5 of Diamonds

- Scorpius: fatality, death
- Mons Maenalus: waste of money
- Musca Borealis: power
- Cor Caroli: overestimation of oneself

4 of Diamonds

- Cygnus: talent, delayed success
- Cassiopeia: soul pain

3 of Diamonds

- Gemini: generosity, diligence
- Pollux: victory

2 of Diamonds

- Pisces: abundance
- Eridanus: small (financial) success
- Circinus: betrayal
- Corvus: lovesick

Ace of Diamonds

- Leo: bravery, honor, wisdom
- Telescopium: message in delay
- Canis major: help from trusted persons

The Suit of Spades

King of Spades

- Quadrans Muralis: no support in difficult times
- Sagittarius: carelessness, passion
- Centaurus: provocation, pain, injury

Queen of Spades

- Lynx: clairvoyance, telepathy
- Draco: malice, deceit
- Musca Borealis: power

Jack of Spades

- Libra: justice
- Gemini: generosity, diligence
- Perseus: egoism

10 of Spades

- Vulpecula: being inconspicuous
- Serpens: courage and urge for action
- Corvus: lovesick

9 of Spades

- Star Alpha Hydrae: greed
- Ophiuchus: wealth through honest work

8 of Spades

- Taurus: hedonism

7 of Spades

- Cetus: temporary separation, short illness
- Cor Caroli: overestimation of oneself
- Cygnus: talent, delayed success
- Eridanus: small (financial) success

6 of Spades

- Serpens: courage and urge for action
- Star Antares: accident, misfortune, loss

5 of Spades

- Sagittarius: carelessness, passion
- Cetus: temporary separation, short illness

4 of Spades

- Star Algol: bad company
- Honores Friderici: lucky youth, scientistic skills

3 of Spades

- Circinus: betrayal
- Scorpius: fatality, death
- Lacerta: painful separation
- Argo Navis: life's work, meaning of life

2 of Spades

- Castor: misfortune

Ace of Spades

- Taurus: hedonism
- Circinus: betrayal
- Ursa Major: emotional chaos

The Alphabet

The meaning of the letters of the alphabet and how to deal with it.

On each card you see a letter in the upper right corner, almost all letters of our alphabet are represented, only the W is missing. According to the system of numerology, each letter refers to a kind of value. The value of the letters, which is important for the Grand Jeu, is taken from the "Wheel of Pythagoras" (page 414). And in the Old Tradition, the letters are only used to calculate a success or failure (see Chapter VIII "The Achievements", page 412).

According to Modern Tradition, there do exist also a keyword for each letter. This can be part of the interpretation of the card and used as an additional meaning for the card. This is not a new core meaning and will never be an independent meaning. From the point of view of Modern Tradition, this underlines the character of the card or shows another aspect.

Here is a list of the letters of the alphabet, on which cards they are represented and a description of the influence of the respective letter on the corresponding card.

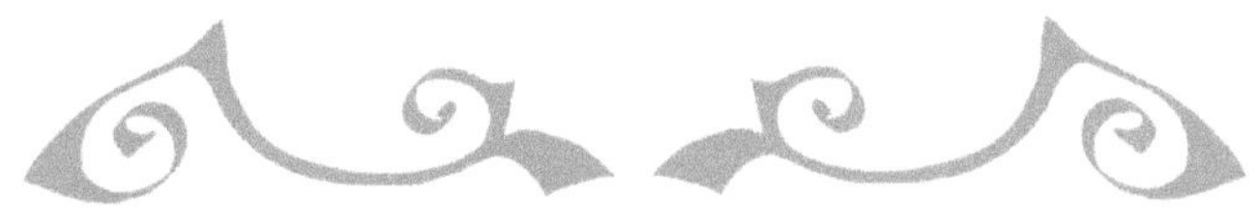

A - Perfection

8 of Diamonds

- Here represented by the perfect profession.

5 of Spades

- Here you can see the perfect skills, even if they are not used.

7 of Spades

- A perfect couple, a perfect togetherness.

B – Duality, opposites, failure

4 of Clubs

- Duality described by togetherness and destruction because of the bad attitudes one has towards something.

5 of Diamonds

- Failure because of superficial behavior.

C – Luck, Success, Achievement

Ace of Clubs

- Luck, happiness, and success are fully reflected in this card.

7 of Hearts

- The happiness and success supported the aspect of the joy of this card.

D – Union, fusion

10 of Diamonds

- The togetherness and cohesion in a company, a project, represented by the union of Jason's team.

8 of Clubs

- This is the card for the wedding & thus represents a union in this way.

E – Personal fulfillment, completion

10 of Hearts

- The various steps of the work lead to completion; one must pass different stages to attain spiritual fulfillment. Something needs to be completed.

Queen of Hearts

- Spirit and soul are filled.

3 of Diamonds

- Two becomes one and thus complete.

9 of Spades

- The only way to achieve spiritual fulfillment is to learn to love.

F – Structure, order

Queen of Clubs

- There are rules and orders by which one lives, in a prescribed ordered manner, and this in satisfaction.

3 of Hearts

- An ingenious, stable, and well-organized existence

4 of Hearts

- In times of unrest, focus on what is stable and orderly.

G – Success

7 of Clubs

- The card gives artists the success they seek.

King of Clubs

- Success only comes from recognizing and learning from mistakes.

H – Perfection

6 of Clubs

- Correct behavior in an uncertain situation leads to a perfect result.

I – Beauty

9 of Clubs

- The beauty is expressed by the unconditional devotion of the Cancer to Hera.

6 of Hearts

- The beauty is shown here by the card's message of deep love

Jack of Hearts

- Beauty depicted in the image of young Dionysus.

J – Beauty

2 of Clubs

- The beauty of the shine of gold.

King of Diamonds

- The beauty lies in the help within a connection, even if it is still new or in the beginning. And even if the persons do not know each other well.

K – Honor, Fame

Jack of Clubs

- With the victory in the race against Atalanta he became famous to the world.

L – Mediocrity

7 of Diamonds

- Even if Pandora had an insight to have done something wrong and she wanted to close the vase again, bad things had already happened. Although diminished and not in full measure, but nevertheless it was there.

Jack of Spades

- Not right, not wrong, sometimes borders blur and it's in between.

M – Healing, improvement

6 of Diamonds

- After a painful delusion there is a slow healing, a slow recovery.

8 of Spades

- A sad soul, a broken heart needs time to recover.

N – Loss, disadvantages

5 of Hearts

- Deals, agreements can have disadvantages.

9 of Diamonds

- Investments, plans, and projects can cause material losses.

O – Structure, order

4 of Diamonds

- Jason has the intention to create stability and order in his realm.

Queen of Diamonds

- There are clear fronts, even if they are sometimes oppositions, but it is still an order.

10 of Clubs

- This word supports the message of the smaller picture on the left that shows the option of peace. The order, the harmony.

P – Mediocrity

9 of Hearts

- With this card you must overcome mediocrity, know your worth, never settle for anything less than you deserve.

2 of Diamonds

- The Card shows that situations that are not necessarily good are not bad at the same time, it is less black/ white - there are also shades. There is something in between.

Q – Appreciation

4 of Spades

- Don't risk anything because of others, appreciate your love.

R – Negative

8 of Hearts

- The negative is described here by the toad, which is removed from the eagle.

6 of Spades

- The bad, represented by the meaning "deception" of this card.

S – Loss, treason, betrayal

Ace of Diamonds

- This aspect is underlined in the smaller left picture by the giant Argus, the spy: the sign of indiscretion and betrayal.

King of Spades

- There is a risk of losing something, a negative judgment.

T – Strength, hope, power

5 of Clubs

- The inner & mental strength to survive a breach of trust.

Jack of Diamonds

- To hope to be able to convince someone.

Ace of Spades

- The power of resistance

U – Pain, grief, darkness (of the present)

2 of Spades

- Difficult situations overshadow life.

3 of Spades

- Pain, grief, death, and darkness can enter life.

Queen of Spades

- The pain and suffering of grief and loss.

V – Pain, grief, darkness (of the past)

3 of Clubs

- The card shows the aspect that before the actual joy in the past was a time of pain.

King of Hearts

- Wisdom comes only through a time of suffering that has been experienced in the past.

W – this letter is not present.

X – Misfortune, fate

10 of Spades

- The card indicates the misfortune that can bring loneliness and theft.

Y – Remorse, regret, forgiveness

2 of Hearts

- In friendship some regret, but some also forgive.

Z – New beginning

Ace of Hearts

- The new beginning: even if it was not possible in the story that tells the big picture; but the very fact that at least one of the daughters did not adhere to the commands of her father is a sign of a possible new beginning.

CHAPTER X

BONUS

The Indiscreet Spread

(for entertainment)

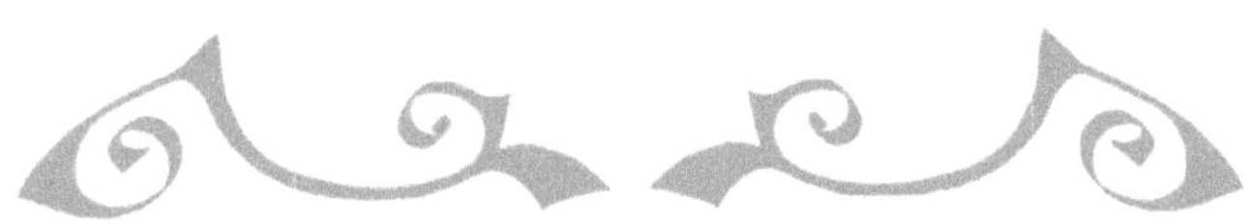

The Indiscreet Spread

A game of thoughts

In the Grand Jeu Lenormand another game is hidden, which can be played with these cards, but is more for entertainment, so this game was added in the original instruction from 1845 as an additional spread, which can be done with these cards, but is not part of the traditional steps of the real Grand Jeu.

One, two, three, up to twelve people can participate in this spread. As a result, it reveals the participants' personal thoughts and everything that comes with them and is thus also associated with the word "indiscretion".

In this method, the table where the people meet is always divided into 12 parts, each of which gets a number and the name of a mythological figure (see the picture on page 457).

At the beginning you write the twelve numbers on small pieces of paper, fold them, and put them in a bag or in a hat as we before in childhood plays.

The persons who participate draw a number indicating the place to be taken by them at the table. Number 1 stands for the place of the god Apollo, the Number 2 for the place of the god Ceres, the Number 3 for the place of the goddess Diane and so on.
Regardless of whether you have twelve participants, you are less or alone, the cards must always be distributed as if all seats were occupied, as if 12 people were part of the game.

GRAND JEU Lenormand

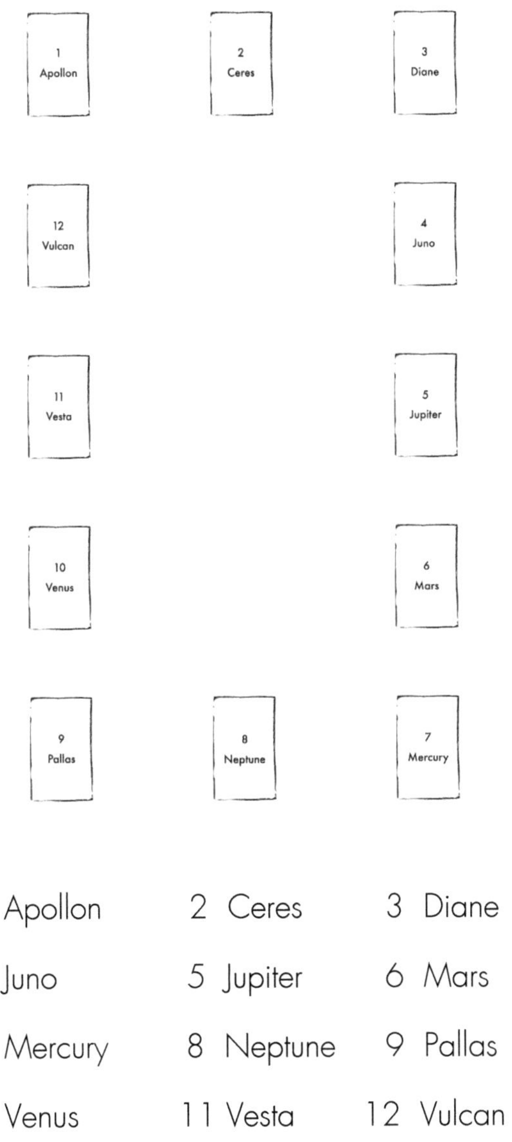

1 Apollon 2 Ceres 3 Diane

4 Juno 5 Jupiter 6 Mars

7 Mercury 8 Neptune 9 Pallas

10 Venus 11 Vesta 12 Vulcan

The person to whom the cards belong must now shuffle the cards and cut them once and starts the distribution from left to right by placing one card on each of the twelve positions, and this is done three times so that in each place, in each position there will be a pile of three cards.

So, 36 cards are dealt, and 18 cards of the deck remain unused.

Each person will always take the pile of cards in their own position for their own pile Number 1, because it is the place that fate has assigned to that person, and the deity that rules that place will represent the person or their thoughts.

NOTE Therefore, even if a person is seated at place Number 3 according to the positions at the "table", for that person the cards in this place are the cards of position Number 1.

Explanation of the Gods, the 12 positions

The initial positions number one to twelve are assigned to certain gods and each of these deities are attributed certain characteristics as follows:

No. 1 or Apollo

He represents a personality with a great imagination, full of fantasy, gifted, well-read and educated. Someone with a strong spirit, loved and sought after by many, because this person knows, how he can make himself useful for others and be an enrichment.

No. 2 or Ceres

Ceres shows someone who always must do hard work, piece workers and anyone who has simple, low, or hard jobs. In the past, you saw those who belonged to the working class, not a person from the upper class, someone who had to always fight for everything. Unfortunately, nothing is a gift to this person in life.

No. 3 or Diane

Indicates a proud, but also a little wild character, which temporarily withdraws from society. This person loves physical exercises, sports, fitness, but in everyday life is often unable to do something conscientiously or to create a safe future for himself in life.

No. 4 or Juno

This is an imposing, somewhat old-fashioned or conservative, strict character who loves regularity, structure, and order. But this character is also very suspicious and is therefore often able to recognize a betrayal.

No. 5 or Jupiter

Jupiter represents a person of great character, noble of heart; his strength of character is comparable to few others; but he is easily receptive to the pleasures and things that bring joy of life, this person receives high honor by his own ambition, gain his own deeds.

No. 6 or Mars

Mars points to a personality with great ambition, always focused on personal fame and it is someone who prefers the chaos, risk and danger of challenges to the calm and security of ordinary life.

No. 7 or Mercury

This person is a worker, a creator with a fine, smart character, but also with a strong need to have control or take care of everything. Sellers, traders, brokers, all professions are good for this person if there is only one profit in it, and as long as the own need, the reason for the ambition, is satisfied.

No. 8 or Neptune

This position points to a fickle, erratic, unsteady or even capricious character doing one thing, then the other, without ever really completing anything: weak in his intentions, inconsistent and completely powerless.

No. 9 or Pallas

Shows a bold character, unwavering courage, receives recognition, possesses wisdom, engages in private life with the sciences and useful arts.

No. 10 or Venus

This is a vain character who prefers the private pleasures over work; friendly, passionate, but fickle, someone who rarely keeps what he promises and unfortunately this person appears to be unreliable.

No. 11 or Vesta

This position shows a character of admirable simplicity, but also sophistication and yet virtue. A personality who opposes the many forms of seduction and who in private life will always be a devoted friend, and in the professional area will always be a loyal employee or colleague.

No. 12 or Vulcan

This is a hard, angry, jealous character, but also an inventive genius, a creative and practical spirit; someone who exercises all kinds of mechanical, technical, and industrial arts with great success.

NOTE And remember, as mentioned before: the place of the deity that each participant occupies is always his personal Number 1, his starting position in the game. And this deity characterizes a person whom the participant (in the future) thinks about, and in the three cards that lie here, the thoughts, the background to the persons, the current or the future situation and what is to expect or fear in this context is described. If no person is meant, a main concern is often presented here, and the other positions provide information about it.

Explanation & meaning of the 12 positions in the game

Suppose a person occupies place Number 3; this place Number 3 (the place of the goddess Diane) is now the place of Number 1 for that person, the starting point of the game. And these cards placed there show the main concern the person is worried about.

Likewise, for a person who occupies place of Number 4 (the place of Juno) will be the starting point and thus stands for place Number 1 of this person, and the cards placed there indicate the main concern of this participant.

The position taken by the person is therefore always the starting point; it is always the personal **Number 1**.

The **Number 2** of the person, the second position in the game, is then represented by the three cards that are in the first position on the left; by the cards that belong to that person who would sit to the left of person 1 (clockwise order, from the person's point of view). In these cards you can see whether there is a change in the situation or a realistic hope for happiness and if so, what happiness consists of.

NOTE Even if no other or only a few other people participate in the game, the cards must always be distributed to twelve positions with three cards each.

It continues clockwise:

The position **Number 3** is represented by the three cards of the second person on the left, at the second position on the left, and this position tells you everything about brothers and sisters, possible friendships, contacts, or even short trips.

The position **Number 4** is represented by the cards at the third place on the left. This position refers to the father and mother, person's secrets, or inheritances.

The position **Number 5** is represented by the cards in fourth place to the left. This position is about possible children, and about the people the person loves the most. The behavior of the person is shown and everything to do with upcoming news, commitments, even what "you get from life and what you give to life".

The position **Number 6** is represented by the cards in the fifth position to the left. At this point, everything revolves around the fellow human beings of the person who have the trust of the person. Likewise, what is related to possible diseases may be mentioned here, too.

The position **Number 7** is represented by the cards in the sixth position to the left. This position refers to private life, home: whether someone is married or not, whether someone is sincere or unfaithful in love. Possible intimate love affairs and relationships of the person are shown here.

The position **Number 8** is represented by the cards at the seventh position on the left. This position denotes all accidents or setbacks that can happen and what they will consist of. On the good side, this position also indicates a long or more distant journey, usually to a foreign country.

The position **number 9** is represented by the cards in eighth place on the left. This position denotes rewards, acknowledgments, and successes of behavior: consequences of wisdom and piety and penalties for injustice or malice; consequences of both good and bad behavior. Unjust trials are also described here, too.

The position **Number 10** is represented by the cards in ninth place to the left. This position represents honor, dignity, pride, and favor the person receives from people who are superior, as well as this position concerns all matters and affairs with administrations & authorities, large institutions, huge workplaces, big companies, and businesses.

Position **Number 11** is represented by the cards in the tenth position on the left, and this position indicates challenges, adventures, situations, encounters, or achievements to be expected.

And finally, the position **Number 12** is represented by the cards in eleventh place on the left. This position gives information about the social status of the person, whether he will live in wealth or poverty, and it can also reveal the state of health in old age.

NOTE As for the positions that refer to other persons, siblings, friends, parents, you will be able to tell by a zodiac sign (see page 281) which gender the person is: A male sign indicates a brother, a father, uncle, or other person of male gender, and a female sign indicates a sister, mother, aunt, or other person of female gender.

All you have to know now are the basic meanings of each card (look up on pages 34 to 250) and you only have to put them into the context of the position they are in and if they do not correspond in any meaningful way to the position, in which they find themselves, they have no meaningful effect in the game; they remain without deeper meaning and without explanation.

Example

Suppose a person occupies place Number 3; this place Number 3 (the place of the goddess Diane) is now Number 1 for that person, the starting point of the game. And these cards placed there show the main issue that concerns the person.

You see, Number 3 is the place that refers to the goddess Diane, and indicates a proud, but also a little wild character that withdraws from society at times. So, the person who has taken place number 3 thinks of someone with a proud, but also a little wild character. And you now interpret the three cards that are in this position:

The first card to the left refers to the type of thoughts it is. What the thought is about or about situation the person is thinking.

The card on the second place, in the middle, refers to the person who is thought of and thus is the origin of the thought. The person or situation that causes the thoughts.

And the card on third place, the card to the right, refers to the Querent and tells what to fear or hope for him.

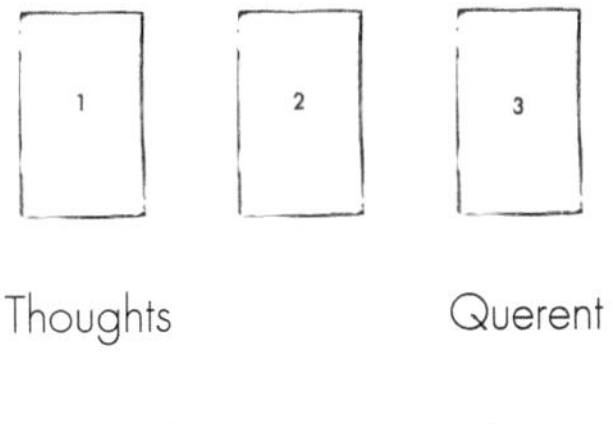

Suppose the card on the left is the 8 of Diamonds, the second card is the 5 of Hearts and as the third card you have the King of Clubs.

8 of Diamonds 5 of Hearts King of Clubs

As you can read on page 165, the card 8 of Diamonds refers to employment, work, and often a secure position offered and guaranteed by someone else.

In this example, this other person can only be represented by the second card, 5 of Hearts. Because on page 123 it is written to this card that it is a person with a great, generous character. And it is also a possible person card.

The third card, the King of Clubs, page 37, refers to applying double standards, self- overestimation; it describes success that does not remain and means instability, and thus happiness of short duration.

So, you could say about the person who is with these three cards: The person you are thinking about or with whom you are hoping for happiness through will get a position that is secured by the support or because of the personal connection to another person. The person you think about will be in a reliable, lasting relationship with someone else.

But in your contact with this person, double standards are applied, and it will not be a permanent contact. Also, because the other person seems more connected to the patron represented by the card 5 of Hearts & 8 of Diamonds.

Now look at the cards in position No. 2, which, as explained above, are in the first position on the left to the person. The position that indicates whether a change is to be expected here and if there will be a fortunate future.

Imagine that these cards are the 8 of Hearts, the 3 of Diamonds and the 6 of Clubs.

8 of Hearts. 6 of Clubs

3 of Diamonds

Among these three cards, you can exclude the 3 of Diamonds and the 6 of Clubs because with their core meaning they do not bring any change of the situation, nor do they announce hope for upcoming happiness. Therefore, these cards are at this point without any influence; they can be ignored because they have no important meaning.

Only the 8 of Hearts makes a small exception: On page 111, it is explained that the card indicates a secret joy and success and that it represents a loss or upcoming distance towards something or someone.

Remember that the first cards indicated that the contact would not be permanent. So, this card, the 8 of Hearts, may indicate that the loss of contact with the person should not be considered negative for the future. It would even improve the situation of the Querent in the long term.

NOTE For all participants of the game, therefore, all personal twelve positions must be interpreted in the same way.

And as said before, it can happen that there are some cards in these positions that show up meaningless and therefore can be seen as less important.

This is the case when the cards take positions with which, in terms of their core meaning, they have nothing in common with the position, the context or do not give any indication of future events.

But the first position, the position of the Querent, his Number 1, is the position of the thoughts, and these cards will always say something - without any exception.

These explanations together with the chapter that contains the core meanings of the cards should make it possible for you to do this special spread without further ado.

FINALE

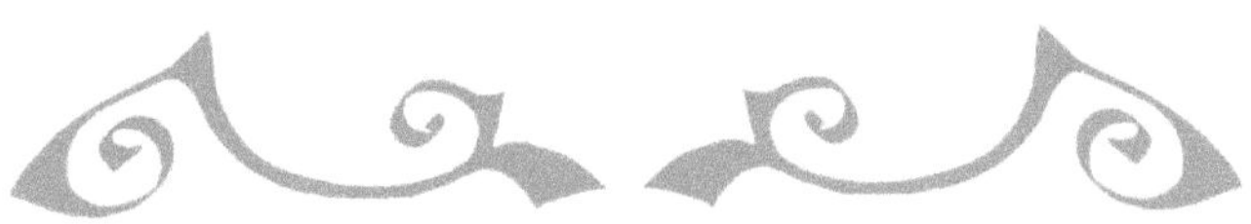

Epilogue

Unfortunately, the Grand Jeu is over now and so is our journey through the world of the 54 Grand Lenormand Cards. I wish that you have been able to collect a lot of valuable information, and that you can now create a good and strong basis for reading the Grand Lenormand Cards.

You are now on your own - now it is up to you what you do with this knowledge and how you will use it. Take the time it needs to get into the Grand Jeu Lenormand - It was, is and will always be the supreme discipline in cartomancy.

And it's not that complicated as it seems, it's just very time-consuming and you should never ever ask the cards in a hurry. Always take your time. Some steps of the Grand Jeu may seem a bit complicated at first, but it is not like that, because it is based on pure logical system, and you can be sure that the way to interpret the Grand Lenormand Cards you learned in this book is the only authentic way to achieve real results with the Grand Jeu.

And remember to treat your cards always with due respect and appreciation. And never doubt their words; trust them, so they always be ready to accompany you and help you. If you have a deep connection with your cards, they will be an amazing advisor to you in every hour of need.

Take care!

Andreas

CONTENTS

About the author, Andreas Nostra Dahm

Andreas Nostra Dahm, born during the 1970ties in southern Germany, is a very spiritual person, and he is very familiar with cartomancy. Andreas follows a tradition of card readers: from an early age he learned to live with the rules of the spirit world and while growing up he was taught traditional divination methods such as using a pendulum, reading coffee grounds and palmistry. And he was taught to pass on the messages the cards. So, he has had read cards since he was 15, looking at upcoming events and unraveling the secrets of the future. Andreas has been working with different decks of cards, always using the Old World's traditional divination methods for more than 25 years now and in the 4th generation of his family. Throughout those years, this has led him to read for clients worldwide and creating a presence on TV, social media, and print media. Besides his main profession as a card reader, he has already published books about traditional fortune telling.

About a reading: Andreas is very familiar with the Old World's divination methods and cartomancy: Be it Skat -, Lenormand -, Kipper-, Tarot Cards of the Gypsy Oracle - he knows reading these fortune telling cards in a very traditional style. Andreas always offers you a classic card reading; nothing more, but also nothing less than that. In his readings, Andreas passes on to you the messages of the cards in a neutral and unbiased way - without mixing the cards' message with his own personal intuition or opinion. The cards' words can be important to find answers to life's questions or to take a closer look at upcoming events or current situations. He does never offer you a general reading because there's always at least one question that led you to the cards and your question should be answered by them. That is what cartomancy is for that is how it works.

"Wise Oracle, from you I do beseech,
knowledge that lies beyond my reach,
hidden thoughts beyond your heart,
pray now, those thoughts impart."

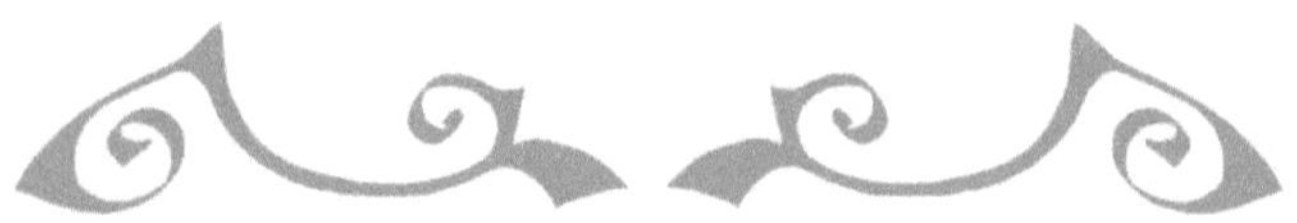

CARD IMAGES

Lenormand
Fortune Telling Cards

Fortune Telling Cards (Material: Premium Linen) - colored; in Box/ Folding Box

54 Cards (5,5cm x 8,5cm; 52 Fortune Telling Cards + 2 Person Cards)

THE END

References & Sources on which this work is based on:

Chapter I to VIII & Chapter X: Instruction Booklet from 1845 "Grand Jeu de Société Et Pratiques Secretes de Mademoiselle Le Normand"

Chapter I to V: Further card meanings and spreads: Traditions of the Ladies Theodora Wilhelmine Rosina Gruteser & Hedwig Margarete Emma Gruteser

Chapter VI: Dicitionaire Emblématique, Chapter IX: star constellations & alphabet: Paul Heinrich Gruteser

Biography "Lenormand – The Sibyl of Paris"

Liability: It is noted that all information in this book is without guarantee and the author's liability is excluded. Questions about health, illness, death, or legal matters will not be answered. The cards do not replace a visit to a doctor, therapist, alternative practitioner, or lawyer.

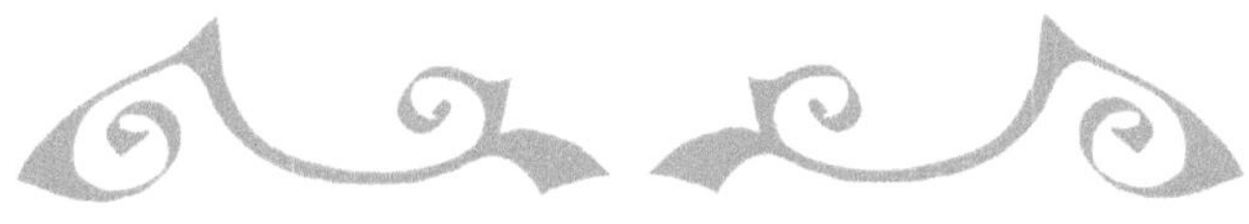

Further Expertise

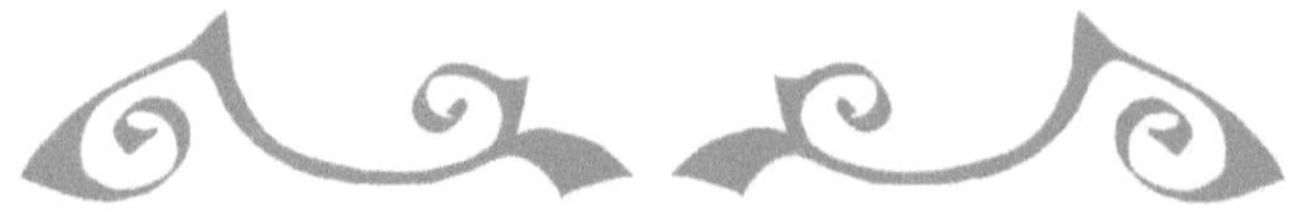

GRAND JEU
Lenormand

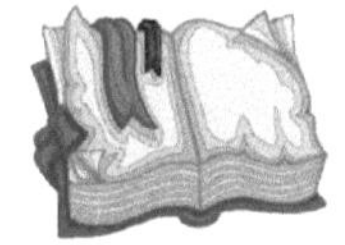

The Lenormand Fortune Telling Book

Fortune Telling with Lenormand Cards

For centuries, many people have felt the need to find out more about their future and their personal fate. In the late 18th and 19th centuries, cartomancy experienced a popular boom in Europe. During this time, 36 small Lenormand Cards were created. With its facts about the origins and origins of Lenormand Cards, this book enables you to learn how to unravel the future with these popular fortune telling cards, just as it was once practiced long time ago. In addition to the traditional and historical core meanings of the 36 cards, a list of everyday themes such as love, work, and finances, as well as other general and explanatory keywords, make it possible to actively acquire knowledge. Explanations on the first steps with small, modern divination methods as well as a description how to read the GT (grand spread) in both a modern and classic way also enable a further understanding of the possible interpretations of the cards. This textbook in the art of card reading may be an inspiration and a dictionary of the language of Lenormand Cards for both beginners and advanced.

275 Pages, Paperback ISBN 978-3758366819, or eBook ASIN B0CXYCNFTL

The
Lenormand Fortune Telling Cards

Lenormand
Fortune Telling Cards

Lenormand

Fortune Telling Cards

Skatkarten

Happy Halloween

Lenormand

Fortune Telling Cards

GRAND JEU Lenormand

'tis the season

Black & White Edition

Fortune Telling Cards (Material: Premium Linen) - black/ white; in Box/ Folding Box

40 Cards (5,5cm x 8,5cm; 36 Fortune Telling Cards + 2 additional Person Cards + 2 Cover Cards).

Color Edition or Color Edition with Playing Cards Inserts

Fortune Telling Cards (Material: Premium Linen) colored; in Box/ Folding Box

41 Cards (5,5cm x 8,5cm; 36 Fortune Telling Cards + 2 additional Person Cards + 1 Cover Card and 2 cards with Listing of the cards – one in German, the other one in English).

Halloween Edition

Fortune Telling Cards Theme Halloween (Material: Premium Linen) – colored in orange/black/white; in Box/ Folding Box

39 Cards (5,5cm x 8,5cm; 36 Fortune Telling Cards + 2 additional cards, that explain the order and name the cards– one card of these in German, the other one in English, + 1 Cover Card).

Christmas Edition

Fortune Telling Cards Theme Christmas (Material: Premium Linen) – colored; in Box/ Folding Box

39 Cards (5,5cm x 8,5cm; 36 Fortune Telling Cards + 2 additional cards, that explain the order and name the cards– one card of these in German, the other one in English, + 1 Cover Card).

The
Skat Fortune Telling Cards
&
Fortune Telling Playing Cards

Skat Fortune Telling Cards (Material: Premium Linen) - colored; in Box/ Folding Box

32 Cards (5,5cm x 8,5cm; 32 Fortune Telling Playing Cards with Suits of Diamonds, Hearts, Spades and Clubs)

GRAND JEU Lenormand

Fortune Telling Playing Cards (Material: Premium Linen) - colored; in Box/ Folding Box

54 Cards (5,5cm x 8,5cm; 52 Fortune Telling Playing Cards with Suits of Diamonds, Hearts, Spades and Clubs)